Everything You Need to Know About Being a Legal Assistant

Other Titles in the Series

Ransford C. Pyle, *Foundations of Law for Paralegals: Cases, Commentary, and Ethics*, 1992.

Peggy N. Kerley, Paul A. Sukys, Joanne Banker Hames, *Civil Litigation for the Paralegal*, 1992.

Jonathan Lynton, Donna Masinter, Terri Mick Lyndall, *Law Office Management for Paralegals*, 1992.

Daniel Hall, *Criminal Law and Procedure*, 1992.

Daniel Hall, *Survey of Criminal Law*, 1993.

Jonathan Lynton, Terri Mick Lyndall, *Legal Ethics and Professional Responsibility*, 1994.

Michael Kearns, *The Law of Real Property*, 1994.

Angela Schneeman, *The Law of Corporations, Partnerships, and Sole Proprietorships*, 1993.

William Buckley, *Torts and Personal Injury Law*, 1993.

Gordon W. Brown, *Administration of Wills, Trusts, and Estates*, 1993.

Richard Stim, *Intellectual Property: Patents, Copyrights, and Trademarks*, 1994.

Ransford C. Pyle, *Family Law*, 1994.

Jack Handler, *Ballentine's Law Dictionary: Legal Assistant Edition*, 1994.

Jonathan Lynton, *Ballentine's Thesaurus for Legal Research & Writing*, 1994.

Daniel Hall, *Administrative Law*, 1994.

Angela Schneeman, *Paralegals in American Law*, 1994.

Eric M. Gansberg, *Paralegals in New York Law*, 1994.

Pamela Tepper, *The Law of Contracts and the Uniform Commercial Code*, 1995.

Jonathan Lynton, *Ballentine's Legal Dictionary and Thesaurus*, 1995.

Susan Covins, *Federal Taxation*, 1995.

Karen Treffinger, *Life Outside the Law Firm: Non-Traditional Careers for Paralegals*, 1995.

Cathy Okrent, *Legal Terminology with Flash Cards*, 1995.

Carol Bast, *Legal Research and Writing*, 1995.

Everything You Need to Know About Being a Legal Assistant

Chere B. Estrin

Delmar Publishers Inc.

I(T)P   An International Thomson Publishing Company

Albany • Bonn • Boston • Cincinnati • Detroit • London • Madrid
Melbourne • Mexico City • New York • Pacific Grove • Paris • San Francisco
Singapore • Tokyo • Toronto • Washington

NOTICE TO THE READER

Cover Design: Douglas Hyldelund
Cover Background: Jennifer McGlaughlin

Delmar Staff
Acquisitions Editor: Jay S. Whitney
Developmental Editor: Christopher Anzalone
Project Editor: Theresa M. Bobear

Production Coordinator: Jennifer Gaines
Art & Design Coordinator: Douglas Hyldelund

COPYRIGHT © 1995
By Delmar Publishers
a division of International Thomson Publishing Company

The ITP logo is a trademark under license

Printed in the United States of America

For more information, contact:

Delmar Publishers
3 Columbia Circle, Box 15015
Albany, New York 12212–5015

International Thomson Publishing Europe
Berkshire House 168-173
High Holborn
London, WC1V7AA
England

Thomas Nelson Australia
102 Dodds Street
South Melbourne 3205
Victoria, Australia

Nelson Canada
1120 Birchmont Road
Scarborough, Ontario
Canada M1K 5G4

International Thomson Editores
Campos Eliseos 385, Piso 7
Col Polanco
11560 Mexico D F Mexico

International Thomson Publishing GmbH
Königswinterer Strasse 418
53227 Bonn
Germany

International Thomson Publishing Asia
221 Henderson Road
#05-10 Henderson Building
Singapore 0315

International Thomson Publishing – Japan
Hirakawacho Kyowa Building, 3F
2-2-1 Hirakawacho
Chiyoda-ku,Tokyo 102
Japan

1 2 3 4 5 6 7 8 9 10 XXX 01 00 99 98 97 96 95 94

Library of Congress Cataloging-in-Publication Data
Estrin, Chere B.
    Everything you need to know about being a legal assistant / Chere
B. Estrin — 1st ed.
        p.   cm.
    Includes index.
    ISBN 0–8273–6518–7
    1. Legal assistants--United States--Handbooks, manuals, etc.
I. Title.
KF320.L4E76   1995
340'.023'73--dc20

94-30139
CIP

P a r t

1

Landing the Right Job

Four articles explain how to market and sell yourself in a very competitive career and hiring environment.

Dedication   xii
Preface   xiii
Foreward   xv
Acknowledgments   xvii

Article 1 • **Power Interviewing in the '90s**   1

Why is interviewing a sales job? Why is hiring a "buyer's market?" What are law firms looking for in employment candidates? Are simple computer skills enough to today's job market? Why is it important to know about the firm you want to work for? Do you know 20 tips for a great interview?

Article 2 • **47 Ways to Find a New Paralegal Job**   13

What do dentists, lawyers, cleaners, and veterinarians have in common? Do you know what a white elephant party is? Interested in writing an article or book or conducting a seminar? How can you use a brag letter to land your dream job? How many types of resumes do you have on hand?

Article 3 • **Standing Out from the Competition**   19

How can you be different from those 300-400 other applicants for the same position? How deadly is a boring cover letter? Is modesty an admirable quality to possess when job hunting?

Article 4 • **In the Name of the Mother, the Father, and the Holy Partner: Looking for a "Family" Atmosphere at Work**   25

Why would anyone want to work in a family? Would you feel more secure working for a parent or a manager? What kind of work environment is best?

P a r t

2

Evolution of the Paralegal Profession

Five articles discuss how the paralegal profession is changing and provides helpful suggestions on adapting to these changes.

Article 5 • **In Search of Role Models**   **33**

Have you ever seen a paralegal portrayed in a television show? What is the media's image of the paralegal profession? Who's responsibility is it to make the paralegal profession widely recognized and respected? Do you have a paralegal role model?

Article 6 • **What to Expect in Your First Ten Years as a Legal Assistant**   **38**

How many years of employment is reasonable before a paralegal can expect to get a window office? Fly first class? Call partners by their first names? Stop Bates stamping? Get respect?

Article 7 • **The Contemporary Temporary**   **42**

Would you like to pick and choose your assignments? Is a temp job a good one? Why are law firms using temps? What are the most important factors in determining which temp agency to use?

Article 8 • **What Paralegals Will Be Doing Tomorrow**   **49**

How do law firms deal with economic hardtimes? Will downsizing spell the end to the paralegal profession? What kinds of duties will a paralegal have in the 21st century? What is a nontraditional career?

Article 9 • **Is a Paralegal Association For You?**   **52**

Have you ever considered joining your local, state, or national paralegal association? What's in it for you? What's the difference between strategic bonding and networking? Do you like politics? How much are the dues?

Part

3 ⬆

Achieving Success on the Job

Six articles explore various motives for and means of achieving success as a paralegal.

Article 10 • **Getting a Grip on Your Career: Strategies for Empowering Your Position**   57

How do you take control of the work place? Is it possible to manage your boss? How important is the firm's policy manual? Past newsletters? Orientation policies? What is career marketing? What are the benefits to being cross-trained for duties other than those you've been hired to perform.

Article 11 • **In Search of Success**   68

How do you define success? What are the pitfalls of self-defeating behavior? Are you willing to risk losing what you have in the pursuit of what you want? What are the best sources of recognition?

Article 12 • **Climbing the Invisible Ladder**   74

Are there benefits to taking on additional responsibilities? What are the steps to alerting the firm that you deserve a promotion? Do you have the gumption to ask for more work? What is the value to continuing education?

Article 13 • **Ten Easy Steps to Leveraging Your Career**   79

How do you increase the chances for your success? How can you increase your visibility in the legal community? Are you bold enough to negotiate for higher level assignments? What's in a title?

Article 14 • **Managing Attorneys to Get What You Need to Succeed**   82

Can you manage attorneys? What does it take to get things you need to succeed? How important is the decision-making process? What are the techniques paralegals can use to get attorneys to make decisions? Can you identify the six kinds of difficult attorneys?

Article 15 • **On the Road Again**   89

Is business travel for you? What are the 10 tips to a smoother business trip? What kind of hotel is best for business travelers? Where can you find information about local vendors?

P a r t

4

Life in the Law Firm

Five articles introduce the reader to the law office environment complete with its evaluation procedures, salary negotiations, outsourcing, and personnel issues.

Article 16 • **How Attorneys Evaluate Paralegals** **97**

What are the factors attorneys use to evaluate paralegals? How do attorneys evaluate paralegals? How important is judgment to attorneys? What's more important quantity of work or quality? How are raises set? How can a paralegal resolve personal conflicts with lawyers at a firm?

Article 17 • **Negotiating Salaries: The Undeclared War** **106**

What's the first step to salary negotiating? How can "doing your homework" increase your likelihood of success at the negotiating table? During a job interview, when should the issue of salary first be brought up? By whom? Is there a positive reaction to being offered a lower salary than anticipated?

Article 18 • **Outsourcing: Cutting Costs and Adding Profits** **113**

What is outsourcing? What are the key issues to outsourcing? Do firms want work completed through outsourcing? How do firms determine which functions are outsourced?

Article 19 • **The Weekend Retreat: A New Benefit for Paralegals** **120**

Why would law firms send their paralegals on a retreat? What kinds of issues are discussed at a retreat? How do paralegals benefit from the retreat? How can paralegals encourage their firms to hold retreats?

Article 20 • **Bay Area Paralegal Administrators Speak up about Personnel Issues** **126**

How are the educational backgrounds of employment candidates perceived by law firms? Do firms prefer career legal assistants or transient legal assistants? How much experience is necessary to getting a job as a legal assistant? How can in-house training improve a paralegal's career?

Part 5

Overcoming Pitfalls and Problems

Four articles discuss the proper manner to resolving employment problems

Article 21 • **Square Pegs in Round Holes**   **137**

How is job discrimination invading the law firm? Is it illegal or just inappropriate behavior? Is gender a relevant criterion in an employment decision? Weight? Number of children? Marital status? Sexual orientation? How does one deal with an interviewer who asks inappropriate questions?

Article 22 • **Expectations for Women on the Job *Are* Different**   **142**

Are women discriminated against in the paralegal job market? How can women raise awareness of their positive value to the legal community? What do men look for in a career? What about women, what are they looking for?

Article 23 • **Office Politics: In-House "Kissing"**   **146**

Should you take part in office politics? How should attorneys and paralegals view personal relationships between themselves? What is the unstated purpose behind office politics?

Article 24 • **Personal Problems on the Job: The Ultimate Conflict of Interest**   **150**

What exactly is a personal problem? How will personal problems affect job performance? How can one determine whether personal problems are consuming too much time? How can personal problems be resolved?

P a r t

6

'90's 2000

Dealing with the Changes of the '90s

Five articles outline how the law office environment has changed in the recent past, including the diminished role of seniority, downsizing, and layoffs.

Article 25 • **Seniority Does *Not* Equal Security**   **155**

What is the impact of downsizing or rightsizing on the status of paralegals? How can you learn about the law firm's financial troubles prior to the initiation of downsizing? How can you survive the downsizing? Do senior paralegals cost the firm more money than they bill?

Article 26 • **Honey, They Shrunk the Firm: Surviving in Today's Law Firm**   **158**

How have the new realities of the legal marketplace impacted the status of paralegals? Should paralegals attempt to specialize in a given legal area or cross-train in others? What are the resources to determine the firm's long-term strategies? What is a support memo? And why should it be used? How can you make yourself invaluable?

Article 27 • **Congratulations, You've Been Laid Off!**   **164**

What are the warning signs regarding impending layoffs? How can you practice safe careering? What are the main reasons for getting fired? When should a fired paralegal begin looking for a new job? How?

Article 28 • **Tough Choices!**   **169**

Why should a paralegal leave a job? What does it mean to be a proactive paralegal? What are the differences between a positive reinforcement firm and a negative reinforcement firm? How should one decide whether to leave the firm?

Article 29 • **Is There Life *After* the Law Firm?**   **175**

What kind of positions are included as "expanded careers?" How can one avoid getting stuck at a career cap? How can a paralegal determine whether branching outside of a law firm is appropriate?

P a r t

7

What It's Really Like

Seven interviews provide the reader with insight into the key issues confronting the paralegal in the latter half of the 1990s.

Interview 1 • **Molly George** 181

How can paralegals capitalize on technological innovations impacting law firms?

Interview 2 • **Jon Montgomery** 183

What kinds of activities does a real estate paralegal perform? How can a paralegal have a profoundly positive effect on someone's wellbeing? Where is the paralegal profession headed over the next decade?

Interview 3 • **Patricia Eyres** 188

What kind of international opportunities exist for paralegals? Who are the best people to train paralegals?

Interview 4 • **Dixie Dunbar** 190

What kinds of activities does an entertainment paralegal perform?

Interview 5 • **Andrea Wagner** 193

What's it like being a paralegal placement specialist? Is it considered a nontraditional paralegal career?

Interview 6 • **Rose Ors** 195

Do law firms need paralegal temps?

Interview 7 • **Deanie Kramer** 197

What are the skills needed to be a successful legal administrator? Are there business opportunities for low-cost non-attorney legal representation?

Suggestions for Further Reading 201

Index 205

*Dedicated to Alvin S.
Gamburd*

1919–1994

*My role model, mentor,
and best of all,
father.*

—CBE

Preface

If anyone had ever told me that when I reached adulthood, I was going to be a member of the paralegal field, I would have instantly discredited them. Let's face it. This is not exactly a field little girls and boys choose to write about in their essays entitled, "What I Want to Be When I Grow Up."

However, either through deliberate selection or sheer accident, you've landed with a splash in this relatively new and inspiring profession. Such was the situation for me. I can't tell you *how* I ended up in the field. But I can tell you I am very glad I did.

Part of the enjoyment of going down this highway has been the many articles I have written over the years. As a national seminar speaker, I have been introduced to paralegals all over the country who hold interesting and absorbing positions. In my many roles in this profession—paralegal, paralegal administrator, president of a national company placing paralegals, author of the PARALEGAL CAREER GUIDE (Wiley Law Publications) and as a publisher—I have been given the opportunity to see the big picture of this profession. As a regular columnist for **Legal Assistant Today** magazine as well as writer of other articles in publications such as the legal newspaper the **Los Angeles Daily Journal**, I have heard about many wondrous opportunities. I have met and interviewed highly motivated professionals with fascinating careers. In addition, I got to stick my own two cents in with techniques for moving up and succeeding in this field.

One day when I was minding my own business, Jay Whitney, Administrative Editor for Delmar Publishers Inc., popped into my office and suggested we put together all my articles for a book. I was, of course, flattered by the suggestion. These articles were based on events and changes in the field as they occurred. Even though they were written over the last five years, most all the information still applies.

This book should be used as an informational guideline for life in the law firm or the in-house legal department. It isn't the gospel. But what it can do is provide a reality check with pointers for enhancing your newly, chosen profession. Just reading about fresh ideas, a paralegal in a similar situation or a familiar predicament can help you adjust to a new field or job. Sometimes, one line that stands out can help you look at things differently. Other times, it's just healthy to have a good chuckle as you recognize yourself and the things you do. But most importantly, it's good to know you're not alone.

I've divided the book into useful sections to help:

- land a new position;
- give you a feel for expectations by demanding legal professionals;
- expose you to techniques others have used to achieve success on the job;
- give you ideas to cope with the pitfalls and problems common to this profession, and
- introduce you to real life paralegals.

All in all, we hope you refer to this book often throughout your entire career. Use it not only as a motivational but a practical tool.

When I am asked by paralegals what's the most important piece of advice I could give, I don't hesitate to quote my favorite line. In the words of business guru Tom Peters; "Do for pay what you would do for play." In order to succeed in any career, you've got to love it. Have fun out there.

I wish you outrageous success.

Chere B. Estrin
The Quorum/Estrin Group

Estrin Publishing
Los Angeles, California

Foreword

The paralegal career can be a difficult one. There is no examination that everyone must take to be a paralegal. Firms require widely varying qualifications to get a job. And many lawyers—who should know better—are unsure exactly *what* it is that paralegals do.

Rarely are legal assistants given much in the way of in-house training. Unless they are fortunate enough to have a mentor who will show them the ropes, learning about the job is accomplished on a trial-and-error basis. And since most firms these days no longer utilize paralegal managers to act as trainers, handle liaison with attorneys, and oversee the daily work flow, paralegals are even more on their own than ever.

Given this limited structure, lack of support, and even misunderstanding, it's *amazing* that paralegals contribute to the success of the law practice as much as they do every day.

The "olden days" in the evolution of the paralegal profession were not much better. When I first started my legal career as a lowly "document dog" on a huge litigation case, I made plenty of mistakes. Not understanding the law firm's power structure (which is *so* different from a business), or how to work with attorneys (who expect you to read minds), I ruffled feathers, disturbed the caste system, and, in general, rocked the boat. Rarely did these events inure to my benefit.

Today, practicing paralegals have come to rely on Chere Estrin's always-insightful "Career Advice" column in LEGAL ASSISTANT TODAY for some much-needed help and guidance. With the encouragement of Delmar Publishers, Ms. Estrin has now collected all these wonderful words of wisdom in one very helpful volume:

- Just getting your career started, and want to know what it's *really* like? Read the very funny "What to Expect in Your First Ten Years as a Legal Assistant."
- Need to know how to successfully travel on business? Check out the many useful travel tips in "On the Road Again."
- Stuck in the same place in your career, and don't know how to move up? Learn all about it in "Climbing the Invisible Ladder."
- Want to learn how to work as a temporary paralegal? Peruse the practical advice in "The Contemporary Temporary."

You'll learn how to negotiate the tricky world of office politics, avoid bringing personal problems to the job, successfully survive a layoff, and effectively manage the attorneys you work with. You'll learn that it's so *very* important to take control of your own destiny. You'll find out all the *real* stuff about being a paralegal that no one told you in paralegal school. For teaching you what you need to know to have a great paralegal career, Chere Estrin is the *best* there is.

(And I'm *not* just saying all this because I work for her!)

Dana L. Graves, J.D.
Editorial Director, Estrin Publishing
April 1994

Acknowledgments

Without the help and support of the following colleagues, friends and staff, we would never have a book. Thanks to:

Dana L. Graves: Estrin Publishing Vice-President and Editorial Director (without her, there wouldn't be a book, much less any articles).

Deborah A. McKibbin: Estrin Publishing Copyeditor (who helped pull this all together).

Jay Whitney: Administrative Editor, Delmar Publishers, (who has been extremely supportive throughout this whole process).

Leanne Cazares: Editor, LEGAL ASSISTANT TODAY magazine (who encouraged me to write, write, write).

Jim Pawell: Publisher, LEGAL ASSISTANT TODAY magazine (who gave me my start as a columnist, acted as a mentor and stayed with me).

Bruce Aho: President, Quorum Litigation Services (who supported me in my publishing ventures and The Quorum/Estrin Group).

Nasser Kazeminy: Chairman of the Board, Quorum Litigation Services (who has been very supportive and encouraging).

The Quorum/Estrin Group Staff: Arlene Finger, Chad Pappenfuss, Jim Harnagel, Liz Elliott, Gina Sauer, Heon Haan, Ron Cogan, Elaine Llanes, Diana Moregon and Julie Rubin—all of whom provided great leads, lots of laughter and the most engaging stories.

Deanie Kramer: President & Owner, Divorce Resources (who provided any kind of help, at anytime).

Tony Polk: Polk Communications (my greatest critic).

Joel Schneider: for being a great son.

Randy Goldner: Publisher, *The Los Angeles Daily Journal* (for asking me to do it again).

P a r t

1

Landing the Right Job

Competing for jobs in the paralegal field can be tricky. Employers look for signs that you can do the job in your resume, cover letter, interview, references and follow-up. You could be tossed out merely because of your cover letter or invited in because you were innovative in your job search techniques.

You never know when you are being tested. The toughest test could be in the recruiting lunch you have with other paralegals and attorneys in the firm.

When beginning your job search it is important to take the time to define your needs and expectations. What may be right for your colleague may not be good for you. Look for the right atmosphere that works for you. Read about insider tips from paralegal administrators and take a new look at the hidden job market. Good luck!

Power Interviewing in the '90s

I nterviewing in the '90s is like opening night on Broadway: you get one chance to satisfy the critics; otherwise they can literally close the show. It is essential that your performance is executed smoothly without any visible snafu.

Your energy must be at its peak. You must be able to recite your lines without any hesitation. Your costume must be tailored for the part. Further, all props (resume, letters, writing samples) must be in perfect working order and your performance has to be believable. You must hit your marks effortlessly, so no one can say you are in need of more rehearsals. The only way you can be certain the reviews are good is if you get the job.

For many paralegals, the prospect of interviewing and "selling" yourself can be intimidating—particularly if you haven't been in the job market in several years. You may come away from the experience baffled as to why you were passed over for the perfect job. On the other hand, you may find yourself in an exciting situation—wined, dined and then signed by the best firms in town. What makes interviewing an easy experience for some and a stressful and anxiety ridden time for others?

 Good research skills are only one of the requirements to be a legal assistant. Yet, it occurs to very few paralegals to research a firm or corporation prior to the interview. Candidates who think they will find out everything they need to know during the interview can be disappointed. They make the assumption that the interviewer has an obligation to tell all.

Case Study

"Ellen Jones" is a litigation paralegal with five years experience from a mid-sized firm earning $35,000 per year plus overtime. She has a B.A. and a certificate from an ABA approved school. At her year-end review,

1

*she was told she was being let go, her billables weren't high enough and she was too slow completing her assignments. The review came as a total shock. Apprehensive, yet certain she'll find **something**, Ellen updates her resume. She's back on the job market.*

Today's legal assistant candidate has more advantages than those of yesteryear. Instead of convincing interviewers why they should hire a paralegal, the job seeker must instead convince the firm why *they* are the very best candidate over and above anyone else. If we were to think of the legal assistant field as a business, then the candidate is no longer creating a market but rather, capturing marketshare.

The four major components for "closing the deal" in today's job market are:

- skills,
- abilities,
- salary acceptance, and
- personality compatibility.

If you score well, chances are you stand a stronger chance of getting the job over other candidates. Yet, scoring well no longer guarantees an offer in the '90s job market.

From entry to senior level, paralegals today are finding a very different job market than that of two to three years ago. Interviews with several paralegal managers around the country confirm these top ten trends and changing attitudes for the nineties:

- The actual interviewing process takes longer than in the past.
- Competition is stiffer because of many more qualified applicants and fewer openings.
- Legal assistants are expected to know more than ever before.
- Some jobs such as paralegal manager have either been eliminated or are now required to bill time.
- Benefit packages are slimmer and many no longer include perks such as fully paid health insurance, parking, continuing education and association dues.
- The days are long gone when a firm hires with the proviso that it will also be expected to train.
- Both senior and entry-level legal assistants are having a harder time finding a position than in the past.
- There are more positions than ever before for paralegals in legal departments of corporations.
- Most positions now require computer skills.
- Some firms now feel compelled to give a writing, spelling or grammar test to entry and mid-level legal assistants.

Joyce Wilson, Paralegal Coordinator for the Los Angeles office of Fried, Frank, Harris, Shriver & Jacobsen explains.

People are being much more careful about making a good fit. You have to be more careful because if you make a hiring mistake, the stakes are higher. Money is very short and is being more seriously tended to. We no longer have the time, the dollars nor the personnel to train a newcomer. It costs too much to have someone turnover. People are inviting interviewees back more times to make sure you meet everyone.

Ellen was exasperated. She has only five weeks left before her job terminates. She sent her resume to at least 25 firms over the past five weeks. Not receiving one call, she decides to call agencies and the local paralegal association job bank. She expands her search to include her school placement service and decides to attend the monthly paralegal association meeting to network. She places calls to all her colleagues asking if they have heard of any openings. She signs up with three reputable agencies and investigates temporary work, just in case. She asks her real estate agent, dentist and therapist if they can refer her to any lawyers. She also looks in the local newspapers for positions that describe paralegal duties without the actual title.

What Do Firms Want?

The prestigious firm of Munger, Tolles & Olson in Los Angeles employs 32 legal assistants. Norma McIntosh, Personnel Manager, looks for top skills, great attitude, good work ethic, and demonstrated effort to stay put. To even get an interview, the resume must have an excellent, professional appearance that stands out from all the rest. It must have a "typeset" look. There must be absolutely no typos. It must reflect stability, and a four year degree. A certificate is preferred, although not mandatory.

"The candidate must be very articulate in order to interface with attorneys. They must possess organizational skills and be capable of independent thinking," said McIntosh.

I like to see an interest displayed in the kind of work, culture, and philosophy in place in the firm. The type of questions the candidate asks in the interview are important: How are the employees treated? What kind of expectations do you have for someone in this position? I have great admiration for ambition.

Wilson also places emphasis on the candidates' questions. "This is not a personality contest. I like to hear questions such as: "What is your day like? What do you like best about this firm? What do you like best about your job? What do you like least?"

While Wilson may not conduct a personality contest to get the job, compatibility with the firm's personnel and philosophy are important. "Companies are looking for competencies and for people to hit the ground running," says Judy Estrin, vice-president of Drake Beam Morrin, Inc., one of the largest individual and organizational transition firms in the country.

> Jobs are going away in all fields. What has not gone away is the work. Firms and corporations are looking at the work differently today. The trend is to look more for contractual assignments. Employers no longer feel that they are signing you up for a lifetime position. There is a misconception that if you demonstrate the girl/boy scout behavior, the company will be loyal to you. Wrong. They won't. Business is business. One of the biggest changes in today's market is that the only loyalty is to yourself and your family. And that's not all bad.

Computer Skills

Just as firms routinely require organizational skills, the trend is to now include computer skills. Few positions do not have the requirement. Sheila Kennedy, paralegal manager of the Minneapolis firm of Dorsey & Whitney and supervisor of 30 paralegals will generally favor a computer literate candidate over others.

> I look for computer literacy that is transferable to our system. It's not so much that the candidate needs to know a particular program, rather that the candidate demonstrates a knowledge of computers and the ability to quickly learn what we have here.

Wilson adds a similar philosophy. "To me, the software programs are not as important because most skills are transferable from one system to another." A few of the most requested programs of paralegals today are:

- InMagic
- Concordance
- Discovery
- Summation
- Basis
- Lotus 1-2-3
- dBase
- WordPerfect
- MicroSoft Word
- PC Docs
- KnowledgeLink (new)

Transition vs. Career Positions

Because employer attitudes have changed for the '90s and many no longer look for lifetime employees, the transition position has emerged for both candidates and employers. There may be instances where you are forced to take a position that isn't the "ultimate" dream job. Instead of being depressed or disappointed with your job search, you may make the decision to accept a position that doesn't exactly fall within all of your parameters, but does, however, meet most of the criteria. You must be able to identify in the interview whether the position is career or transitional. Some factors that determine whether to take a transition job over a career position are:

- the length of time you have until you must take another position,
- the job market, and
- the lack of qualifications, experience, or education for the position that you are ultimately seeking.

You may, for example, desire a Litigation Support Manager position. However, your computer skills in case management, training or finance may not be strong enough for the management position. You decide to take a transition position which will enable you to gain the expertise necessary. This position may last one or two years. At that time, armed with more education in computers and on the job training, you set out to seek the management position.

Or, you may have just been laid off and time and financial constraints do not permit you to land precisely the job you want. You end up taking a position you may not have taken under other circumstances. These are transition jobs. However, be careful how many times you take a transition job. A resume that indicates a job hopper is not likely to attract too many takers.

Some firms like to hire transitory paralegals. These firms believe that the legal assistant career offers a limited vertical climb. They feel a paralegal who is on their way to somewhere else such as law school or graduate school make the best employees. The firm does not expect the paralegal to stay more than two years or so. Hiring requirements are usually a four year degree with no certificate. This type of hiring, strong in the late eighties, has not lost steam with many of the larger New York or Washington, D.C. firms today.

Other firms believe hiring a career paralegal, one that will stay as long as possible, is the best route. The assertion there is either a demonstrated vertical climb upward or enough horizontal advancement to keep good people motivated and in the field. Still others will have a combination, their "transitory" paralegals enter the program as paralegal assistants or document clerks and career paralegals enter the program as legal assistants.

It's up to you to find out in the interview whether or not the firm's philosophy toward paralegals fits in with yours. And don't be fooled because you are interviewing with a corporation! If you want to make a vertical climb up the ladder, find out how many vice-presidents or department heads came up through the legal department. If the answer is none, and that is your career goal, this may not be the place for you!

Ellen was still optimistic. The last interview, she felt went well, although the rejection letter she received did not indicate why she didn't get the job. Perhaps she shouldn't have refused to take their test--even though she strongly felt that if the firm didn't test attorneys, why should they test paralegals? Perhaps she shouldn't have mentioned her firm was in financial trouble. It may have been better just to say she was being laid off and moved on to another topic. And, she didn't really discuss how her particular skills fit in with the firm's needs. "Of course", she thought, "I didn't really know very much about the firm and expected the attorney to give me more information. If I hadn't asked what the hours were, maybe they would have thought I was more professional and less clerical. My comment that the salary was a little low probably should have come when we were in negotiations." "And", she thought, "emphasizing how important the benefits were was probably not a good move either. It may have been better to have just listened to the package and analyzed later whether it met my needs."

The Interviewing Process: Beating the Competition

Scoring an interview these days can be a major victory. You have been selected over many other applicants. Once on the interview, however, it is important to emerge as a victorious candidate, even if initially you don't want the job. After analyzing the pros and cons of the position, it could turn out this is what you wanted after all or this job has very viable transition possibilities.

The key to a successful interview today is to sell your accomplishments and competence. During your meeting, it is up to you to draw the parallel on how your accomplishments meet the needs of the firm. You can use phrases such as:

- "When I was the lead paralegal on the Acme case, I coordinated 15 paralegals and document clerks. That sounds very much like what is needed here on the Jones case."
- "If I understand you correctly, you will need someone to work closely with various government agencies. I worked extensively with state and federal agencies when I was with the Brown firm. I can save you time and money because I can get in quickly and know precisely which source to go to."

"If you say you can do something on your resume, you had better be able to do it. God help you if you can't," emphasizes Estrin. "The buzz word today is "value-added." You need to convince the firm that you can do more than what the job calls for and the hidden agenda is you'll do it for less money.

Because of right-sizing, budget restraints, and smaller staffs some entry-level paralegals have a tough time finding jobs. Many firms no longer have the budget to train new personnel. And, entry-level paralegals are competing with experienced candidates who may be willing to work for less money.

Charlotte Callegari, director of graduate placement for Phillips Jr. College in Carson, California advises newcomers to the field to get involved in an internship. "Not having an internship hinders the job seeking process," she says.

> I have recently completed a mailing asking if firms would like to participate in the internship program. I got a great response. Most of the firms are asking for at least a 3 month commitment and for a student in the final quarter in school. Students need to understand that many firms don't have the resources to offer on the job training. The internship then becomes a valuable training vehicle.

Patricia Curtis, is the legal assistant coordinator for the Kansas City, Missouri firm Polsinelli, White, Vardeman & Shalton. Her opinion on hiring entry-level paralegals may not win points with educators.

> There are so many schools nowadays that the quality of education has actually gone down. Graduates from certificate programs are not well equipped. Maybe my expectations are higher, however, I have found new paralegals require more training. I have great concerns that the basic steps are missing.

Senior-level professionals also have a tough time because firms would much rather hire paralegals for less dollars. "The market in Washington, D.C. has been pitiful," states Elizabeth Hardwick, legal assistant supervisor for Finnegan, Henderson, Farabow Garrett & Dunner. "While the market is better than in the past few years, it is really only better for people with a couple of years experience. Too much experience and they don't want you."

This is particularly true if no growth nor sophistication in assignment level is evidenced in the senior-paralegal's work history. Perceptive interviewers assessing senior-level paralegals find many stuck at mid level. The fear is they may be paying for longevity in the career rather than expertise. Estrin explains:

> If a senior-professional's assignment level is that of a mid-level paralegal and the firm can hire a person at the same level of expertise for fewer dollars, it only makes good business sense to do that. However, on the other hand, if a senior-level person brings in a particular expertise, can do the job faster, and bring added value for the dollars spent, then the firm does well to hire the senior-level expert. During the interview process, it is up to the candidate to demonstrate growth, expertise, and a unique ability equal to no other candidate.

Curtis tests candidates regarding procedures by giving them sample case studies such as, "Here's the Jones Corporation. How do you qualify it in Florida?" The best candidates demonstrate abilities by stating what the next step would be.

> Using a commercial litigation case as an example, I may toss out that the case is going through deposition. If the candidate asks if

summary judgment has been filed, I know I have someone here who is knowledgeable. I like someone who carries on a conversation about the actions and doesn't wait for me to tell them what's happening.

While we've all read hundreds of resume writing and interviewing books, actually executing those techniques can be a talent in and of itself. Rhonda Rice, CLA and legal assistant for the Anchorage firm of Atkinson, Conway & Gagnon is a whiz at the interviewing process.

"When I interview, I let the prospective employer know they are better off with me than without me. My attitude is: I can take the load off. I use action words on my resume or when speaking with people. I go the extra mile — always."

How does she close the deal? "I use body language. I lean forward. I speak positively and I talk about my personal philosophy on life in addition to working skills. I convey a "can do" attitude."

Paralegals need to be intuitive, insightful, and ambitious. By this I mean they need to know what needs to be done before the attorney does **and** have the guts to do it. I think too many paralegals are waiting for things to be handed to them and are not assertive enough. I strive to make myself indispensable. I'm not afraid to say you need me.

Have You Done Your Research?

Good research skills are only one of the requirements to be a legal assistant. Yet, it occurs to very few paralegals to research a firm or corporation prior to the interview. Candidates who think they will find out everything they need to know during the interview can be disappointed. They make the assumption that the interviewer has an obligation to tell all.

One paralegal came to see me not too long ago. She had recently made a lateral move from one major firm to another. The impetus was billable hours. "My former firm required crazy billable hours from me. Little did I know, that the new firm asked even more."

Frankly, I was astounded. Didn't she know her new firm was notorious for the amount of hours it required? Apparently, she didn't do her homework.

Interviewers are always impressed when a candidate is able to speak intelligently about the firm. Comments such as "I've been following the Acme case and. . ." or "I read about the firm's merger with the Smythe firm. Can you tell me if that affected the firm's . . . . " prove your interest.

"Know who you are interviewing with," states Wilson:

> It is much more impressive to sit across from someone who is already knowledgeable about you or your firm. Having to explain who we are or the types of clients we have is sometimes insulting. This is a very prestigious firm with well-known clients. I shouldn't have to try to educate the candidate about the fact we are a fine, upstanding organization.

Don't go overboard, however. One manager relates the story about a candidate who called up and asked for a written job description prior to the interview. The manager canceled the interview. Another manager received a phone call from a candidate who said before she sent in her resume, she wanted information about the company. The manager asked for her name but didn't send the information. When the company advertised again a few weeks later, the candidate sent her resume anyway. The manager immediately sent a rejection letter.

You can find several resources for information such as:

- Nexis Search,
- InfoAmerica,
- Dialog (or other on-line programs),
- local newspapers and periodicals,
- Martindale-Hubbell,
- the annual report of the corporation or firm's brochure or resume, or
- networking may give you an informal source of information.

Knowing the firm or the interviewer works well. I was once extremely impressed with a candidate who had read all of my articles and books. She sat in front of me and let me know a particular article of mine had helped her with a difficult client. While I didn't know if that was at all true, I was impressed she took the time to conduct the research and could **actually quote** the article. She alerted me to her resourcefulness, which was good because I may not have considered hiring her. While I recognized I was getting my ego stroked, I did look at her as a more serious contender for the position.

As an earnest candidate, you must understand the job you are applying for. Liz Elliott, former UCLA attorney assistant placement coordinator and currently attorney recruiting manager for the Los Angeles based firm, Of Counsel, recalls an embarrassing but amusing incident.

> I once sent a telegram to the vice president of marketing which was a technique unheard of. Consequently, I was interviewed by the president of one of the largest publishing houses in the United States. Because of the sophistication of my presentation just to get the interview, I found myself interviewing for a major western states marketing position. During the interview with the president, I found I was in way over my head. When he asked me how much money I wanted, I quoted a salary probably 3 times **lower** than I should have, and I saw his face drop. I disappointed him as a candidate. I was aggressive, but I couldn't follow through for the level of job I was being considered.

> *Ellen was excited. She had a second interview with a prestigious firm. She was certain she could land this position. While the firm originally wanted a more junior level person, Ellen was able to sell herself by pointing out the associate level assignments she has performed.*

"By hiring me, you end up with a person who can cover a much broader scope of assignments. And you only will pay me slightly more than the junior-level paralegal and significantly less than an associate. You can bill me out at a higher rate. In the long run, you save money and have virtually no downtime because I don't have to be trained."

She followed up with a dynamic thank-you letter to everyone she interviewed with pointing out how her experience benefitted the firm. She couldn't wait to hear.

Go for the Brass Ring

Even though the '90s may be perceived as an employers' market, remember you have a choice in where you land. No matter if you accept a career or transition job, be cautious and commit to a worthwhile employer, one that can advance your career in the manner you want it advanced. When you go on an interview, remember the top five points firms look for from the '90s legal assistant:

1) You must now have superior organizational, communication, and computer skills.
2) You must demonstrate an eagerness for the job.
3) You are open to salary negotiations.
4) You know your job better than anyone else.
5) You are compatible with the firm's personality, culture and philosophy.

Think carefully of the advantages and disadvantages of the position and how it works for you. Each job is a stepping stone in your career. And when you interview, above all else, be yourself. When all is said and done, this is what employers buy.

The phone rang. A now familiar voice was on the other end. "Hello, Ellen", it said. "We'd like to make you an offer." "I'd love to work with you," said Ellen. And the rest is paralegal history.

20 Insider Tips For a Great Interview

1. Ask good questions that are job related such as:
   - What is your day like?
   - Could you describe a few assignments I will be undertaking?
   - What is the status of paralegals in this firm?
   - What is the average length of employment for paralegals?
   - What is the firm's philosophy?

2. Research the firm or corporation **before** you get to the interview. Get an annual report or brochure from the firm, if available. Know something about their clients and history and relay that information to the interviewer.

3. Know who you are talking to:
   - what their position is,
   - hiring authority,
   - length of time with the firm, and
   - whether they are partner, associate, paralegal, or administrator.

4. If the interviewer has written any articles, read them before the interview and let them know you were impressed.

5. Follow up with a typewritten, professional thank you letter to everyone you interviewed that reemphasizes point-by-point why you are uniquely qualified for this position.

6. Know when the interview terminates. Don't try and drag it out.

7. Be clear about salary expectations and signal your willingness to negotiate under the right conditions. Giving a range gives the interviewer permission to offer you a salary at the lowest end.

8. If you find an article, news story, or announcement of a meeting the interviewer may be interested in, send a copy of it with a note: "Thought you might find this of interest."

9. Always bring extra resumes, references and writing samples with you to the interview—in a briefcase or portfolio—not an envelope or folder.

10. Computer skills (more than word processing) are more crucial now than ever. Be sure you are user friendly.

11. Communicate an instance where you were the hero. Do it in such a way that you are not bragging but rather demonstrating your abilities.

12. It may not be a good idea to admit you "just fell into the field." Even those firms that hire transitory paralegals like to know your career isn't an accident.

13. Writing skills are more important than ever before. Even if your position does not require drafting documents, you must be able to write intelligent, comprehensive letters and memos.

14. Language skills are critical. Valley girls and boys are out. Articulate, intelligent conversation is in.

15. Foreign language skills are desired by more and more employers. If you speak another language, let the interviewer know, even if it is not a requirement for the position you are applying.

16. Let the interviewer know that you are aware of the latest in technology, changes in the law and anything else that may affect your position.

17. Even if you are being considered for a position with another firm or corporation, the interviewer wants to know that you want their job and their job only.

18. Sell yourself and what **you** bring to the table. Not your husband, wife or significant other.

19. Some interviewers have no problem if you take notes during the interview, others find it threatening. Always be sensitive to the situation.

20. Smile.

Interviewer's Top 20 Turnoffs

1. Candidates who don't look at you or keep looking away.

2. Asking too soon in the interview about the benefits. (A "what's in it for me?" attitude.)

3. Candidates who lean on the interviewer's desk or touch the interviewer's copy of their resume.

4. Candidates who talk too much, not at all, or pause as though they are pondering each question.

5. Routine cover or thank you letters.

6. People who don't appear to take the interview seriously.

7. The dressed down look.

8. Candidates who give the receptionist a rough time or act "very important."

9. Asking the interviewer to validate your parking.

10. People who gesture to indicate "quote" "unquote".

11. Typos of any kind on resumes, letters, or writing samples.

12. The "Dear Gentlemen" salutation.

13. The reply, "It's on my resume," in response to a question.

14. Not giving a direct answer regarding salary; whether you're still on the job; or reason for leaving.

15. Going into great detail about "what really happened" on your last job; talking about how bad your situation is; or, giving insider information such as "the firm is in trouble" or "the partners are fighting."

16. Taking too long to fill out paperwork or objecting to filling out an application.

17. Negativity of any kind.

18. Using the term "certified" paralegal when you mean "certificated".

19. Leaving off dates on the resume; sending your picture; or a copy of the ad with the resume.

20. Gigglers, wimpy handshakes, poor posture, or closed body language.

47 Ways to Find a New Paralegal Job

inding a job in today's market is no easy undertaking. Reports have been heard from East to West Coast and up and down the middle of the country about the stiff and voluminous competition for each opening. Traditionally, it has taken recent graduates up to three months to find a position. In today's market, those three months have escalated into six months and even one year. And, because many law firms have cut back on salaries, senior level people earning over $45,000 per year are having a particularly rough time finding a new position quickly.

Finding a new job now requires imagination, creativity and just plain old-fashioned street smarts. More than ever before, it is necessary to stand out from the competition. To give you an idea as to what you are up against, some employers who have run ads in the local journals have actually complained that these ads will pull between 300-400 responses. A pretty dismal thought to those competing for those spots.

> *Go where attorneys go. Bring cards with you. Bite the bullet and go up to them during breaks and introduce yourself. After the initial chit-chat, hand out your card and tell them you'll give them a call for lunch.*

However, all is not lost. Paralegals can and do find jobs in this market. In addition to the standard job search strategies, listed below are a few innovative suggestions you might wish to consider using.

1. **Paralegal White Elephant Party:** Gather up all the paralegals you know who are looking for jobs, may know of a job or have friends in the field and throw a party. To get in, each paralegal brings a job lead. These are leads that didn't work for that individual but may be good for someone else.

2. **Ask your dentist:** Every dentist has a lawyer for a patient. Ask him/her for three lawyers. Use the dentist's name to get in the door. You can always break the ice by comparing root canals.

3. **Ask your doctor:** Ditto for the doctor.

4. **Ask your cleaners, real estate agent, and veterinarian:** Lawyers have sick puppies, soiled suits and houses on the market.

5. **Alumni:** The alumni from your college or paralegal school is always a good source. Letters sent to alumni at least get a response or special attention, even if there are no jobs available. No one wants to alienate a fellow alumni.

6. **Agencies:** Try to use only those that specialize in paralegal placement. Clerical agencies have slots to fill and may end up sending you on positions that require typing tests.

7. **Trade associations:** If you are seeking a position outside of the paralegal field, one of the best sources of information are trade associations. Write to the association for information regarding newsletters and association meetings. Go and network to find out about the career. You may have transferrable paralegal skills.

8. **Newspapers:** Always read the ads not only in the legal newspapers but your local newspaper. Read the listings from A through Z. Don't stop at the legal section. Be sure you read the Business Section for information on what's happening with firms and corporations.

9. **Editors:** Get to know some editors in legal publishing. Not only can this be a good alternative career path for you, editors know lots of lawyers and paralegals. They may be able to make introductions to just the right person you need to know.

10. **Corporations:** The jobs right now are in the corporations such as insurance companies, banks, health care, pharmaceutical, and anywhere corporations are building in-house legal departments.

11. **Looks likes, talks like, walks like, must be a. . . :** Many times you'll see an ad that describes a paralegal position but simply doesn't have the title. Apply for that position. Be sure your cover letter and resume strongly resembles the position and points out the similar job duties.

12. **Read articles for what's happening in cases:** Read, read, read. When you read an article about a certain case that's hit the media or is bound for trial, send a letter along with your resume pointing out **why** they need you. Illustrate your expertise and how it correlates with the case. Even though the firm or attorney may not be looking, they may consider you.

13. **Who's hiring associates:** Check out who is hiring associates. This is an indicator that the firm is growing. If the firm is growing, they may need

paralegals. Get to them before they start a highly visible search. If they are hiring partners only, they may be looking for new business.

14. **Temporary to permanent:** This is the age of temping in America. You may get on a long-term temporary assignment which could convert into a permanent position. This also gives you an opportunity to look over the firm before making a commitment.

15. **Interview potential employers for an article**: Write an article. Go out and interview several hiring authorities. Everyone wants their 15 words of fame.

16. **Write a book**: Nothing else establishes you as an authority in the field like having a book published. Not only will your mother be proud of you, but it sets you apart from the competition and puts you in a whole other league. It's amazing how desirable you suddenly become.

17. **Give seminars:** Again, establish yourself as an authority in the field. You also never know who you're going to meet.

18. **Ad in paper:** You could always advertise.

19. **College placement office:** Even though you may have graduated as much as 10–15 years ago, you can always go back to your college placement office.

20. **Attend bar association meetings:** Go where attorneys go. Bring cards with you. Bite the bullet and go up to them during breaks and introduce yourself. After the initial chit-chat, hand out your card and tell them you'll give them a call for lunch.

21. **Go where attorneys hang out:** gyms, golf, tennis, volunteer groups or pro bono work. There's something about meeting people in a social scene that puts everyone on an equal footing.

22. **Big Suits listings: Federal Reporter:** Follow the "Big Suits" listings in local and national publications such as *The American Lawyer*. Cases heating up may need additional assistance. Put the thought out there before the employer thinks of it and calls everyone in town.

23. **Who's rented new space:** Find out who has rented additional space through real estate agent friends or PR notices in the paper. If they need new space, they may need more personnel.

24. **Lottery winners:** I once knew of an entry-level paralegal who read in the St. Louis paper that a paralegal just won $18 million. She immediately sent a letter to the firm and said, "chances of my winning the lottery are next to nil.

Therefore, I can promise you that I won't be quitting anytime soon." Okay, it's a long shot.

25. **Brag letter:** Instead of a resume, consider sending a brag letter. This letter highlights (on one page) your qualifications and teases the employer to find out more about you. Send it where there are no openings listed anywhere, yet the firm may be perfect for you because of a like background.

26. **Send your published articles to potential employers:** Get an article published (even in your local association newsletter). Send the article to potential employers. Ask for an interview.

27. **Attend recruiter and paralegal coordinator seminars and meetings:** The best place to meet recruiting coordinators is at seminars. Attend their seminars and network, network, network. You'll meet them on a one-on-one and may even learn about a new position.

28. **Start a new business:** If you have the talent and are ably financed, consider using your contacts in a new venture. Be your own boss for a change.

29. **Look for firms laying off associates:** Firms laying off associates may entertain the thought of hiring paralegals at lower salaries and billing rates.

30. **Lose weight, gain weight, get a new hairstyle, change your image:** In other words, build your self-confidence. Feeling better about yourself means that you'll sell yourself better on the interview. You'll also be more creative and aggressive in inventing new ways to find a job.

31. **Redraft the cover letter:** Most cover letters are boring, boring, boring: Dear Prospective Employer: I-am-sending-my-resume-in-response-to-your-ad-in-the-Legal-News. I-am-a-six-year-litigation-paralegal-at-a-major-firm. I-will-call-you-next-week-for-an-interview. Ugh! Get creative. Your writing skills are being tested here.

32. **Take a class to meet people:** Take a class to meet new people in the field. Even something you wouldn't ordinarily attend such as: "101 Ways to Use a Law Degree." Here's an informal way to meet attorneys.

33. **Check out the legal vendors:** Here's the best kept secret in the field—the vendors know more about what's happening in town than almost anyone else. They are also generally high on hiring paralegals for their own businesses.

34. **Get interviewed:** Get a story written about you. Start your own PR campaign, start attracting attention and building name recognition.

35. **Listen for people who are leaving their jobs:** Someone you know leaving their position? Get there before the advertising starts. Ask that person to introduce

you to the hiring authority the minute they give notice and before they leave. It will make them look good to have filled that position. Also, don't be put off if your years of experience are not in line with the person leaving. If they are a senior and you're junior, sell lower salary and billing rates. If they're a junior and you're a senior, sell expertise, quickness to get the job done and higher billing rates.

36. **Look for new start up firms — read the professional announcements:** New firms don't even know who they need yet. Read the professional announcements and go sell them on the concept of hiring you.

37. **Draft three or four different resumes:** Slant the resume according to different positions. (However, **never** lie on the resume.) If, for example, you are a senior level paralegal searching for an administrative position, highlight your personnel and financial skills. If you are looking for a case manager position, highlight your organizational and computer skills.

38. **Get introduced to the paralegal coordinator:** You've got friends at other firms. Simply ask them to introduce you to the hiring authority at their firm, even if the firm isn't looking. Referrals are the best possible source of getting a job.

39. **Go first class on trips:** Let's face it. The people with the most power go first class, not steerage. You'll meet the people at the top. (Unless of course, you end up next to the person who's using their frequent flier miles to get bumped up.)

40. **Use information directories:** Using the *Martindale Hubbard* is still the standard. However, *Standard & Poor's Moody's, Ward's Business Directory of U.S. Public and Private Companies, Of Counsel 500, Association of Legal Administrators Directory* are only a few of the directories you can use to find firms and corporations.

41. **Find a federal job:** Ever think about working for Uncle Sam? Even though there may be a hiring freeze in certain sectors, there are agencies and government branches that do have openings. The Army, Air Force and Veteran's Administration hire paralegals.

42. **Get promoted:** Simple enough.

43. **Attend seminars, conventions:** Legal Tech, ABA convention, Association of Legal Administrators conference, Legal Assistant Management Association, National Federation of Paralegal Associations, National Association of Legal Assistants, your local paralegal association, National Association Law Placement, State Bar Conventions, and the Paralegal Educators Association are only a few of the conferences where you are apt to find employers.

44. **Reunions:** Nothing like your old cronies to help you find a job.

45. **Make sure you have computer skills:** What's hot, hot, hot now are computer skills. You need more than word processing knowledge such as WordPerfect, however. Lotus, DBase, InMagic, Concordance, Summation, Quatro, and Basis, are only a few of the software packages you may need to learn.

46. **Other paralegals:** Really, the very best source of information.

47. **Join a law firm softball league:** Nothing like sliding into first base and knocking over a potential employer. At least it's an ice breaker.

Keep in mind that you can't make a pest out of yourself or do anything foolish. However, since the industry is relatively small, your connections can take you far. The first thing you have to do is **get** those connections. Then work them wisely, all the while having fun and keeping your good name and reputation in tact. You will always have to deal with good markets and bad markets. The ups and downs are not within your control. However, you can make your own destiny and determine your own flight pattern. Good luck and happy hunting!

Standing Out From the Competition

I can't remember ever seeing a tougher job market than the one currently facing job seekers. Regardless of the cause—the overall poor economy, downsizing of law firms, increase of in-house counsel or just plain consumer awareness—the fact remains that it now takes legal assistants almost twice as long to complete a successful job search as it did two years ago.

Paralegal schools report that entry-level legal assistants look for positions for three to six months (or even longer). Gone are the days when new graduates had to spend only one to three months' time in serious job hunting. Worst of all, senior-level paralegals are experiencing six to twelve-month job searches that were once accomplished in four to six weeks.

Law firms relay reports of receiving hundreds of resumes for one position. In past years, many paralegals had the luxury of picking and choosing the exact job they really wanted. Now, with the fierce competition, choices have narrowed.

> *A cover letter is very often the first impression the employer has of you. If you don't "wow" them with your letter, but they still bring you in for an interview, you might still need to overcome the stigma that you are either lacking in originality, writing skills or creativity.*

How do you overcome obstacles such as these? The fact that a law firm receives an overwhelming volume of applicants is certainly not within your control. But you do have a weapon—you **can** stand out from the crowd.

The traditional advice you've heard before, like "always have a well written resume" and "don't worry, your outstanding qualifications should see you through" isn't good enough. Almost everyone today has a well-written resume and outstanding qualifications.

What potential employers **don't** necessarily see—because this isn't presented well by candidates—is the means to **differentiate** those qualifications over and above other outstanding candidates. What you must produce are resumes and accoutrements to the resume (cover letters, "kudos" letters, writ-

19

ing samples, etc.) that differ from the norm. You need to make the employer sit up and take notice. After all, just how many boring cover letters (like the one below) can one employer read?

October 27, 1992

Dear Prospective Employer:

Enclosed please find my resume in response to your ad in the *Daily BoomTown Legal Journal* for a senior paralegal with computer experience.

I am a litigation paralegal with six years' experience. I received my paralegal certificate from the Legal Assistant Institute and my B.A. degree from Collegetown University. I am looking for a position that offers new challenges for a senior paralegal such as myself. I am diligent, hard-working and a team player.

I will give you a ring next week so that we may set up an interview. I look forward to meeting with you soon.

Sincerely,

Karen L. Smith

If the employer hasn't already dozed off during the second paragraph, your letter just have arrived early in the resume-reviewing process. If the employer has only started recruiting and hasn't already read hundreds of letters just like yours, your submission might be put in the "to be followed up" pile.

Cover letters are **critical**. They represent not just a sample of your writing style, but can provide very clear information about your ability to communicate with attorneys, clients and colleagues. A cover letter is very often the first impression the employer has of you. If you don't "wow" them with your letter, but they still bring you in for an interview, you might still need to overcome the stigma that you are either lacking in originality, writing skills or creativity. So far, your cover letter has provided no indication that you are distinctly superior to the next candidate in skills or enthusiasm for the career.

Many resume writing books will tell you how important it is to keep your cover letter brief. While this is certainly true, many people mistake "brief" for "unoriginal." The sample letter above presents nothing inspiring about this paralegal's background or, more importantly, her attitude about herself or why she is seeking another position. No information about her accomplishments, eagerness to meet with the firm's representatives, knowledge about matters the firm has handled or even ability to write original compositions is provided.

Yet employers see this same letter over and over again. Paralegals should not be reticent about their accomplishments. Modesty is **not** an admirable component of a job search.

With the need to catch attention, and provide real information on why an employer should pick your letter and resume out from hundreds of others, let's rewrite Karen's cover letter. Remember, we want to highlight her actual experience and skills, while at the same time cultivating the enthusiasm she needs from the prospective employer:

October 27, 1992

Dear Ms. Jones:

With the increasing trend toward computerizing legal services, I am sure that an individual with analytical skills, fluency in computerized litigation support, along with a practical business management perspective, would be an asset to your law firm.

I have spent my entire professional career as a problem solver for law firms. As a senior legal assistant, I specialize in computerized litigation support for a medical malpractice firm in Chicago. Because of this experience, I have developed working relationships with influential clients and legal vendors. I am now ready to transfer my skills to a firm such as yours that is interested in strengthening its emphasis in computerized litigation support services.

I have developed the ability to see what needs to be done in any assignment, mapping out a strategy for accomplishing these goals and then following through. I have implemented proven techniques to accomplish projects more efficiently. A few examples of those projects are:

* Reorganized and computerized the process finding crucial information for the Doe Commission;

* Designed and implemented databases for a $6 million case;

* Established and implemented training programs for support teams to organize over 100,000 documents.

I possess a B.A. degree and have completed post-graduate work at the Legal Assistant Institute. I am also an adjunct professor at the Paralegal Studies University.

I look forward to discussing the opportunity of contributing to the important work of your firm. I will give you a call early next week to determine when we may meet for an exploratory discussion.

Sincerely,

Karen L. Smith

I don't know about you, but I certainly would call this candidate. This letter has sophistication, it reflects confidence and provides examples of the writer's ability. Prospective employers receiving this kind of letter would most likely schedule an interview, just because the cover letter provides more impressive information. And, of course, the interview is what you need in order to **really** sell yourself.

Job search candidates also fail to show originality—and thus distinguish themselves from the average interviewee—in the use of letters of recommendation. Most recommendations follow a tried and true, but definitely time-worn, pattern:

October 27, 1992

To whom it may concern:

Jane R. Holmes was with our firm as a litigation paralegal for six years. We hired her right out of paralegal school. We found her to be a loyal, diligent, hard-working individual whose responsibilities grew over the years.

It is with great sadness that we acknowledge Jane's desire to move on. We will miss her terribly and give her the highest recommendation possible.

Sincerely,

Managing Partner

When I receive these kinds of letters, I'm never sure if Jane was the family puppy or a family member who has passed on.

With all the laws governing the employment relationship, many employers are reluctant to put anything about an employee in writing, even if it is praiseworthy. As a result, letters of recommendation can be both hard to get and actually suspect, because they may be written about someone who was terminated. They no longer have the power they once had because most employers now prefer "underground networking": the technique of soliciting "off the record" comments from past employers of potential employees.

Instead of a letter of recommendation (or in addition to it), use a "kudos" letter. These are "brag" letters someone else has written about you. They can be used both as a letter of recommendation and as an addition to your resume. If you have done a great job on a project, ask your department manager or the supervising attorney to write a letter thanking you for a job well done. Often, because of their heavy schedules, attorneys will ask you to write the letter for their signature. When this happens, you can tailor the letter to match the job skills you want to highlight and use most in your next position. Keep in mind that you can also obtain kudos letters from volunteer work. Ask the person in charge of the effort or the volunteer organizer to write a kudos letter for you.

Kudos letters are ageless, and the more you have, the better. When you have a number in your collection, you can pick and choose the ones that really meet your job hunting needs. Start collecting kudos letters now, **before** you start looking for another job.

Keep the letter short and sweet. Most employers don't have the time to read everyone's long and glowing reports. Also, if the letter goes on and on, you run the risk of making the letter less believable.

October 27, 1992

Dear Jane:

I would like to thank you for a "job well done" on the *Acme* case. Without your superb organizational abilities and attention to detail, we would never have found the "smoking gun" that made our case. Your diligence and hard work really paid off.

It is a pleasure to write this letter; I wish you luck and success in whatever you do. I will highly recommend your services to other attorneys in the firm. You're really the best.

Sincerely,

3rd Year Associate Attorney

Don't be shy in asking for this kind of letter when you receive compliments about your work performance from supervisors. Sometimes, in response, someone will ask: "Why? Are you looking for a new position?" You can simply say something like "attorneys have short memories" and you would like the letter for your personnel file or your next performance review. This response is quite legitimate—most reviewers only remember the performance in the past two to three months.

Another great accoutrement to your resume is a "knock their socks off" writing sample. While legal writing samples are often required, many law firm employers are also interested in employees with good business writing skills. Memos, letters, committee reports, status reports, deal memos and request for proposals may all be appropriate for this purpose. Use published articles, even those published in paralegal newsletters, to further establish your writing credibility.

Be sure, however, whether you are using legal writing samples or business samples that **all** confidential information is **redacted**. This includes removing **all** names, parties and numbers of cases, places, dates, any internal law firm information and all references to the specific matter or parties involved. It is also a good idea to have your firm's permission to use the sample. Because you should not, under any circumstances, violate client confidentiality, many employers first look to see if you have removed all confidential information. If not, you have flunked the test, and they won't even bother to read your writing sample.

On the other hand, if your writing sample is an exercise from school, leave the instructor's comments on the sample. Comments like "Good effort with difficult subject" or "Great job" only serve to enhance the B+ you received, not detract from it.

Be sure to keep your writing sample **brief**. Believe me, no one is going to wade through a 32-page treatise, no matter how good you think it is.

The impression you make during your job search—both good **and** bad—is all in the **packaging**. In today's job market, experience, educational background and ability to communicate is a given. However, if you cannot present your "sales" materials in an impressive package, the employer (or "consumer") is not going to be so anxious to "buy" what you're selling. To be successful, your efforts must go beyond the traditionally accepted level.

Whether you're a trailblazer who's clearing the path, or the engineer who is paving the road, you're not going to get a chance to "prove yourself on the job" if you can't get the job. So start now and go that extra mile. Good hunting!

In the Name of the Mother, the Father, and the Holy Partner: Looking for a "Family" Atmosphere at Work

magine a utopia of next-to-no problems, a fantasy land of raises and bonuses, a dreamscape of rising job prospects and new opportunities, a plethora of coworkers who understand and fully support your every career move.

Sound like a Hollywood production of an Andy Hardy movie? Or is this the kind of work place you envision when you hear a potential employer say, "We're just like a family here." Both employers and employees frequently describe their perfect working atmosphere in these terms.

Curious isn't it? Most people I know are not particularly interested in recreating their childhood or current family situation in the work place. This is true even for people whose present family scene is sensational. After all, most families—even the healthiest ones—harbor some well-kept secrets.

Those work places emphasizing a family atmosphere may actually have one. There may be parental figures: the mother, the father, even a grandparent. Coworkers may rival for attention. Sibling rivalry may exist. You may find yourself "grounded" for a length of time as punishment for a violation of the house rules. (Translation: Not the right attitude, and no raise.) You may be ostracized by not receiving choice assignments. You may get the message when you screw up: wait until your review. (Translation: Wait until your father gets home.)

So, while some people look for a "family" atmosphere at work, others run for the hills. Regardless of your own response, one thing is clear. No matter where you work, you are bound to create close and (hopefully) comfortable relationships with many of your coworkers.

Looking for a "Family" Atmosphere at Work

Why is it that some prefer to infuse business with family values and conditions? Are these people really looking for a family in their job environments?

When workers describe a family atmosphere they are generally talking about fun, togetherness, closeness, trust, and friendships. The phrase "family atmosphere" generally applies to a small firm or small business work place. The larger the business, the less likely you will hear the work place described as family. The president of a $500 million corporation would be hard pressed to name every employee in her domain. Employees of mega-firms and huge corporations very seldom describe their work environment as family, although many times individual departments may qualify.

Understanding the typical hierarchy of the work place explains why some confuse family with the work place. There are pecking orders and authority figures. There are close relationships and the proverbial bonding. However, there are major differences between the family unit and the work place.

All families contain common elements. There is an authority figure, usually a father or mother, or both. There are children and sometimes siblings. You'll find varied pecking orders. Each family member makes certain contributions to the family, although not equally, depending on each person's age.

Of course, you're simply handed your family. You cannot choose your family members or the family's pecking order. You also cannot simply choose to occupy a position of power and authority in a family.

It is only when you grow up, and move OUT OF THE HOUSE, that you become equal to the parental authority figures. Eventually, even the baby of the family gains equal input. For this to happen, the dynamics of the family must change: children must grow up and move out. Until that time, there is an unequal distribution of power and contribution.

Work is not Family; Family is not Work

Major differences between work and family do exist. Your family is your family for life. Whether you want them or not. With very few exceptions (that little boy in Florida), no one divorces their parents. This is not the case with a job, even if you think "I'll be here forever."

On the other hand, you choose your work environment. You can move up a career ladder, thus changing the pecking order. Each worker can contribute equally to the common goal of the firm. While each work place utilizes authority figures, the particular person in authority may not be in that position forever. And you may not have to leave the environment in order to become an authority figure with equal status.

The reality of the work environment also requires that you NOT share all of your innermost thoughts. You cannot show your worst moods or share your personal problems. It is not okay to burst into tears in your office over the latest drama in your love life.

A recent article in *Working Woman* magazine asked the question, "Which of these relationships can you not have with your boss: helper, follower, colleague, pal, equal, close friend?" The answer, of course, is that you cannot have an equal relationship with your boss. The company's organizational chart clearly says you're not equal.

Sometimes, women have a particularly hard time understanding that they cannot be their boss's equal. Some women translate the leaps of faith that are inherent in a friendship to the work place. Mixing the personal with the professional will almost certainly be difficult.

Experts say that female friendships tend to have a tighter emotional weave than male friendships. A woman is more likely to share information about herself, along with her vulnerabilities. This is very much like the atmosphere at home where you can be yourself, whether you're on top of the world or falling apart.

Because men's cultural experiences while growing up involve hierarchical structures, they may have a less difficult time trying to accommodate friendships within the professional pyramid. This is partially due to an emphasis on team sports. If you play sports, you always know who the captain is. He may be your best pal, someone you share a beer with after the game, but everyone knows he's the one who calls the shots.

Women have more often been encouraged to handle things on a one-on-one basis. Fortunately, young girls today are taught differently.

A "Family" Atmosphere is not Always Healthy

According to Mark Gorkin, a Washington D.C. psychologist and corporate therapist in Washington D.C., you should acknowledge the differences between healthy families and dysfunctional ones. Gorkin believes that when a company or firm looks to recreate a family rather than a team, what usually gets recreated is a *dysfunctional* family unit.

Those work places emphasizing a family atmosphere may actually have one. There may be parental figures: the mother, the father, even a grandparent. Coworkers may rival for attention. Sibling rivalry may exist. You may find yourself "grounded" for a length of time as punishment for a violation of the house rules. (Translation: Not the right attitude, and no raise.) Or, you may be ostracized by not receiving choice assignments. Further, you may get the message when you screw up: wait until your review. (Translation: Wait until your father gets home.)

One of the primary causes cited for job change is personality conflict. While many employees can live with some kind of inadequacy or imperfection in their jobs, most cannot live with the emotional distress caused by personality conflict. Yet, many people experience the same disappointment time and time again. They don't like the way that they are treated. Consequently, they may blame the entire field with such edicts as "paralegals are always treated poorly."

What they may be doing is recreating their family scene in the work place and are actually comfortable with the discomfort because it feels so familiar. Employees experiencing personality conflicts originally came to the job scene each time with different expectations. This time, you tell yourself, things will be different.

Being in a family atmosphere isn't necessarily a bad thing. But is it really the atmosphere you are after? Or are you seeking what the "fantasy family" represents: nurturing, coddling, support, fun, picnics, friendships, strong ties, lifetime commitments, chicken soup?

Familiarity lulls employees into a false sense of security. Intimacy, discussions about one's personal business, the feeling that your coworkers understand the total you can set unrealistic expectations. Your supervisors become your best friends. As a result, the lines are now blurred between employee and family member. In a dysfunctional family atmosphere, boundaries are not set and employees end up in unproductive and unpleasant work situations.

What are You Really Looking for?

Recently, I had a very interesting conversation with Dona Tanaka, a senior legal assistant with American Golf Corporation. Our discussion led Dona to reassess her priorities in the work environment. Tanaka first emphasized that a family atmosphere was important to her, saying "I like to feel that I am contributing equally to the company."

I asked Dona if she was looking for a mother or father figure or a hierarchical situation. "Do you want someone to provide for you?" I asked. "No," she replied, "I want my contributions recognized." When I asked whether this would look more like a team, she said yes, adding:

> I would rather feel that I am part of the team moving in the same direction as a family. When I say family, what I think I am asking for is someone who will support my career—be fun to work with. But upon reflection, I guess what I'm really asking for is a good working team.

Dr. Patricia Wisne, a Los Angeles based psychologist, offers this theory: "Just as we learn to speak English rather than some other language, we learn an emotional language." Wisne claims people will gravitate toward an environment with which they are familiar:

> If you grew up in a family where there was only one way to think or there was one dominating figure, you may gravitate toward that same type of atmosphere in business. Unless you become aware of your pattern of expectations, you will keep recreating the same scene, whether you intend to or not. For example, you may surround yourself with employees or employers who refuse to hear you or who are rigidly controlling. You may end up being supervised by a bully. Most people ordinarily activate the emotional climate they're familiar with. It's a natural response to the "recognition" factor.

This explains why many firms and companies appear to hire certain "types" of employees: cheerleaders, tough guys, lady-like matrons, sales experts or warriors. If a firm is considered liberal or conservative, this says something about what kinds of people you'll typically find working there. Underneath the surface of most organizations, you will most likely find one or two dominating themes.

Choosing a "Family" or "Team" Environment

Contrast the "family" atmosphere with a work environment based more on a "teamwork" approach. In a teamwork environment, the leader functions more like a coach. No one person is solely responsible for the success of the team. (Compare this with a parental figure, who tell the children what to do, and how to do it.) Workers are not punished for bad behavior. Instead, they are coached into good performances.

- each member of the team contributes equally;
- a team leader is the authority figure, not an autocrat;
- leadership positions can change to any member of the team;
- there is no "sibling rivalry," or efforts by others to attract attention from above;
- everyone works together for the common good of the company;
- each member of the team is recognized for his or her efforts and judged independently;
- members of the team are equal and acknowledge the team leader.

The only way to break the cycle of joining the dysfunctional family work place, according to Wisne, is to become aware of what constitutes positive emotional language. For example, some people are taught that criticizing is a way to handle conflict. "When someone criticizes or bullies you, and bullying is all you know," she says, "you're not going to recognize something different. You have to learn a whole new emotional language: body language, thoughts, and words."

When you hear someone describe a work place as a family atmosphere, a warning flag should go up. First, ask whether it's a family that you're after. Or are you really seeking a professional team environment. Always dig deeper:

- Is there clear communication? Are employees heard?

- Where are the employees in the pecking order? Can that change?

- Are there parental figures here or team leaders?

- Would you be recreating my childhood scene?

- Will you be expected to "share all" and if not, will you be ostracized for not playing the game properly?

- Will you be coached to improve performance or punished?

- What kind of "family" is involved here? Healthy or dysfunctional?

Learn to surround yourself with a group of people who will contribute to the common goal. Remember, you do have the power to create a happy, healthy work environment around you. And you *don't* have to take out the trash.

[1]   "Power Interviewing in the '90s," was first published in the May/June 1994 issue of LEGAL ASSISTANT TODAY.

[2]   Liz Elliot is currently an attorney placement coordinator for the Quorum/Estrin Group in Los Angeles.

[3]   "47 Ways to Find a New Paralegal Job," was first published in the September/October 1993 issue of LEGAL ASSISTANT TODAY.

[4]   "Standing Out From the Competition," was first published in the January/February 1993 issue of LEGAL ASSISTANT TODAY.

[5]   "In the Name of the Mother, the Father, and the Holy Partner: Looking for a "Family" Atmosphere at Work," was first published in the July/August 1994 issue of LEGAL ASSISTANT TODAY.

P a r t

2

The times they are a-changin'. And so is the paralegal field, at a rapid pace. Whether you're just beginning in the profession or you're a seasoned professional planning to make a change, it's important to know what firms expect and to know what opportunities exists for you.

Evolution of the Paralegal Profession

It's helpful to pinpoint role models early in the career. Find out who the success stories are and how they got there. You may find new avenues available to you. How they evolved may give you clues as to what to expect as you embark down the road of your profession.

In Search
of
Role Models

I have never heard anyone say that what they wanted to be most when they grew up was a paralegal. While the field didn't really exist when I was a child, we did have all kinds of lawyers who served as role models. Every Monday night we could say hello to Perry Mason and his right-hand person, Della Street; Robert Kennedy was the attorney general; and there was F. Lee Bailey, the famous criminal attorney.

In later years, when we were making career decisions that were supposed to last an entire lifetime, we had Sandra Day O'Connor, Alan Dershowitz and Archie Bunker. There were rumblings of something called a "paralegal," but no one at that time seemed to have a ready definition as to what that was.

Once, there was a glimmer of public acknowledgment: A TV series called Hill Street Blues *created a character named "Hector," a convicted felon turned paralegal. At last, some recognition of the field. But the series wrote him out by getting him killed in a gang fight. (Hmm, not exactly representative of most of the other paralegals I had ever met.)*

Somehow, after trying out other careers, I landed in this profession. It was a brand new field, it had a professional ring to it and I didn't have to go to law school to be one. I was so elated, I thought someday I would make partner.

The profession caught on quickly. Positions developed as firms and legal departments found they couldn't practice law without paralegals. Studies showed that it was the fastest growing profession, etc. But still, there was little public knowledge as to who we were.

The Media Image

I began to notice that television was paying a lot of attention to other "helping professions." Shows were centered around nurses, paramedics, and teachers. Even male housekeepers like Tony Micelli were heroes. The movies offered us secretaries like the ones in *Nine to Five* and *Working Girl.* (O.K., so *we* knew that a couple of laws were broken when the secretaries tied up the boss in *Nine to Five* and a few securities violations were committed in *Working Girl.*)

Once, there was a glimmer of public acknowledgment: A TV series called *Hill Street Blues* created a character named "Hector," a convicted felon turned paralegal. At last, some recognition of the field. But the series wrote him out by getting him killed in a gang fight. (Hmm, not exactly representative of most of the other paralegals I had ever met.)

So we continued on in a field that basically had yet to develop a career path, had no real promotions, and somewhat vague job descriptions. Even the name of the position was in question: legal assistant or paralegal?

But I didn't much care about all of that. I was loving every minute of this profession. I jumped from litigation paralegal to paralegal administrator to owning my own paralegal business. New fields, after all, take time to develop, and surely we would receive public recognition and develop real-life role models sometime soon.

A few years ago, I attended a Los Angeles Paralegal Association seminar where the technical advisor, a real lawyer, to the TV series *L.A. Law* was speaking. During the question and answer period, a paralegal raised her hand and asked why in this day and age the show did not have a role for a paralegal. In fact, it appeared to her that the show didn't even mention the position.

Well, it seemed that the technical advisor was of the opinion that paralegals didn't have interesting positions and, to add insult to injury, the producers felt it wasn't possible to build a love story around a paralegal. A couple of seasons later, the series had a minor story line involving a law clerk/paralegal who had this tiny drug problem.

About a year later, my colleague, Molly Burns, and I attended the ALA conference in Toronto. One of the vendors had hired an actor who played a senior partner on *L.A. Law* to hand out autographs.

Molly and I stood in line patiently waiting for our turn. When we reached him, he asked us where we would like his signature. "Oh, thanks anyway," we told him, "but what we really want is for you to take a message back to your producers to put paralegals in your show."

We went on to tell him the role paralegals play, that there are more than 80,000 out there and how it would add reality and credibility to the show. Actually, he was a very nice person with a great sense of humor. He took us seriously and told us the reason for omitting a full-time role for a paralegal was it wasn't an interesting position and the writers couldn't build a love story. What, did these guys rehearse this?

The Exciting Realities

Not have interesting lives? Can't build a love story? Obviously, these guys weren't clear on the concept. I recalled working on a case with customs officials, snooping around newly-arrived 747s from overseas looking for contraband. I recalled other paralegals, those who were:

- working with political refugees, finding hiding places for them while working with the government to get status in this country;
- assisting day and night on discrimination cases that would make *L.A. Law* stories look like a mild case of indigestion;
- involved in toxic waste cases that LIFE magazine would find too gruesome to photograph;
- involved with billion dollar takeovers that made the film *Wall Street* look tame;
- working on the infamous Michael Milken case;
- tracking the Marcos fortune;
- defending a mass murderer;
- living overseas in England, Malaysia, Hong Kong, France, Switzerland, and Puerto Rico on exciting cases;
- involved in product liability cases that changed laws; and,
- risking everything they owned, and even imprisonment, to deliver low-cost legal services directly to the public.

The Public Needs to Know

Lately, with all the new lawyer shows, I have been hearing bit mentions of paralegals. *The Trials of Rosie O'Neill* once referenced the position with something like "having the paralegals research it." But no real roles center around a day in the life of a paralegal. It is true, however, that most of the TV and movie stars portraying lawyers seem to do a lot more hands-on factual investigation than most lawyers I know.

I don't know where the stars get time to draft any pleadings, being at the crime scene so many times. And it's amazing what with all the chitchat that I haven't heard any of their supervisors complaining that billables are down.

It's important to be included in these shows because it demonstrates the respectability of the profession. Nurses are portrayed as people really in touch with what's going on. They are not portrayed as under the doctor's thumb. Rather, they are shown to be independent, strong people with colorful, interesting lives.

Even though we know the stories that the television and film media give us are generally hype, the public has come away with a strong image of that profession through positive reinforcement. After all, since one of the foremost reasons a paralegal is in a firm is to save clients' fees, it seems the public would want to be fully aware that this position even exists.

Why Don't We "Promote" Ourselves?

While I was thumbing through a few of the newsletters and publications geared toward legal assistants, I noticed that there was little mention, if any, of *real* role models in any of the publications. Sure, there were lots of columns and articles (about changes in the law, seminars to attend, who moved where, and how to use the latest software program), but nothing that spoke to the audience about the field's own heroes.

I researched further into in-house newsletters and read about attorneys who won certain cases, landed important clients, and gave noteworthy speeches, but none of the in-house organs spoke to its audience about contributions by legal assistants.

I attended a few seminars for paralegals and heard about significant cases but interestingly enough, *none* of the seminar leaders spoke to the audience about the contribution from the legal assistants! I wanted to know what the legal assistants did, what evidence they uncovered, what methods and techniques they used, and what happened.

I was searching for role models. I quickly realized that it is possible that paralegals hesitate in creating their own role models. It is small wonder that the public hears very little about the actual role of the paralegal. It's almost as though a certain modesty exists within the field. Is it because attorneys get all the credit? Are we confusing "supporting role" with "invisible role?"

Because the rise to stardom and seniority in this field is faster than most (in many firms you are considered a senior by having only five years in the field), the turnover rate is high. Litigation paralegals have been known to burn out within one to three years. Paralegals who are disappointed with lack of advancement and repetition leave the field. Yet, there are thousands of paralegals who have fascinating, exciting careers.

Building Role Models

Paralegals need to know about other paralegals. Describing a position's job duties isn't nearly as colorful and "real" as hearing about the paralegal who does it. This means that in our newsletters, magazines, and seminars we need to point to role models. We need to not get discouraged with the entire field simply because one job that we may presently hold is uneventful or unexciting.

Paralegals need to know what other paralegals are doing. Where are the highest paid paralegals and what do they do? Who are the paralegals sent to work in a foreign country? How was it to work on a case where you were followed by the press? What was it like to work on the biggest movie deal of the decade?

Paralegals need to know that there is much more to this career than number stamping and summarizing documents. There are paralegals in the field right now working in our dream jobs.

Many paralegals leave the field in search of exciting opportunities that exist right here. But because there seems to be little field recognition and a great deal of downplaying the role, a stereotyped version of the field can exist in the paralegal's own mind.

Shatter the myth. Talk about your role models in association meetings, seminars, and newsletters. Write to this magazine and tell them about interesting and exciting positions. If you are wondering whether someone qualifies as a role model, ask yourself these questions before allowing yourself to be influenced:

1. What is this person teaching you about your field?
2. What is this person teaching you about yourself and your capabilities?
3. Why do you feel good when you are around your role model?
4. What are your role model's characteristics and traits?
5. What is this person's significant contribution to the field?
6. Why is this person's background significant to you?
7. Do you admire this person from afar or do you have a mentor relationship?
8. What makes this person stand out from the crowd?
9. Why is it important to you what this person says and does?
10. Is there a significant event involving this person that stands out in your mind?

We can perpetuate our own myth of an uninteresting career. However, facts point otherwise. As a group we need to promote ourselves to ourselves, highlighting existing role models and staying enthused about a very rewarding career. After we establish our role models, perhaps then the profession will gain more recognition and acceptance through media such as TV and movies. Although, I don't know how to answer the question of interesting love lives. I think I'll leave that to the producers.

What to Expect in Your First Ten Years as a Legal Assistant

omehow, when you are in paralegal school, someone forgets to tell you about real life as a legal assistant. Oh sure, they bring in the typical "real life" working paralegal on career day, who tells you all about "a day in the life." and it all sounds so very glamorous. Who wouldn't want to go to trial, meet with clients, travel with attorneys and be a real part of the legal team? Armed with this "inside" information, you breeze through the interview for your first position, not listening too closely as the interviewer describes your duties. You are wonderfully optimistic and refreshingly positive.

This situation is a little like your first kiss. You spend months daydreaming about what it is going to feel like, certain that the boy (or girl) will fall instantly in love with you, knowing that bells will ring and fireworks explode. And then you discover that the kiss was a little wetter than you planned, your braces bumped together and you were not entirely sure whether you actually did it right.

 You're given a new office. One of the partners comes in and starts counting ceiling tiles (a time-honored way of judging the all-important size of the office). You then lose your new office.

Ten years is considered a long time in this field. A senior partner used to tell me that being a legal assistant builds character. I often wondered if I could do with a little *less* character.

At some point, the question crosses everyone's mind as to whether they've made the right choice. This is due, in part, to the peaks and valleys, debits and credits of the career. Don't panic. The legal assistant career does offer a certain exciting progression that almost everyone experiences. Walk with us down the paralegal career path and we'll show you what we mean.

Year One: You find yourself Bates stamping, summarizing depositions and checking closing binders. One of your most challenging assignments is to put these tiny little tabs on documents. You wonder if the firm hired you for your brains, your potential or your skill with an Exacto knife.

No one told you that when you summarized a deposition, you had to talk about the exhibits too. After all, they were only some handwritten notes and didn't seem very relevant. Even the defendant said so.

You're scared of every attorney who comes toward you. You start thinking of your day and your life in terms of tenths of an hour. You find yourself telling the kids that they have exactly .6 of an hour to get home. You had no idea that the firm's required 1800 hours didn't include lunches, vacations or sick days. And it would have been really nice if someone had taken the time to explain that you aren't going to get part of the $75.00 an hour the firm charges the client for your work.

You find out that your definition of "private office" and the firm's vastly differ. Before taking this job, you were unaware that four 6 x 9 movable felt "walls" could be called an office.

Year Two: You finally learn that you **can** delegate some tasks to your secretary. Associates are looking less scary and the partners no longer grunt at you in the hallways—they actually nod hello. The firm's power structure inexplicably begins to make some sense to you.

However, you realize you probably won't get that corner window office you've been dreaming of. On the other hand, you are actually introduced to a real live client who calls you on a regular basis. Every day, in fact. You realize there was a reason (beyond your keen intelligence) that you were introduced to this person.

You learn that the day you wear your new Chanel suit--the **white** one with the gold buttons--is the day you are sent to a client's warehouse for the firm's largest document production, ever. Forty boxes have to be stamped, in **red**, with the legend "Sealed Under Protective Order." And, the stamp must be re-inked every half hour.

Year Three: You learn not to bill time for locating lost documents, even though it means giving up close to 100 or more billable hours per year. And, on your time sheets you now call Bates stamping "source coding." Someone actually helps you move boxes.

Your mother **still** thinks you're in this career to marry an attorney. You're just happy to hear a rumor that other people actually have social lives.

You're given a new office. One of the partners comes in and starts counting ceiling tiles (a time-honored way of judging the all-important size of the office). You then lose your new office.

You are asked to interview an entry-level legal assistant. This person tells you about the "real life" paralegal she met in paralegal school, and she's wonderfully optimistic and refreshingly positive. She then asks for more money than you made all of last year. You change jobs.

Year Four: The attorneys are still mostly intimidating, but you actually call an associate or two by their first names. Two-day weekends are now a mere memory. You convince the administrator you have to have a computer on your desk. You are designated the expert. You train attorneys, paralegals, and staff. You spend an entire weekend recreating the database you lost.

Your article on cite checking is published and suddenly, you've become the expert. Now, you can't find your desk, although it may still be there, somewhere under 20 feet of briefs.

You see glimmers of working on a "team" with attorneys one of these days. You get to travel on matters with attorneys. Yes, the attorneys are seated in first class and you're relegated to steerage. They do, however, wave to you as the cabin attendant pours them another glass of champagne.

Year Five: You are seriously considering therapy. Stress management classes start looking very appealing. You finally figure out why they call first year associates "baby attorneys." Because of all your hard work (not to mention "character"), you are starting to be considered a senior legal assistant. You have formed alliances with some key partners, or at least they know your name. When you fleetingly consider becoming a lawyer yourself, your mentor does you a big favor, and hands you an article titled, "Mama, Don't Send Your Kids to Law School."

Your work doesn't automatically go to the bottom of your secretary's work pile anymore. The firm seems to be hiring attorneys who are looking a little younger. And the summer clerk extravaganza is definitely losing its luster. In fact, you dread the month of June and can't recall why, in the past, you were so insulted that you weren't invited to all the parties.

Year Six: You are asked to speak at the firm's retreat, and this year, the firm doesn't make you "double up" with six other paralegals. You even get to bring a significant other. You find out he left last year.

You might be asked to work on firm committees, although you don't understand why you are the one expected to take the minutes. In your last telephone call to your mother, she tells you that your cousin Minnie is engaged to a lawyer. The firm assigns you your very own paralegal assistant or case clerk. You now get introduced to clients on a regular basis. Your office is no longer in the basement and someone Bates stamps for you. You're asked to assist at trial on a regular basis. As a result, you earn the distinction of getting abused in front of the Judge, the Jury and everyone, instead of just in the privacy of the firm.

Year Seven: You are now the most senior legal assistant in the entire firm. If you were an associate you'd be up for partner this year. Alas, there is no partnership or even career track for legal assistants in most firms.

Although you do get to act as if you are the paralegal manager, the firm doesn't make it official with a tittle or even any authority. Your billable hour requirements stay the same, but you're expected to increase your administrative time 300 to 500 hours per year. You give up lunches, dating, banking, dentists, haircuts and most bathroom privileges.

Year Eight: You realize the firm needs a full-time legal assistant manager and a bona fide, structured paralegal program. You start campaigning for change. You join the Legal Assistant Management Association (LAMA) and commiserate with other paralegal managers.

You're now responsible for profit margins, and you had **no idea** the firm could make that much money from paralegals. You rethink your last salary increase. You get to deal with attorneys who either can't work with paralegals or work them to death.

Attorneys are still getting younger. In fact, they now even sport pimples. You, on the other hand, just bought a new moisturizer that promises a youthful, dewy complexion. You're also saving your bonus for a down payment on liposuction.

Year Nine: After a lengthy campaign (you really know how to work the committees to get what you want), you're named the official Legal Assistant Manager. And, at last, there is an official paralegal program.

Of course, now's the time that all your experienced people quit. The firm doesn't want to pay decent salaries, they increase the minimum billable hours requirement, bonuses go down and recruiting is hell. In your last telephone call to your mother, she tells you she's glad you're doing so well in this career —married life isn't everything. You now call senior partners by their first name—and they call yours back—usually very loudly. You start thinking about "life after the law firm."

Year Ten: You've arrived. Your paralegal program is working, you've developed a great staff, and you can pick and choose your own assignments. You have a decent office, with a decorating budget, no less. And, you've finally been given a parking spot **in** the building.

You're a frequent guest speaker at important seminars. Your articles are published regularly. The firm will do anything to make sure you're a happy camper. They implement your ideas. They never question your hires. They make sure your bonus is terrific and your raises outstanding.

You have a great reputation. Associates come to you to find out how things "really" get done. You choose which attorneys you want to work with, and you can easily avoid those you don't. You discover what vacations mean (and have even found another significant other).

Then, one day, the firm's most senior name partner calls you into his office. You think he's going to ask about those management reports that are still sitting on your desk, waiting to be finalized. But instead he asks you to "Please put these little tabs on these documents, and oh, if you have an extra minute, summarize this deposition and Bates stamp these exhibits."

"No problem," you reply. And you promptly introduce this name partner to your best first-year paralegal, the one with the brightest rising star. Because after all, you're now responsible for the management and profit margin of the entire paralegal department, and you recognize some attorneys will **always** need nudging when it comes to the proper use of legal assistants.

The Contemporary Temporary

The Way Things Used to Be

It's funny how attitudes change. It used to be that temporary employees were often looked at as "radicals." They were certainly tagged with the "job hopper" label.

Remember the movie "The Temp?" That certainly was not anyone you would take seriously. People working as "permanent temporaries" were enigmas. After all, why on earth would anyone *not* want to settle in at a regular job somewhere?

In the '90s environment, temping in America has changed the face of the work force. Traditionally, our parents, our parents' parents, and their parents took a job and stayed with that company for as many years as was humanly possible.

 This arena of the paralegal field can be lucrative, stimulating, fun, and not at all boring. It all depends on how you choose to drive your career. It is no longer considered a detriment to your career (or a problem with your resume), to have worked as a temporary employee.

And not so very many years ago, lawyers also signed on with firms for the duration of their careers. Changing firms—for *any* reason—was practically taboo. (Actually, bouncing around on any level—attorney, paralegal, or legal secretary—was suspect.)

People bought houses and lived in them for their entire marriages. They shopped at the same stores, banked at the same banks, stayed with the same hairdresser, and definitely didn't leave their spouse.

Changes in Attitudes

Then, along came television, jet planes and computers. Attention spans began to shorten. As the years went on, the criteria for how you were judged professionally began to change. Suddenly, if you were in a job for more than 10 years, you were "not a risk taker" or worse, you were "unmotivated." This wasn't your father's world of employment—where staying in the same job was considered a *virtue*—anymore.

Noticeable climbs up the ladder began to be more important. Fast-trackers were making names for themselves. How much you made, who you worked for, the model car you drove, and the designer clothes you wore took on monumental significance. The age of decadence was upon us.

The '90s have brought a different value system. Buzzwords such as "alternative careers" and "lifestyles" took on real meaning. To rectify and excuse the colossal '80s, "downsizing" (and the politically correct "rightsizing") terminology surfaced. Employees no longer made commitments to their firms for life, neither did the employers.

Paternity leaves and househusbands were in. Family leave policies took hold. Time and cost saving mechanisms came into play even in the legal world:

* fast-track litigation,
* alternative dispute resolution,
* value billing, and
* "blended" rates.

With the recession in full swing, budgets were slashed, resulting in the layoffs of hundreds of associates, paralegals, and sometimes even entire departments.

Temping in the '90s

Enter the '90s temp: hero in a crisis-driven environment and winner of the "skirt around the budget" award.

According to the National Association of Temporary Services, the temporary help industry fills more than 1.3 million jobs daily. In 1992, temporary help generated an annual payroll in excess of $16.7 billion, and revenues of nearly $25 billion. Approximately 46.6% of all temps went to work as office/clerical employees, 10.2% worked in technical fields (computer programmers, engineers, etc.), and 5.3% worked in professional roles (accountants, doctors, lawyers, paralegals, middle and senior management). Studies show that between 90% and 100% of U.S. companies use temporary help.

The NATS survey further found that:

* approximately 80% of temporary employees choose this route to earn additional income;
* 67% reported they gained new skills working as temps, and

- a whopping 54% were asked to continue working in a full-time capacity by the companies to which they were assigned.

In the legal world, temping also gives you excellent avenues for:

- looking for a permanent position;
- reentering the work force;
- investigating the type of firm or corporation that appeals to you;
- obtaining important experience for entry into the field;
- building either new skills or further developing the skills you already have;
- meeting a variety of interesting people; or
- just to experience more freedom in when you want to work and with whom you want to work.

Law Firms and Temping

Law firms and in-house legal departments have been using paralegal temps since at least the early '80s, and the need for temp legal assistants continues. "[For employers today,] it's the only way to go," states T. J. Pendergrass, manager of litigation support for the Northrop Corporate Law Department in Los Angeles.

This arena of the paralegal field can be lucrative, stimulating, fun, and not at all boring. It all depends on how you choose to drive your career. It is no longer considered a detriment to your career (or a problem with your resume), to have worked as a temporary employee.

Jeanine McKeown, paralegal coordinator for Gibson, Dunn & Crutcher, can't say enough good things about temporary paralegals. "They help the in-house paralegal tremendously. I'm an avid supporter because they have been really good workers."

McKeown, in charge of a substantial program with a major international firm, has noticed that the experience and education levels of temporary paralegals are different today, compared with just two years ago. "The face of the temps has changed," she says:

> You're getting more "oomph" for your buck. Instead of document clerks right out of college, you're getting people out of paralegal school who have some work experience. You're also getting J.D.'s instead of certificated people. There is no longer discrimination against the J.D. who wants to work as a paralegal. Everyone used to think that people with J.D. degrees would only be there until they took the bar. Not so. They also make *great* temps.

Choosing a Temporary Agency

There are many advantages to using a temporary agency. Spending time and money looking for the next job can be difficult and time consuming, especially while you're already on assignment. Using a good agency can help you work continuously and ensure that you will receive a regular paycheck promptly. (Some independent contractors have to wait thirty days or even longer to receive payment for their work.)

Look for an agency that has a reputable background in the legal community, one that demonstrates this company understands the paralegal field. The agency's recruiters also must be able to expertly match your skills to the assignment. Don't be afraid to ask questions:

- How long do temporary employees stay with the company?
- Does the agency have an aggressive recruiting program?
- What is the permanent staff like?
- Do the recruiters have paralegal or legal backgrounds?
- Does the agency have adequate insurance to protect you in case of a workers' compensation claim?

Many general personnel agencies have entered the paralegal field, thinking they can succeed because, after all, "placing is placing." This approach can fail for two very important reasons.

- The agency that has a strong clerical base may not acknowledge the differences between paralegal (professional) and clerical (support staff) positions.
- They may not have recruiters who understand the intricacies of legal project management and thus cannot make appropriate staffing recommendations.

Another *very important* factor to consider when choosing an agency is one that temps often overlook. This is the financial stability of the agency. Just because job orders roll in, this does not mean that all agency owners are able to finance that rapid growth. The agency must pay you *first*, before it gets paid by its client for your services. If the agency grows too quickly and does not have adequate funding, the company may have trouble meeting its payroll.

Working with a Temporary Agency

First, put together a resume that shows off *all* your skills. Just as you would with another employer, remember that your resume is your first introduction to the agency. If your resume has typos in it, is poorly written, or doesn't contain pertinent information, you may not even get called in for an interview.

It helps the agency make a determination about whether it can place you if you provide a very detailed resume. Even if it takes more than one page to list all your skills and experience, that's okay. For the purpose of providing the agency with a complete picture of the types of jobs you'd be perfect for, the more detail, the better.

Details are especially important when it comes to listing your computer experience. These days, a general comfort level with different computers and programs is necessary. In the legal field, you will be more marketable if you have experience using word processing, spreadsheets, and database software. The broader your experience—both the number of software programs and their applications—the better.

Provide a clearer picture of your background by listing specific usage details, for example: "Utilized InMagic for designing and building litigation support database of 15,000 documents." Simply listing the various software programs you've used, without any background about the extent of that experience, is not as helpful to the agency when making matches with specific jobs.

Share any letters of recommendation you've received with the agency. These are impressive for temporary employers, and you will provide the agency with a better picture of how you can perform on the job.

Once you're on an assignment, keep the agency informed of how the job is going. Be sure to let your recruiter know whether it looks like the job will end sooner, or last longer, than expected. This way, the agency can better anticipate your availability for other assignments.

Picking and Choosing your Assignments

You certainly have the option of turning down assignments. Remember, though, recruiters are only human, and they will respond to those temps who are easy to work with. Rudeness, failure to return calls promptly, late time cards, and being overly picky about accepting assignments, are all factors that can turn a recruiter off when deciding about working with you.

When clients call, it is usually an emergency. The agency's reputation depends in large part on how fast and how accurately it fills assignment. If you consistently turn down jobs for which you are qualified, the agency may hesitate to call on you again.

The same tenet holds true if you market yourself without going through an agency. Turn down a firm one too many times, and that firm may not be inclined to call you back. Flexibility is a key ingredient in temporary staffing.

"You Want Me to Go Where?"

Temp assignments can range anywhere from dreary and dull to exhilarating and invigorating. For paralegals, the bulk of temporary work is in litigation. The nature of the assignment can vary from reviewing millions of documents to chasing down factual information and traveling to parts unknown. You can be assigned to a terrific firm with coworkers you absolutely adore, or you can be assigned to the jerk who gets a temp because he can't keep a permanent paralegal. No matter what, expect the unexpected.

They Love You, They Love You Not

Oh, those office politics. You can either walk in as a hero or as a threat to the permanent employees. Here are some guidelines that will help you avoid being caught in the middle:

• Don't get involved in the permanent employees' fights, causes, politics, relationships, tussles or struggles with management.

• Don't try to prove there is a better way of doing things. That may be so, but the best approach is to coach or suggest. Try not to use the following phrase: "At my last job, we . . . ." You'll only antagonize the client, who will probably respond with: "Yes, but *HERE*, we . . . ."

• Try to find something out about the firm's culture *before* you arrive. Ask the agency for background, or pay close attention to the people who work there. Find out the following information:
    — style of dress,
    — formality with partners and coworkers,
    — extent allowed to deal with clients,
    — how the work product is produced,
    — policies on personal phone calls and doctors' appointments (usually taboo and particularly frowned upon for a temp), and
    — do people go out for lunch or is it an "eat-at-your-desk-work-through-lunch" kind of atmosphere?

Follow all written policies and procedures provided by the firm/corporation and the agency. If you are on a long-term assignment, it is a good idea to review the firm's employee manual. A good temporary agency will also provide you with a copy of its employee manual.

Assignments vary. You may be given an excellent office, a good secretary, and all the tools you need to do the job. On the other hand, you may arrive to find there isn't even a desk or phone for you. Be prepared for *any* situation.

Because you are "The Temp," attitudes toward you may vary. You may be judged by harsher standards than those applied to permanent employees. Or, you may be easily forgiven for mistakes. Be prepared for *both* attitudes.

Conflict of Interest

You have a professional obligation to make sure that you have no conflict of interest when you go from firm to firm, case to case, matter to matter. Ask the agency representatives if they know to what matters you will be assigned. If they don't know, and you arrive to find there is a conflict, you must declare it *immediately.*

To Bill or Not to Bill

Even though you are not a permanent employee, you will probably be expected to turn in timesheets, even in some corporations. Every firm has its own standard of billing. Be sure you get complete instructions as early in the assignment as possible.

Ask for a sample of a completed timesheet used by the firm so you know exactly what work codes or abbreviations, billing units, terminology, client/matter numbers, and administrative numbers are used. Find out when timesheets are due and to whom they should be presented. Just because you are "the temp" does *not* mean that you aren't expected to know how to bill your time. Make every minute count. Your time is being billed not only to the client (by you), but also to the firm (by the agency). Misuse of your time results in complaints. Too many complaints about your billing practices, and neither the firm nor the agency will be anxious to give you more assignments.

Do You Have What it Takes?

"What I look for [in a temp] is a paralegal who needs only minimal direction," says Pendergrass. "Someone who looks at the document, analyzes it and puts some thought to it. I need people who take their jobs very seriously."

As a Manager of Litigation Support—dealing in volumes of highly technical documents—Pendergrass puts teams of temporary paralegals together who can take supervision well from his staff. He is an advocate of paralegals, and particularly temporaries. Once, on a research project, a temporary paralegal found a very important document which resulted in resolution of a litigation matter, a fact Pendergrass often cites.

Pendergrass has dealt with literally hundreds of temporary paralegals. His advice: "Listen but don't be afraid to ask questions. Above all, don't overanalyze—especially in a temp situation. Keep your mind open."

Susan Scott, president of Paralegals Plus in Dallas, and president of the Dallas Legal Assistant Association, gives some pretty good advice to temporary paralegals.

> Not all paralegals see themselves as professionals. Some are on their way elsewhere and are what I call transitory paralegals. My advice is to view your attorneys as clients rather than bosses. Clients purchase professional services. Bosses direct activities of employees. I would bet that the best paid and most valuable paralegals are those who embrace new technologies and take chances—not the paralegals who merely wait for direction.

What Paralegals Will Be Doing Tomorrow

What's clear about paralegal profession of the future is that it will differ from the present. Just two decades old, it has already undergone extraordinary changes and that will only continue.

Indeed, long dubbed the fastest growing profession in the '90s, it might now better be called the fastest changing profession of the decade.

Just how it will change is the million dollar question. Interviews with a wide array of experts and managers in the field certainly suggests no unanimity of prognostication.

> *It is quite possible, for instance, that while paralegals will be pulled back from attorney-like tasks, such as drafting complaints, they may well move into other areas like marketing, budgeting and other management tasks. The role may evolve into an administrative role, such as litigation executive or case manager.*

There is one school of thought whose vision of the paralegal future is so bleak that no one will utter it for publication. That thinking is that there is no future for paralegals, that the abundance of attorneys will drive paralegals out of the marketplace as associates no longer on the partner track assume what has traditionally been paralegal functions.

To that, I say nonsense. Fifteen years ago physicians were predicting that the new role of nurse practitioner would disappear because there were so many new doctors coming into practice. What's occurred, in fact, is that the abundance of physicians notwithstanding, the nurse practitioner role has expanded and flourished as economic realities forced the medical establishment to use the most inexpensive means to provide the necessary levels of care.

That is already occurring in the legal industry. Linda Broker, paralegal administrator at Paul, Hastings, Janofsky & Walker, said clients are already aware of paralegal capabilities. "Savvy clients are recognizing the cost savings and specifically requesting paralegal services." In an effort to compete for clients, law firms are marketing their paralegal programs in their collateral materials such as brochures and firm resumes.

Still, the medical model differs from the legal model in that during the period of expansion of nurse practitioner usage, demand for health care grew extraordinarily. If the legal field expands similarly--then paralegals will in all likelihood follow the nurse practitioner model.

But what if the legal industry continues to contract and is forced to become far more cost effective, as so many experts suggest? My view is that's likely to reduce the number of attorneys, rather than paralegals. If potential attorneys believe they face careers without partnership, doing work that does not use their educations, and pays at paralegal levels, law school enrollments will drop. At the same time, almost all the experts agreed that stiffer educational demands will be made on the paralegal.

But in the name of efficiency alone, firms will still have to use paralegals. Meg Charnley, legal division manager, Advanced Business Assistance, San Francisco, said that like attorneys, paralegals will need to cross train into other specialties to follow the legal action. With transactional work drying up, they will move into health care, aviation and environmental law. "This recession has taught us that in order to survive you must be cross-trained. Business paralegals will need to be aware of litigation, litigation paralegals will need to have knowledge of real estate and corporate."

Kathleen Call, of Kathleen Call & Associates in San Francisco, a recruiter who once served as senior paralegal at Brobeck, Phleger et. al., predicts that the economic realities of the future will stymie what has been the continual expansion of the paralegal role. "Paralegals may not necessarily get more sophisticated assignments such as drafting as they would like, rather, the role of the executive will emerge. Paralegals possess extraordinary organization and management skills which will not only finally be recognized but utilized appropriately as the practice of law changes."

But whether that actually occurs—and how it will play out—will depend largely on the severity of the constriction in legal. It is quite possible, for instance, that while paralegals will be pulled back from attorney-like tasks, such as drafting complaints, they may well move into other areas like marketing, budgeting and other management tasks. The role may evolve into an administrative role, such as litigation executive or case manager.

"With the globalization of the American economy, there will be far more demand for paralegals with foreign language skills to work internationally," said Andrea Wagner, a veteran legal recruiter, whose first book, "How to Land Your First Paralegal Job" (Estrin) has just been published. "Japanese,

Chinese, Russian, German and Korean language skills are in demand now. The more American lawyers are working internationally, the more paralegals will follow."

Joyce Wilson, Los Angeles paralegal coordinator at Fried, Frank, Harris, Shriver & Jacobson sees paralegals becoming more heavily involved in law firm computerization, specifically in the areas of management, human resources, case management, and information management. "The paralegal without computer skills will become obsolete", states Wilson.

Shelley Widoff, director of paralegal studies, Boston University, believes that the movement of paralegals into the corporate environment will not only continue but increase to the point that many positions will require a paralegal background but not necessarily carry the title, such as the contracts administrator position.

Widoff also said that corporations will increasingly use paralegals in nontraditionally law related areas. "Banks are now innovators using paralegals. However, this wasn't always the case. They may have done better in the past if all of their loan officers were paralegals. Loan officers don't always know how to read titles or contracts and may not know what they gave away," Widoff said.

Dixie Dunbar, a senior entertainment law paralegal at Ziffren Brittenham & Branca, in Los Angeles echoes that sentiment. She foresees paralegals playing an increasingly important role in entertainment. With their legal knowledge and comparatively low cost, they will be perfectly situated to handle an increasingly wide array of negotiations. Dunbar even foresees independent entertainment paralegal firms profiting handsomely by providing lower cost legal services in an industry that historically pays highly for them.

Richard Granat, former president of the Institute of Paralegal Training and current president of the Center for Self-Help Law in Philadelphia, has doubts about the continued upgrading of the paralegal role in the law firm environment. But he sees them increasingly providing a wide array of affordable legal services to the American public.

"The future of the paralegal movement lies in providing certain routine legal services and other legal information services directly to the public without supervision of attorneys. New computer-based legal expert systems will enable paralegals to create and operate 'Legal Information Centers' as a practical and economical alternative to the present patterns of legal service delivery," Granat said.

Gazing in the crystal ball to predict the future is difficult and dangerous at best. Therese Cannon, Dean of Paralegal Studies at University of West Los Angeles put it aptly, "We had no idea 20 years ago that paralegals would be doing what they're doing now. The way we practice law has changed drastically. It's almost impossible to predict where we'll be even five years from now. But what's clear to me is that role of paralegal will continue to evolve. It is a profession that's here to stay."

Is a Paralegal Association for You?

" **I**'m just not the association type," claim many paralegals or paralegals-to-be. I wonder just what is the association type. What kind of vision does the stereotype conjure up? Conservatives? Radicals? Traditionalists? Cool dudes? Dyed-in-the-wool fundamentalists? And just what motivates professionals to join or stay away?

If you are new to the field, your local paralegal association can be the place for you to make valuable, lasting contacts. You may be nervous about going to a meeting or seminar where you are virtually unknown. But in the long run these contacts can become a cornerstone for building precisely the kind of successful career you are seeking.

> *Holding an office in an organization can help your career zoom. High visibility, a larger circle of contacts, being "in the loop" and building a solid reputation in the community, are only a few of the discernable benefits to your career—not to mention long lasting friendships and incredible support.*

Strategic Bonding

Experienced paralegals understand how to use association contacts as a tool to market yourself in a career where word-of-mouth is far more valued than an unsolicited resume. Who you know and how you know them becomes your key to opening doors. It is networking at its optimum.

When most people think of associations, they also think of networking. However, the term networking has been overutilized and misunderstood. Has anyone really figured out exactly what networking means? A more descriptive and attention getting term would be strategic bonding.

Strategic bonding allows you to utilize great contacts if you are job searching, information gathering or friendship building. "Dana Graves suggested I give you a ring about your paralegal position" has much more impact than just sending a letter without any prior knowledge of the receiver or common link. It makes your job so much easier to be able to call your contacts for referrals to find out the best vendors, court peculiarities, expert witnesses, or the "inside" info on computer software programs. Many lasting friendships are born through the networking process.

Politics

If you are passionate about politics in your field, associations are an excellent vehicle to voice your opinion and persuade colleagues to take action. Sometimes it works, sometimes it doesn't and sometimes you are just way ahead of your time.

I recall an instance sometime in the mid-eighties where I was asked to speak to a paralegal association about the possibility of licensure for paralegals: what it could do for paralegals, the pros, the cons and how a comparable field, nursing, survived a similar endeavor (salaries increased over $10,000 per year in 1970's dollars). Little did I know at the time how the group felt about the issue.

I walked smack into a room full of 40 riled up people. The concept was very new and under no circumstances would this organization consider licensing paralegals. I thought I was going to be tarred and feathered. Now, ten years later, licensing has become a hot topic for just about every organization in the United States.

Benefits

Associations offer members benefits such as:

- regular meetings with networking opportunities,
- seminars,
- membership lists,
- discounts for students,
- speakers bureau,

- group health insurance rates for freelancers,
- schools lists, or
- newsletters.

Dues

In past years, membership dues were part of the benefits package for paralegals. Now, most paralegals are expected to be responsible for payment. Dues can run anywhere from approximately $25.00 to $100.00 per year. Most organizations will give a discount if you are a student.

Some organizations have rules for membership such as you must be working. In some states you must have a certificate or CLA designation. If you don't qualify, you may be able to join as an associate member which means that you are not a voting member. However, it's still valuable to join for all the other benefits.

Holding Office Benefits Your Career

Holding an office in an organization can help your career zoom. High visibility, a larger circle of contacts, being "in the loop" and building a solid reputation in the community, are only a few of the discernable benefits to your career—not to mention long lasting friendships and incredible support.

Much has been made of the mentoring process. Usually it's how someone goes about getting one. Holding office in an organization is a statement that you have arrived. Colleagues look to **you** to be **their** mentor. Here's a nice acknowledgment of how far you've come in your career.

Make Yourself a Leader

All associations are borne out of a need. Usually the need is based on a desire to find others who have similar experiences in your chosen career and who can support you. Those who start organizations are leaders.

Because the paralegal field cannot exist without an attorney's guidance, and the field is classified as a helping occupation, paralegals are not considered to be principals. You cannot own a law firm, sign documents (for the most part), or argue or single-handedly win the case. However, the lawyer can.

Being a paralegal, playing a supporting role, can cause you to be overlooked as a leader. Creating an association or holding an office in one helps to establish yourself as a leader in the field. It also teaches you basic leadership skills that can help you throughout your life.

[1] "In Search of Role Models," was first published in the September/October 1992 issue of LEGAL ASSISTANT TODAY.

[2] "What to Expect in Your First Ten Years as a Legal Assistant," was first published in the November/December 1992 issue of LEGAL ASSISTANT TODAY.

I received help from Dana L. Graves and Joyce Wilson in brainstorming this article. Also, I was inspired to address this issue in the first place by Kathy E. Mount's article, "What to Expect in Your First Decade," which was published in *The San Francisco Recorder* (May 27, 1992). Ms. Mount addressed the topic from the viewpoint of an attorney.

[3] "The Contemporary Temporary," was first published in the January/February 1994 issue of LEGAL ASSISTANT TODAY.

[4] "What Paralegals Will Be Doing Tomorrow," was first published in the December 2, 1993 issue of the LOS ANGELES DAILY JOURNAL.

Part
3 ⬆

Achieving
Success on
the Job

No one enters the field with the attitude "I'm going to fail". Everyone wants to be successful. How you plan to achieve it can be critical in how you move ahead.

In today's climate, a horizontal climb up the ladder may not be as easily reachable as in yesteryear. Due in part to the recession in the early '90s, law firms and corporations have flattened the pyramid.

A horizontal climb is now achieved and rewarded through increased responsibilities, knowledge and capabilities rather than title and how many people you manage. This is particularly true in the paralegal field.

Getting a Grip on Your Career: Strategies for Empowering Your Position

I just read about three new emerging careers for the 21st Century: underwater archeologist, cryonics technician, and automotive fuel cell battery technician. Well, these jobs sure beat the shyness consultant job I originally had my eye on.

Why, you may ask, would *I*, of all people, be considering a career change? Me, the career advice lady, the ultimate optimist, the Paralegal Pollyanna? It's such a mixed up story, you wouldn't believe it if I told you.

O.K., I'll try.

> **Law firms are finally learning the value of cross-training for paralegals, and many paralegals have saved their jobs during these recessionary times because they have more than one skill. And the better paralegals are at looking beyond their immediate job, the better for both the firm and the paralegals' career.**

I'm expected to follow certain policies of the corporation. My position as president of a multi-million dollar division of a significant and well-respected player in the legal field cuts me no slack when it comes to having to abide by those policies. O.K., I really don't mind so much. And, I want to say, before anyone thinks ill of me, that I work for an outstanding company with super people.

But last week, I had a great learning experience. I was informed that I was going to be paid an incentive to get me to better conform to company policies.

Huh? This decision assumed that:

57

a) I had received proper training and orientation,
b) I knew what those "hidden" policies were, and
c) I chose to ignore them.

None of these assumptions was correct. How did I get myself into this pickle?

(Now, I also need to throw in my emotional state at this time. While the sharing of an author's most intimate details is not generally done, it's extremely important to understand how personal events in your life can influence your state of mind about your career.)

The past six months have been particularly eventful and tragic for me. I had: lost both of my parents; been evacuated in the Malibu fire; lived through the L.A. earthquake, lost a cousin in a quake-related car wreck; started up two new offices; and yes, it's true, my boyfriend dumped me. I was totally over my limit in personal tragedies—probably another company policy I had overlooked.

I sat down with my friend Bernie. Now, Bernie has known me for quite some time and is pretty familiar with my philosophies. He asked some pretty hardball questions. It was a moment of truth.

"When you found out you didn't know enough about company policies, did you go back and demand proper training and orientation?"

Well, no. *I didn't want to rock the boat. I was new in the organization. There wasn't any formal training for execs.*

"When you discovered that the manner in which you proceeded slightly bent the rules, did you justify yourself in a memo, getting the proper department heads to understand why?"

No again. *I didn't want to appear to be pointing fingers because I couldn't get the system to work the way I needed.*

"Did you attempt to change corporate policies to make things run smoother?"

No, not really. *I wanted to be perceived as a team player.*

"When you saved the corporation over $8,000 by going outside the system because going through proper channels would have doubled the expenditures, did you blow your own horn?"

My answer was "No" one more time. *At that time, I just wanted to get the job done as quickly as possible.*

And finally, Bernie asked: "What effect has the past six months had on you?"

Uh, oh. Caught. He had made his point.

It's true that the corporation could have done things differently. It's also true that personal tragedies out of my control strengthened a desire for lots of comfort and support from those around me. Further, those events were forcing me to reevaluate my lifestyle and take a hard look at where I was headed.

However, the message was clear: Was I taking control of those things I **could** control? The answer was no. As a result, I was becoming a victim of the system. Clearly, it was time to get a grip on my career.

Learning the Ropes

Whether you are new in the firm or there have been significant changes going on about you, it is imperative that you "learn the ropes." Just about every firm or corporation has some sort of policy manual. Unfortunately, most are written in a style that would put the dead to sleep. This results in most employees looking at such manuals as if they had the following warning label: "Do not remove from the shelf for at least five years."

Even if your firm's manual doesn't make sense when you first go through it—because you may not be familiar with all of the firm's in-house abbreviations or new lingo—be sure you **read it carefully**.

Some firms provide in-depth orientations which offer a stockpile of information. However, some firms only allot an hour for this process. Quickly meeting with the Human Resource Director, filling out the W-2 and health insurance forms, and learning about the vacation policy is NOT an "orientation."

In such short indoctrinations, employees learn about their firm or corporation only by what is NOT said at the orientation. They also learn important information only when they've made mistakes "by not following company policy."

Ask to read all of the firm's collateral material. Such material includes the firm brochure, company annual report, firm's resume, rainmaking letters, and even the "face" book (that so-informative directory with everyone's picture and educational background).

Also ask for copies of all of the firm's newsletter back issues. Reviewing these documents will give you a feel for the progression of the firm, who was promoted from where, what significant clients the firm handles, and who exactly are the important players. Your firm may publish in-house and client newsletters, be sure to get copies of both.

Find out whether the firm has a videotape library of previous seminars and other events. There may even be photo albums of past holiday parties and company picnics.

If your firm doesn't have an orientation process, you may want to draft a set of procedures (going through proper channels, of course). Volunteer for handling the orientation itself. Emphasize how much money you'll save in employee mistakes and turnover. This participation in firm management can broaden your horizons and step you into other valuable arenas in the firm.

Career Marketing

One of the problems paralegals face is being part of the backstage process. When a case is won, a matter settled, a merger completed, it usually isn't the paralegal who is the primary source of praise and attention, it's the attorney. And while many attorneys will acknowledge the help and assistance of the paralegal, more often, paralegals are the "unsung heros." If you rarely receive praise for a job well-done, don't be afraid to reach out and claim it. How you claim your rightful share of the spotlight, however, can be a very sensitive matter. For example:

MEMORANDUM

TO: Jane Doe, Esq.

FROM: Mary Smith, Paralegal

Congratulations on winning the *Smith* case! It was great to work on such a dynamic team as ours turned out to be. I want to personally thank you for allowing me to "stretch." I have never before had the opportunity to attend the trial of a case on which I had worked. The experience and exposure to these kinds of sophisticated assignments will enable me to advance further in my paralegal career.

Of course, don't go overboard saying things such as "and wow, those 15-hour days just whipped by." And be careful of sounding phony. Telling someone what a great team player they were when the most you ever got was a growl (on a good day), won't pass muster.

Another simple, yet effective, career marketing tool is to find out who lunches—and get yourself invited. This technique will enable you to:

- find out what is going on in the organization that may pertain to you or your assignments;
- communicate to others what you are doing, thus marketing your skills in the process; and
- give you exposure to other cases and other projects.

You may find out that Attorney X has been assigned to a matter you're already working on without your knowledge. You can approach Attorney X for additional assignments or you can act as a liaison between Attorney X and the trial team. You begin to make yourself invaluable.

Communicating to others what kinds of matters on which you are working and what level of assignments you are handling gives others an opportunity to promote your career for you. Assignments may come up, additional paralegals may be needed and your colleagues will be able to suggest you because they are familiar with your capabilities. Make it easier for your colleagues to support you. Many are the times we see paralegals sitting at their desks day after day as we walk by, and we haven't a clue what they do, how they do it or who they are doing it for.

The "That's Not My Job" Syndrome

I once hired someone who refused to pick up the phone when the receptionist was away from the front desk. This was bad enough, but what really annoyed me was when she also let us know that she didn't make coffee. I always got the feeling she sneaked in, drank the last cup and then waited to see what I would do.

Now, most offices I know revolve around that coffee pot. You come in, get your coffee, start your day, go back, get more coffee, maybe making the next pot, and face the rest of the day. Then you can go home. It's really a *very* simple ritual. But in her mind, this just wasn't part of her job. This "not my job" attitude unfortunately spilled over onto other, more important areas. Needless to say, she was a mere memory in a very short period of time.

Doing one's own job is often not enough. Many times, it's necessary to step in and go the extra mile. According to a 1990 *Fortune* magazine article, some Federal Express clerks spotted a problem that was costing the company $2.1 million per year. These employees were motivated to go beyond their specific jobs and dig deep to solve in-house problems.

Companies have learned that putting employees in just one spot with only one job can be quite counterproductive. Law firms are finally learning the value of cross-training for paralegals, and many paralegals have saved their jobs during these recessionary times because they have more than one skill. And the better paralegals are at looking beyond their immediate job, the better for both the firm and the paralegals' career.

To avoid the "that's not my job" syndrome, it is wise to understand the big picture of the firm or corporation. According to Terrence E. Deal and William Jenkins in MANAGING THE HIDDEN ORGANIZATION, "By routinizing work, [companies] believed relationships between specialized activities could be tightly prescribed and vertically managed." The problem, according to Deal and Jenkins, is that "[A]s people become highly skilled at a particular task, they quickly become extremely bored. Tight regulations and micromanagement do not motivate people. Nor do they keep people from finding ingenious ways of covering up mistakes and passing them down the line."

Having a problem getting paid by the firm? Sorry, that's not my job. You need to talk with someone in Accounts Payable.

Stepping in and helping out can give you new career options. You may find yourself lending a hand during a rush. Supervisors and colleagues may—for the first time—notice your leadership or your ability to respond in a crisis situation. These actions translate into enthusiasm and a great attitude on the job.

"Great attitude" is something we hear we're supposed to have, but not everyone knows how to demonstrate it. Luckily, everyone knows a "great attitude" when they see it. So ask yourself what it was that impressed you the last time you received great service at a department store, or when a DMV clerk helped you more than you expected. Going beyond the bare minimum to provide assistance in a friendly and efficient manner: this is the beginning point for achieving a "great attitude."

Career Advancement in the Changing Workplace

Legend has it that Lee Iaccoca always carried a special 3x5 card with him. On this card, he had listed the dates, types of promotions and salary increases he expected to achieve until he reached president of the corporation. Not a bad idea, actually.

However, the look of today's workplace has changed. Rather than a vertical climb, promotions and raises are now based on horizontal moves and increasing responsibilities. Corporations and law firms have flattened the pyramid, eliminating many management-only positions. Fewer middle managers are required today to manage the "knowledge workers." The trend is to reward employees based on their specialized knowledge and skills rather than power, job title and number of people managed.

According to Samuel Cypert in THE SUCCESS BREAKTHROUGH, the SEC has initiated an executive compensation plan that links pay to performance. The goal is to pay people based on their abilities to contribute and continuing to learn so they can contribute even more. The "pay-for-skills" approach which values continued learning may redirect the career paths of employees. "Instead of being penalized for horizontal moves," states Cypert, "they will be encouraged to gain knowledge and acquire expertise in a variety of subjects in order to advance in the company."

Many paralegals feel that moving into upper management would take them away from their preferred hands-on work. And, there are just as many who are either unsuited for or uninterested in management positions. These are employees who thrive in the trenches and have no desire to command the troops. Having a plan of action for those who desire and seek horizontal moves is just as important as for those who look to move up the career ladder.

One approach is to target where you would like to be in yearly segments, up to five years. Your plan of action for horizontal moves may look something like this:

Year one	Increase computer expertise: learn DOS, spreadsheets, litigation support packages, Dialog. Become more familiar with the Federal Evidence Rules and U.S. copyright laws.
Year two	Learn patent and trademark prosecution specialty.
Year three	Make jump to patent and trademark firm, increasing salary by 12%.
Year four	Become assistant to senior partner. Gain actual trial experience.
Year five	Become firm's patent and trademark expert.

Another approach is to network within the firm. Include all levels and all divisions. Remember that people working at lower levels have information you may need. Members of my staff have been in firms where none of the paralegals in the firm have any idea what other paralegals are doing.

Having more information available gives you the ability to pick assignments with potentially great impact. Become more well-informed, obtaining a larger picture of the firm or corporation. Anticipate the needs of supervising attorneys and your clients.

Of course, people will expect you to exchange information too. But this doesn't mean engaging in rumor or gossip. Above all, don't pass on confidential information. Maintaining a good network *takes* work.

Doing the "Right Thing" Rather Than "Doing Things Right"

According to Deal and Jenkins, having to follow rules rigidly can be especially frustrating. "Emphasis on doing things right rather than on doing the right thing can shift attention from an organization's more important vision and values," they claim. Fortunately, law firms can be somewhat more lenient than corporations in forcing employees to follow strict policy.

While I'm not suggesting that you risk your job, I do know that with emphasis on client satisfaction and "customer service," there are times you may find yourself wishing you had the authority to make certain decisions on the spot when the options affect service, the budget or the client.

One example of slightly bending the rules stands out. A paralegal in a law firm received a frantic call from the firm's client, a small corporation. The corporation's own paralegal was stuck in a new computer program and could not find her way out. Nor could the vendor provide much help. After several phone calls, the law firm paralegal went over to the client's offices after working hours and talked the other paralegal through the program. She bent the rules because she never charged for her time. But the client never forgot the favor.

When the firm discovered what the paralegal had done (she documented her trip in a memo), they recognized her extra efforts in an article prominently placed in the firm's in-house newsletter. This paralegal gained respect, recognition and acknowledgment of her excellent computer skills.

If you find yourself in a situation where you've chosen to bend the rules, make sure that your actions are appropriate and that all persons involved understand the reasons for your actions. If the paralegal in the above example *had* charged the client for legal services performed, chances are the law firm would not be citing her for her extra achievements. The would probably hand her a disciplinary action instead.

You Need the Right Assignment

The parameters and opportunities in many assignments are not within your control: a client matter that should have been tricky and difficult ends up being resolved with a routine form; a case that would have attracted media attention ends up settling immediately. And so on and so on. However, when you can, it behooves you to pick assignments that will bring you to the attention of your supervisors and senior management. Safe and routine assignments will *not* get you noticed.

Using your network within the firm or legal department, scout out the places where you can make an impact. Seek out challenges rather than wait for the plum assignments to come to you. By familiarizing yourself with the power players and the up-and-comers in the firm, you can put yourself in a position of knowing about opportunities *before* they are assigned to someone else. Find a place where your competence and skills will bring results that coincide with your yearly plan. You are *not* at the mercy of the firm. You *can* guide your own career.

When taking a new assignment, extract commitments from your supervising attorney or manager that you will be able to accomplish certain goals. For example, when tackling a difficult and time-consuming project—such as an extended trial in a remote area—spell out exactly what you want to achieve: additional experience in a particular area of expertise, new and more sophisticated levels of assignment, or whatever is beneficial to your career. It isn't a particularly good idea, however, to hold anyone hostage to these goals.

The attitude in many organizations is "this is what we pay you to do." Use skillful negotiation to continually upgrade your knowledge and increase your competence level. If you are negotiating with attorneys for upgrades in assignments, be advised that these folks didn't just go to law school to learn the practice of law. Oh, no. They went to learn how to negotiate. You can take that one to the bank.

On the other hand, be sure you are open to new assignments. Adopting the "it's not my job syndrome" will only hurt, not help you. Getting labeled as someone unwilling to cooperate in the best interests of the firm is one way of winning first place in the unemployment line.

Managing Your Boss

Because the very nature of the job of the paralegal is to perform routine and repetitive tasks, many paralegals get stuck in a rut, a certain lack of movement and expansion of the career. One way of breaking this monotony is to *manage your supervisor* so that you are able to advance quickly.

Let's face it. You're going to be told what to do and how to do it. You can perform magnificently on all your assignments and never get noticed.

Dr. Adele Scheele has written many articles and books on the subject of Achievers and Sustainers. The Sustainers, she writes, go through school doing their work, turning in their homework and showing up everyday. And, they are *automatically promoted* to the next grade. When Sustainers reach the adult world, they take this background and attitude into the work force. They are looking for that automatic promotion. However, they either fail to get noticed or promoted.

Achievers, on the other hand, work the system, take control, and move ahead.

If you work strategically with your supervisor, you are likely to get noticed and rewarded. However, managing your supervisor should be apparent to no one but yourself. Here are a few suggestions.

Get to know your supervisor. I particularly enjoy it when the managers or staff in my organization ask what's going on with me. I travel a great deal, and when they show interest in what I have been doing or the direction I am taking the company, I appreciate it.

I also enjoy having staff members who stand out because of their own contributions. Be careful, though. Some supervisors may feel threatened.

Establish clear lines of communication. If you keep your supervisor advised of everything that is happening, there are no surprises. Your supervisor then becomes an ally because he or she participated in key decisions and will be prepared for any bad news. A weekly status report can be an excellent tool, particularly if your supervisor or managing attorney is not accessible or does not invite an open door policy.

Anticipate their needs. My publishing house staff anticipates all my needs for every seminar I conduct. They have my schedule down, a form they fill out for providing the speaking tools I'll need, appropriate handouts and any other possible seminar needs. My temporary placement staff anticipates my every need for budget control, client calls, recruiting, marketing and travel. Of course, they don't know that *I* know they're managing me. It's great.

Get decisions made in a timely manner. Some supervisors can make split-second decisions, shooting from the hip. Others, particularly attorneys, need to deliberate every little thing. Some will avoid the process altogether or delegate. I absolutely abhor the ones who "need a second opinion." What I even hate more is when a committee is set up to arrive at a decision. More important decisions are lost in the committee process than anywhere else in the world.

One way of combatting the slow decision maker is to not ask for a yes or no answer. Instead, give the decision maker a choice between A and B. That way, you'll have cut through most of the process.

Another method is to issue the ultimatum memo. Now, be careful about this. By putting it in writing, "Unless we pin down the date for the document production with the *Acme* firm, we will lose our last opportunity for discovery.. . ." should get their attention. Do not, however, use threats or any derogatory language whatsoever.

Don't be afraid to praise. In some firms where caste systems exist (you can work with attorneys until midnight, but you're not allowed to eat with them), it is more difficult for some paralegals to hand out praise. Be aware that attorneys need their egos stroked just like anyone else. In fact, when they go head to head with another attorney, frequently it's not who has the best lawyering skills who wins, but who has the strongest and most durable ego.

You don't have to be flowery, but an acknowledgment of a matter resolved, a case won, or a brilliant brief filed could go a long way. Always be sincere. You'll be found out otherwise. When I lie, for example, my left eye crosses in.

Don't tie your future to your supervising attorney or supervisor. It used to be that attorneys stayed with the firm for life. Not so any more. People leave, are laid off or retire. And, the truth is, they may not be able to take you with them. You must be able to stand on your own and by your own merits.

Create Good Relationships with Vendors

Some people have very funny attitudes about dealing with vendors. They say the word with a small "v" and under their breath. I urge you to take another look at the value of the vendor. By vendors, I'm referring to any company that sells a product or a service to the legal community.

In addition to your local copying service or stationary store, don't overlook the fact that large and well-respected corporations such as IBM, Xerox, Quorum Litigation, Apple Computer; publishing houses such as Wiley Law Publications, Clark Boardman Callaghan, Delmar; and more are actually vendors to the legal community. These companies are loaded with important "intelligence" you can use. They have vital information that you need to do your job. And many of the professionals in these companies started as paralegals. Vendor representatives are degreed, sophisticated, educated and savvy about today's market. They frequently are on top of the latest trends. Because law firms are generally the last to get on the bandwagon for anything (i.e., the use of computer technology), vendors can be your best resource for introduction to valuable tools you need to more efficiently and competently do your job.

Take vendors to lunch. Pick their brains. You don't need to buy anything nor do you need to give out any confidential information. They recognize that selling to a law firm is generally a crisis-driven action and are not expecting you to sign on the dotted line. I doubt that you'll be sorry for the contact you made.

Don't Be Afraid to Rock the Boat

Wayne Gretzky once said, "You miss one hundred percent of the shots you don't take." By not stepping up to the issue of managing your career, you may miss one hundred percent of those chances to give yourself the best possible course. Taking risks may mean that you make a mistake—and making mistakes is just a part of life. Hopefully, you'll minimize the results of those mistakes, hurt no one—including yourself—in the process, and learn through life not to repeat them.

You must create a positive atmosphere for yourself to get rid of nonproductive fears and eliminate the possible role as victim to the system. Your career strategy must be constructive, cautious, planned and flexible in order to make quality leaps forward. Some suggestions here may work for you, others may not. You choose one, and mold and shape it to fit your personal scenario. Whatever you do, use your best judgment and consult your peers and mentors for feedback.

As I look over my career, from paralegal to paralegal administrator to entrepreneur of a successful company to president of a corporation, I understand now that while I have made some classic mistakes along the way, I was rewarded in my career for not being afraid to rock the boat. I've also seen others who demonstrated this same ability and were rewarded. On the other hand, I have also seen some people self-destruct, because in the process, they managed to alienate everyone around them.

Law firms and corporations have, for many years, shared in the mistaken belief that only those who don't rock the boat will succeed. That's not true. The system *does* reward those who rock the boat and those who take their careers in their own hands, benefitting not only themselves but their organizations as well.

Nothing can stand in your way. Not office politics, not corporate policy, not personal events, not difficult bosses, not colleagues who want you to keep a low profile. Take charge of your own career. You owe it to yourself, your family and your profession.

In Search of Success

"*I* can't imagine a person becoming a success who doesn't give this game of life everything he's got."

— Walter Cronkite

No one, in my recollection, has ever expressed to me that their goal in life was to fail in their career. In fact, in the literally thousands of legal assistants I have met during my tenure in the legal arena, most people have asked, "What can I do to improve my situation, get ahead in my career or succeed beyond where I am now?" It seems that the desire to succeed in your career is a universal goal—basic in instinct, one that everyone wants.

To succeed means you must become a risk taker— trying new responsibilities, new expectations and, risk losing what you have in the pursuit of what you want and need. It is very important to tackle these risks in a realistic, sensible and organized manner.

Success has a new definition for the nineties. It used to be that success meant "being a winner". In order to be a winner you need to have triumphed over something. Success today, I believe, has as much to do with fulfillment as it does with victory. Each individual has the right to define success according to his or her needs.

I have a very good friend whose wife views his career as unsuccessful. When I questioned him closely, it turns out that he never really came close to **her** definition of success. For example, at one point in his career, he earned around $65,000 a year as a paralegal administrator. But in her opinion, "success" started at $100,000 in salary. She wanted him to reach for a Director of Administration position in a major firm. He was never promoted further than the paralegal manager position, having no real desire to leave the paralegal field at that time. His background included several careers with a stop in between at film school. After abandoning that (only a few credits away from a Master's Degree), and entering the legal field, he opened his own business. I think his wife would have been happier if he'd become a civil servant, not necessarily making big bucks, so long as he stayed in one place for a long time with some kind of upward mobility. He always felt that he was letting her down.

I have quite a different view of that very same fellow. I see him as a highly successful individual who tackled a new career and had the spunk and courage to open his own company. The business today is taking off, offers many possibilities and is an obvious reflection of his combined past experiences.

If you define your success according to someone else's criteria, it can be impossible to meet expectations. You are setting yourself up to fail simply because the vision is not yours. Success is one thing you and you alone can envision, claim and own as yours.

Self-Defeating Behavior

Sometimes we create our own failures. I'm sure everyone has an area in which they wish to achieve more success. Take, for example, my total lack of athletic ability combined with my strong desire to ski. I have always fantasized about zipping down the slopes, hair blowing in the wind, RayBans plastered against my face, my skin glowing with Retin-A. Although I have never skied before, I heard that in order to get fitted for skies, you must inform the attendant of your weight. Now, you can rest assured this is the one area that I'm going to lie about. It's a given. I don't care how perilous the situation is, I'm going to lie.

So, there I'd be, on the bunny slope in my "to-die-for-outfit," watching four-year-olds whiz past me, as I desperately grip my poles and sink slowly down into the snow. Self-defeating behavior? You bet. Will I change? Probably not.

This kind of behavior translates into the job scene when we do seemingly inconsequential things such as avoiding particular assignments we're not good at it, dodging colleagues or attorneys we can't deal with or putting off making important decisions because we're not confident enough we'll make the right choice. Self defeating behavior can affect our success and limit our lives.

Before you can succeed, you must closely examine the subtle, circuitous and complex techniques you can use to assure your own failure. Have you chosen the wrong job for yourself? Are you in a masochistic relationship with an employer who behaves in ways which are guaranteed to ensure that you will not get a raise or promotion?

To succeed means you must become a risk taker—trying new responsibilities, new expectations and, according to Michael Korda, (author of the best-selling book, *Success!*), risk losing what you have in the pursuit of what you want and need. It is very important to tackle these risks in a realistic, sensible and organized manner:

- Ask yourself: how much responsibility am I willing to take?
- Set realistic expectations—not so high that you set yourself up for failure.
- Assess just how willing you are to leave behind your failures, an untenable situation, or just plain undesirable scene in order to rise up the next step and get what you've always wanted.
- Absolutely allow yourself the freedom to fail.

Separating rational fears from the irrational allows you to gain a more realistic picture of your success possibilities. It is sensible to accept a new job based on the career path it can lead you. On the other hand, if you feel that in order to move up, you'll have to get lucky or that the promotion will only bring you trouble, headaches and possible retaliation, then you're holding yourself back out of unnecessary guilt and fear.

Step one to success is to learn to accept the consequences of your decision. Korda teaches, "it isn't a matter of assertiveness or being right so much as giving up a comfortable cocoon of apologies and guilt in which most of us have chosen to live."

Get Recognition From the Right Source

It's crucial to be recognized for your accomplishments. It's equally important to seek recognition from the right source. One of the paradoxical things about success is that those who love you may unconsciously want you to fail. They may also conspire in our failure. We are all aware of marriages that can withstand failure, (no matter how miserable both partners are) but success has a tendency to destroy the relationship quickly. We have heard of or experienced relationships that endured years of poverty and broke up the moment one partner succeeded.

Korda contends that in these kind of relationships, one partner maintains control over the other. As one partner begins to succeed, the other's control begins to slip. The successful partner begins to experience benefits from this success but the life the couple maintains together doesn't improve. Success becomes betrayal.

The same kind of attitude can be found in law firms. Some colleagues have a difficult time when someone else has been promoted. Attorneys or supervisors may dismiss stellar accomplishments from paralegals because, after all, "the paralegal was just doing her job." The recognition giver may feel he or she is losing the ability to control the paralegal.

Many law firms offer negative reinforcement environments. There are no "atta-girls or atta-boys," few praises and no recognition. In an attempt to validate their very existence, many legal assistants seek recognition only to discover the undertaking backfired. This has a great deal to do with the source from whom the paralegal seeks recognition. Is the person from whom you are seeking recognition capable of giving it to you?

It may be that the person or firm you choose will not now nor will it ever, be able to bestow upon you the proper recognition you deserve. You need to decide whether it behooves you to move to another source that will give you what you need, or whether you can continue on in a dead-end situation and accept it for what it is. If that is the case, ask yourself what price will you pay for your happiness or fulfillment?

I am reminded of one time I sought recognition for success (albeit through material possession). It was the late '80s, the era of divine decadence, and my paralegal businesses were doing extremely well. I had come up through the ranks as paralegal, paralegal administrator and was now a paralegal entrepreneur. I had several offices across the country, had just won a prestigious award and was finally, finally, making some nice dollars. In Los Angeles, where the car is king, I decided to treat myself to a symbol of the times, the Mercedes. Did I dare? Me? (Nowadays, of course, with the new '90s attitudes, when we drive a luxury car we say our Pinto is in the shop.)

So with my '60s upbringing getting further and further behind me, I bit the bullet and went out and bought the prettiest car I could find. I was so excited as I drove it home. After all, I remembered starting my first paralegal job at $1500 per month. (But really, I'm sharing way too much with you all.) The next day I decided to show my brand new car to my mother. She walked over to the car, ooohing and aaahing at it. We got in. She ran her fingers over the dash board. She giggled over the strange symbols on the radio. She purred over the color. She played with the sunroof. Then she turned to me with this quizzical look on her face and asked, in all innocence, "Honey, is this a Toyota?"

When was I going to learn? I went to the wrong source for recognition and confirmation that "I did good."

Paralegal of the Year Award

I had an opportunity recently to encounter a group of paralegals who reached out and claimed their success. I was very honored to be part of a panel for the "Paralegal of the Year Award" given by Security Reprographics in Los Angeles. The panel had a very difficult decision because the quality of nominees was remarkable. Here were 17 finalists who had moved their supervisors into a position of acknowledging their success. They achieved status and recognition by motivating the right person to notice and speak out about their performance.

What was quite interesting was the extraordinary ratio of men to women that were nominated. In a female dominated field where statistics show us that there is only a 5% to 8% male population, approximately 50% of the nominees were men!

Two questions arose immediately. Were attorneys more apt to recognize outstanding achievements by men? Or, were men more likely to claim and seek recognition?

Those Who Reach Out and Claim Success

It's very difficult for most people to acknowledge success. Women, in particular, are generally not raised to acknowledge success as openly or willingly as
men. Many women will tell you that their success was due, in most part, to luck
or "being in the right place at the right time" or even "due to the talents of my
team, my employer, my firm, etc." While this may be true on many levels (we
always want to acknowledge those who helped us), the fact remains that many
women have a hard time claiming and owning their success. They wouldn't say
to themselves, "I'm successful because I strived for it, achieved it and earned it."

Since the paralegal profession is dominated by women, it is no surprise that
very few legal assistants reach out and openly claim success. This is what we
have been taught all of our lives. No one wants to be accused of being
boastful or arrogant. Men, on the other hand, have been taught since birth
that it is their duty to be successful. They learn this through competitive
sports, attitudes about boys vs. girls in school and family value systems. Fortunately, attitudes toward women and success are changing, slowly but surely.

The paralegals and paralegal managers nominated for the "Paralegal of the
Year Award" in my opinion, are all winners. I want to emphasize that they
motivated me to the point of mentioning them in this column: They are:

Jack Jessup; Cummins & White
Constance L. Howell; Rogers & Wells
Charles Speed; Gipson Hoffman & Pancione
Julianna Kim; Fried, Frank, Harris, Shriver & Jacobson
Winston S. Keh; Waters, Mcclusky & Boehle
William Koller; Lewis, D'Amato, Brisbois & Bisgard
Kemper R. Chafin; Sidley & Austin
Laura Hill; Sidley & Austin
David Studhalter; Long, Brown & Weisberg
Patrick Lin; Gartner & Young
Gwen Bauer; Keck, Mahin & Cate
Michael A. Blake; Los Angeles County District Attorney's Office
Karin A. Brietrich; Transit Casualty Company in Receivership
Norman P. Ejan; Office of the District Attorney
Mirta Ocana; Litt, Marquez & Fajardo
Janet M. Walker; Ivanjack, Lambirth & Aranoff
Winner: Susan L. Miller; Reisch & Luftman

Common Bond for Success

The prevailing theme throughout the nomination review process concluded that
in each instance, the paralegal had an unfailing ability to support attorneys
without letting them down. Each person gave others the feeling that **no matter
what,** they would be there to get the job done. *In a position specifically created to
support another position, this attitude was the key to success.*

Michael Jackman, president of Security Reprographics, said he put together the award ceremony because, "We think the paralegals are the unsung heroes of the legal profession. This is our gesture toward acknowledging the sterling work they perform. The quality of nominee was exceptionally high and a measure of this can be gleaned from the enthusiastic nominations from their firm's senior partners. The thought and effort that had to be applied to the nominating procedure reflects the attorneys' endorsement of the paralegals' efforts."

This profession has many Michael Jackman's of the world who willingly take these steps. The responsibility rests with every legal assistant to seek out those attorneys, firms, schools and vendors who will work in tandem to openly acknowledge success. Each stride the field takes toward getting long deserved recognition of successful paralegals increases its chances for advancement and improvement.

You Have a Right to Succeed

It is natural to want to succeed. Success is not an abnormality, it is a healthy drive to achieve, in a productive and fulfilling process, your right to the kind of life you are entitled. You have to want success in order to get it and understand that if another person has it, so can you.

Everyone has the power of self-motivation. To succeed is to take that first courageous step. Break out of the common ranks and take the risks to grow, to challenge, to confront change, to live your life as you want it to be. The journey to success will lead you nowhere if it isn't satisfying, challenging and exciting.

Taking the steps here: creating your own definition for success; overcoming self-defeating behavior; going to the right source for acknowledgment; and reaching out and claiming your success is a start in the right direction. Only a small difference exists between those who succeed and those who are just getting by. But that difference is the key to success—the critical edge that makes us winners.

Climbing the
Invisible Ladder

Reviews for many paralegals are just around corner and, once again, we are prepared to ask for increased responsibilities and upgraded assignments. Unfortunately, it's a little like using the phrase, "bless you" when someone sneezes. It becomes rhetorical, without true meaning, something we are automatically programmed to say.

This is not to say that we shouldn't think in terms of improving our careers and reaching past our comfort zone. Just how that can be accomplished is the question. Many articles and books advise us to "take the initiative" or "take on additional responsibility" and "be positive" but I wonder just what that really means.

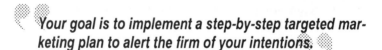

Your goal is to implement a step-by-step targeted marketing plan to alert the firm of your intentions.

By smiling as you walk down the hallways, will you convince a senior partner to ask you to sit at counsel's table during trial? By "taking on additional responsibilities" will you become a victim of empty loading—instead of summarizing six depositions a week, you goal is now twelve?

For many years, poorly thought out job planning has caused many paralegals to leave otherwise wonderful firms and legal departments. When we accept a new position, we accept the "dream" that life will somehow be better with this new position and the upward mobility it is sure to bring. Rarely do we attribute disappointment or growing frustration in the position with our own lack of personal responsibility for career planning.

In order to increase responsibilities and receive upgraded assignments we must first target job duties that enable us to move up. Expecting to climb a nonexistent ladder by relying on vagaries is as effective as receiving a nondirective to improve from your supervisor. "You'll have to improve your job performance," she says. "Great," you say, "I'll do just that." What on Earth was just said here? Improve? Improve what? Writing skills? Ability to use the computer? Research skills?

The same vague and useless exchange happens when you ask supervisors or attorneys to upgrade your assignments. Upgrade? Increase? "Okay," says attorney Jones and nothing ever happens. Why? Because now not only have you given control of your job to someone else, you have given him nonspecific directions on how he should proceed. Consequently, you sit and wait, your frustrations mounting.

Have a Plan of Action

What is your plan of action? If you are looking to upgrade your assignments, what is it that you plan on doing? Make a list of your current responsibilities. If you are an entry-level paralegal, it may look something like this:

- index documents,
- summarize depositions,
- calendar deadlines, and
- prepare witness lists.

Now list those specific assignments which automatically upgrade your position. Your goal is to implement a step-by-step targeted marketing plan to alert the firm of your intentions. The next step up in assignments may look like this:

- prepare answers to interrogs,
- draft summons and complaint,
- draft responses to discovery demands, and
- supervise document production.

Peruse the Master Calendar

It is useless to sit and wait for those assignments to fall into your lap. You're going to have to go out into the firm and get them. Review the firm's master calendar. Let's say that you notice that in three weeks there is a document production in the ACME case. Bingo. Who do you have to go to in order to request the assignment? Is there already a paralegal assigned to the case? Can you ask to assist?

If you are not stepping on any toes in your firm by sending a written memo, send a "Calendar Memo" to the attorney on the case. The memo may read:

According to the master calendar, there is a document production scheduled in the *Acme* case on December 3rd. Please check the areas where I may be of assistance to you:

_____ Supervise Production

_____ Attend with document clerks

_____ Arrange for microfilming

_____ Prepare indices

_____ Prepare database

_____ Respond to demand

_____ Organize documents

_____ Other

_____ See me

The power of the written word is in play here. Even if some of the assignments you are requesting are not ordinarily given to paralegals in your firm, the written word reinforces the concept that these particular assignments belong to paralegals. If paralegals do not, for example, automatically prepare the response to the discovery demand, the memo is a tool to educate attorneys on just what assignments you are capable of doing. If you have targeted this assignment as one of your next steps up, the memo is a good tool to use in going after that responsibility.

Once you have completed an assignment and have targeted the next step up, use that assignment as a request to upgrade. For example, you have just completed a Shepardizing assignment. You know that the next step is a motion to compel. When returning the completed assignment, add a memo that states,

> I can prepare the motion to compel for you and have it on your desk within 72 hours. Can you meet with me on Tuesday at 9:00 a.m. or would 1:00 be better?

How to Handle Resistance

If you meet resistance due to your inexperience, ask for assistance with the assignment. Merely asking someone to "help out" may not get you what you need. Instead, find out what the objection is related to. Is the attorney afraid that the client may be billed too many hours by an inexperienced person? Ask the attorney how many hours he thinks a first-year associate would take to complete the assignment.

Let's say the attorney estimates six hours. Now is your time to negotiate. Take a shot at how many hours you think it will take you to complete the assignment, perhaps ten, and inform the attorney of your estimate.

You may require one hour of attorney time to review and evaluate your project. If the work product is acceptable, you will then bill the client for six hours and account for the other five under the non-billable administrative number or, if your firm doesn't have one, write off those hours. The client will receive excellent work product at a lower cost (a prime marketing tool these days) and the firm will have a paralegal trained in these procedures. Everyone wins.

Continuing Education

Taking a continuing education course to upgrade responsibilities only works if the end result is that you receive new and exciting assignments. Unfortunately, in today's recession, law firms are reluctant to pay for many legal assistants' seminar courses. If you take a course in order to expand your responsibilities and your firm is unaware of that fact, alert the firm by giving a sample of your course work to one of the attorneys you have targeted as a potential resource for new assignments. The memo might say:

> I am enclosing a sample of the commercial lease agreement I drafted for the Real Estate Transaction course I am taking at the university. I feel confident that upon completion of this course I will be able to prepare agreements for our clients. Please let me know how I can assist you with the Smith agreement due on December 15th.

Stay away from using tentative suggestions such as "I was wondering if..." or "I was hoping to..." Don't wait to be called. Scout out a potential use for your skills, name the assignment and claim it.

Supervising Vendors

Legal assistants looking to get into management can prove their management skills by supervising vendors on projects. These types of projects include microfilming, large-scale photocopying, initiating new computerized projects for the firm, financial printing, relocating offices, overseeing temporary paralegals, and more. The process of interviewing and selecting new vendors calls on your ability to make judgments, evaluate skills, compare costs and act as a liaison for the firm.

Drafting a request for proposal to a vendor positions you as a person capable of organizing and supervising complex projects. Don't overlook this technique as a stepping stone to more sophisticated responsibilities.

Taking Charge

Taking charge of any career is difficult and that is particularly true with paralegals. You are trying to fit into a highly structured world—the legal industry—in a role that is still trying to define itself. That inherently makes for conflict—both with attorneys who have done things a certain way for years and with others who perceive that doing things differently is somehow rocking the boat or cheating instead of making things better.

On top of that, you are engaged in an intellectually oriented career without the same status as some of the other players involved. Had you chosen to go to law school and become a lawyer, the playing field would be more level. But the reality is that no matter how smart or experienced you are, a paralegal always seems to be in the process of proving him or herself. Some of you may thrive on that kind of challenge but most of us prefer a level of comfort and confidence that is beyond proving yourself on an ongoing basis.

I have outlined only a few techniques for a disciplined method of taking the difficulties in this emerging career and using them to your own benefit. If you are patient, smart and strategic, you can chart your progress toward your goals with confidence and, in most cases, speed. All it takes is the willingness to clearly think through your career and your goals and then apply what you know to the task of getting what you want.

I have seen hundreds of paralegals do this. It is a process that never fails to excite me because it is another way for people to take charge of their own lives. My message to you is, have faith, you can do it, too.

Ten Easy Steps to Leveraging Your Career

What have you done lately in terms of planning for your professional future? Many legal assistants, once they accept a position, let the position guide their careers.

The steps you take now will have a great impact on your future. How do you increase the chances for your success?

> *Too many legal assistants respond with "I don't know" when asked where they'd like to be in five years. Many look surprised even to be asked. Even in a field where you're considered senior with five years of experience, it's still essential to have a five-year plan with flexible goals.*

1. *Word your resume to reflect your next career move.* Don't give a laundry list of every kind of assignment you've ever had. If you're looking to upgrade your position, for example from an entry-level legal assistant to a specialist, don't emphasize deposition summarizing if it's not what you want to do. Emphasize substantial duties in a priority order relevant to the position you're applying for. Remember, the skills you list will guide your future employer's level of expectations.

2. *Focus on a conduit to power.* Some experts advise you to go to top management and convince them of what you can do. Easier said than done in many law firms and corporate legal departments. Getting to the managing partner may be next to impossible. However, you can determine who has the authority's ear. Perhaps it's an associate who works directly with the managing partner. Pay attention to the power structure around you.

3. *Take an attorney to lunch.* In firms where an unofficial caste system exists between attorneys, management and legal assistants, the assistant may work side by side with attorneys into all hours of the night and on weekends, yet never be allowed to eat with the attorneys. Many meaningful and powerful business deals are born during an otherwise unassuming lunch. Your career is business! Be assertive. Give attorneys and management the opportunity to get to know you. There are very few people in a position of power who will turn down your lunch invitation—most will be pleased you asked.

4. *Increase your visibility.* Get out into the community by accepting speaking engagements or teaching assignments, and by writing articles or agreeing to be interviewed. As you do, your reputation as a credible source builds. This leveraging technique means that new employers will consider it a real coup to hire you, and you will gain recognition among your present employers. Keep those who are important to your career informed.

5. *Develop a master plan.* Too many legal assistants respond with "I don't know" when asked where they'd like to be in five years. Many look surprised even to be asked. Even in a field where you're considered senior with five years of experience, it's still essential to have a five-year plan with flexible goals. This plan outlines where you're going and how to get there. From your plan, establish a list of goals every year and review them every six months or so.

   If you have difficulty with the review process, you might try the letter technique. Write a letter to a good friend, dating it one year ahead, and outlining everything you intend to accomplish for the year:

   > "Dear Carol:
   >
   > This was a very successful year for me. I learned how to use the personal computer in my plan to become a litigation support expert. After I learned the basics, I became very knowledgeable in the four top litigation support programs in the country. My firm recognized this expertise by giving me the litigation support team leader position in the LKD case. I'm on my way!"

   Actually give the letter to a close friend and ask him or her to pull it out to review it with you in a year. You may be surprised at how close you've come to accomplishing your goals.

6. *Attend seminars.* Increased knowledge is only one reason to attend. Seminars are where others who are key to your career goals—contacts, mentors, teachers and future employers—are gathered in an informal setting.

7. *Negotiate for higher level assignments.* Sometimes easier said than done. Those who have the courage to ask for the big assignment are still often refused because the attorney fears there's a lack of experience. Or, worse yet, the

attorney trained in negotiation will become defensive, and your demands may produce negative results.

One way to combat this is to target a specific assignment, and ask the responsible attorney how long it should take to complete it. If the attorney thinks it would take four hours, claim that you can do it in eight on the first try. Offer to charge off four hours (or do it on your own time) and charge the client for the expected four hours, at the assistant's rate.

Ask the attorney to invest an hour or two to review the project with you (offer to meet for breakfast if you have to). This method provides you with training and a higher-level assignment, the attorney with an experienced assistant and the client with lower fees.

8. *Go for the title.* Titles are an important leveraging tool. As a critical need for specialists develops, there is less and less emphasis on the legal assistant as part of a team. A title is a springboard to the next step in your career. If you obtain the title of litigation coordinator, for example, it helps to pave the way for promotion to legal assistant administrator.

9. *Take charge of a new firm activity.* This is always an ideal way to advance yourself and gain recognition. If, for example, your firm has never had an educational retreat for legal assistants, you may demonstrate your leadership and training skills by organizing the event.

10. *Keep an eye on what's next.* New challenges should always be a part of your plan. If things feel really comfortable, you're probably not growing.

Be good to yourself by keeping yourself motivated, excited and rewarded. The legal assistant career is still a relatively new field. Here is the perfect opportunity for you to help shape the future of a powerful industry.

Managing Attorneys to Get What You Need to Succeed

The other day I had lunch with one of the most charming and wise managing partners I've met in a long time: Ralph Williams of King and Williams in Los Angeles. We sat in the California sun, eating the latest in nonfat, no cholesterol, no calorie, no food cuisine.

As we talked about how to manage attorneys, Ralph struck me as a not-at-all-run-of-the-mill manager, because his ideas were innovative, fresh and applicable to **anyone** who works in the legal environment. During this discussion, I realized that even though paralegals are technically in a subordinate position in law firms, they are **no less responsible for managing the attorneys** they work with.

 Paralegals needing decisions from attorneys may do well using these two techniques. The first approach is to walk in with the answer and give the attorney a choice on how to proceed.
The second technique is to present two well researched and preselected choices and leave the decision to the attorney.

You're Already Managing Attorneys

Now, before you snicker, it may be prudent to remember exactly what you may have to go through in order to get a promotion, an attorney's attention or help, an assignment completed, or a decision made. Think about the steps needed to accomplish these things. I think you'll find that in many instances, you're already applying proven management techniques and strategies to get your job done. Without using these techniques, we may as well be puppies on linoleum floors: lots of motion with no movement. . . unable to control the outcome of our own careers.

As the profession evolves, more and more legal assistants have management duties, even though they do not have the title "manager." Paralegals are charged with responsibilities for purchasing equipment, recruiting, evaluating, and assigning work flow. The day-to-day management of your individual career includes managing the attorneys you work with to get:

* timely responses,
* documents filed on time,
* events coordinated,
* the necessary tools for the particular project researched and purchased, and
* clients handled.

Macro vs. Micro Management

In most cases, you will put your managerial skills to work on individual attorneys. But you may also occasionally need to manage a group of attorneys—or even all the attorneys in the firm—toward a particular decision.

Because law firms are governed by committee, getting what you need quickly is often impossible. Decision-making by committee is definitely an arduous process. And the committee structure isn't your only problem. Because lawyers generally don't like to be solely responsible for decisions affecting the entire firm (or even a department), it is even more difficult and time consuming to get a consensus of opinion. This is particularly the case if speed is required.

Getting what you need may require campaigning, documenting, arguing, and most definitely, enlisting your key power sources. According to Williams, moving attorneys along the path to a group decision "is a lot like herding cats." Getting from point A to point B may not seem all that difficult, but just wait until you try to move all those attorneys in the same direction at once.

Using the "Experiment" Approach

"Jack," a 35-year-old paralegal administrator for a mid-size insurance defense firm, describes his frustrating experiences trying to get the firm to update its 20-year-old calendar and docket system:

> I couldn't seem to convince them that not only did we have potential malpractice problems, but the wasted time involving paralegals manually checking dates was outrageous. I simply couldn't get the practice management committee to make the necessary commitment to the dollars and training time.

The solution? Understand and react appropriately to the mind-set of an entity in which no one person wants to undertake full responsibility. If the firm makes a major commitment to change, and that change fails, the peer pressure and criticism can be so severely shame-based that attorneys may fear to make another change-oriented decision.

Williams' answer to moving law firms toward quick decision making is to suggest the proposed change as "only an experiment." Even though the experiment may require the allocation of money, viewing the decision as only an experiment, allows the chance of failure to be more acceptable. Experiments also don't entail a total commitment to the decision, thus psychologically relieving everyone of responsibility.

If the decision is a final one, it had better work. If, on the other hand, the experiment fails, no one person is at fault. After all, it was "**just** an experiment."

It's Not Necessarily the Answer That's Important: It's the Process

One of the best techniques for getting what you need is to involve yourself in the **decision-making process**, rather than focusing only on the answer. Attorneys have been heavily trained to look carefully at both sides of an argument. They will most likely review all aspects (without prejudice) of a so-called black or white, yes or no situation. You'll get what you need from attorneys if you understand that the decision evaluation process is just as important as the decision itself.

"Jack" also told me that he was involved with his firm's recent attorney retreat. At the event, the managing partner wrote a list on the blackboard which consisted of next year's goals for the firm. These goals had not been discussed with the firm's partners; they were simply determined in advance and announced by the managing partner. Goals such as bringing in 20 new cases per month, increasing revenue by 15%, increasing utilization of paralegals, and developing a new training program for new associates were highlighted.

"What was interesting," said Jack, "is that no one argued about the goals themselves." But long discussions over how to **achieve** those results did occur:

> One attorney argued that the firm must bring in 20 "quality" cases, so the firm would not turn into a "mill." This prompted discussion of exactly what was the criteria for "mill"? At what point can a firm be reasonably deemed a "mill?"
>
> Other attorneys debated whether increasing the utilization of paralegals meant one paralegal for every associate/partner team, or one paralegal for every attorney.
>
> When the managing partner stressed "more team playing" as another goal, a 45-minute debate erupted over what **kind** of team should they be? Hockey? Baseball? Basketball? Finally, the attorneys deter-

mined that they were a golf team: everyone played their own game, yet they all ended up on the 18th hole together. "No one argued about the end result," says Jack.

Techniques for Getting Decisions Made

Paralegals needing decisions from attorneys may do well using these two techniques. The first approach is to **walk in with the answer** and give the attorney a **choice on how to proceed.** For example: You need a new litigation software package to summarize depositions. After conducting your research, you determine that package A would best suit your needs, even though package B offers a better training program and price. You tell the attorney your recommendation for purchasing package A and then suggest the following options for proceeding with this decision:

> We can purchase package A now and request additional training from the company with a 30-day return policy. We can then experiment and evaluate our findings. Or, we can have John, Mary and Susan evaluate the demonstration disk for package A over the next two weeks and report back. Which option would you prefer?

The second technique is to **present two well researched and preselected choices** and **leave the decision to the attorney.**

> We can purchase both packages A and B with a 30-day return policy. We can then experiment with both programs and evaluate our findings. Or, we can save time by spending the few extra dollars on purchasing software B, and get all the bells and whistles now **before** we expand this department. Which approach would you prefer?

Managing Difficult Attorneys

Let's be honest. Every office has at least one difficult attorney, and everyone knows who it is. We try to be polite about it. We even try to joke about it. But the fact remains that in every law office resides at least one monster euphemistically called the "difficult attorney." Getting the decisions you need from this person can be burdensome at best. But you need to manage difficult people so you can, in turn, manage your own career. Here are a few ways to handle these people.

The Nonlistener: Nonlisteners consider themselves very busy people. They give you the impression that they have very little time to hear what you have to say. Your meetings with them are interrupted by "important phone calls." To get their attention, you find yourself chasing them down the hall. Pressure mounts as you try to race through your request. You feel guilty because you're taking up their valuable time.

Timing is everything with Nonlisteners. Find out when is a good time to capture their attention. Perhaps they are not so frazzled in the morning when they first walk in, or after hours when the phones stop ringing is a good time to talk. Walk in with an agenda. Write it out if you need to, so you can present your request in an orderly fashion. Tell Nonlisteners you need six or twelve minutes of their time. (Because people ask for five or ten minutes so often, that phrase has become meaningless.) Pay attention to your watch and stick to that time frame.

Be direct. If you feel the Nonlistener is slipping away, call him or her on it: "Jane, I need your full attention on this matter." Don't get intimidated if they have rank over you. Speak in short sentences, and elicit a response from the Nonlistener every few sentences. You are attempting to have a two-way conversation so you don't lose their attention. Always follow up with a short memo memorializing the conversation.

The Time Waster: Time Wasters are aggravating because most often, it's **your** time they've wasted. Time Wasters will have you do unnecessary tasks such as sit in their office waiting while they talk endlessly on the phone to someone unrelated to any of your assignments (all on **your** billable time). Or, they will have you redo an entire assignment because they "changed their minds" and forgot to inform you. Time Wasters stop **your** clocks.

It's up to you to set boundaries. Let Time Wasters know that your time is valuable. If they are on the phone, smile, get up, indicate you'll be back and leave. Or let the Time Waster know that you have a more efficient way of doing things: "Tom, I understand your request. However, if we computerize these documents instead, we can save six to eight hours of time. Here is how I propose we start."

Time Wasters seldom recognize that they have a time management problem. People who delve into time management books are generally organized to begin with and simply desire to improve their present systems.

The Deadline Deviant: These people start projects late, keep you working weekends and ask you to pull all-nighters because they don't seem to be able to complete **their** work. They frequently ask for continuances and extensions, and routinely reschedule appointments. The Deadline Deviant has a time management problem, but it affects **your** work. If you are involved in a project with this person, **don't** try to manage all of their time. Manage only those aspects that involve you so you're not victimized by working unnecessary, crazy hours.

Don't wait to be told when to start a project. Take the initiative and start the Deadline Deviant on the project: "Here is an outline of your jury presentation. Can I meet with you tomorrow at 9:00 a.m., or would after lunch be better?" Or, "I see you need these documents on Tuesday. What time on Tuesday? What will you need the documents for?" Be sure to ask if this will result in another assignment and prepare accordingly.

The Mixed Messenger: This person sends out mixed messages and sets unclear goals. For example, "Dena" was a corporate paralegal who had heavy client contact. However, "Bruce," the attorney she worked with, didn't want her spending time on the phone with clients. (Bruce wanted his clients to feel that he was easily accessible.) At the same time, he was very upset over having to bill attorney time for what were clearly paralegal duties. Dena was confused about her role, but the person to really hold responsible was Bruce.

Since Bruce was incapable of giving clear signals, it was up to Dena to define the goals: "Bruce, let's educate our clients about what they can ask me for and what is clearly an attorney function. Each time the client asks for information in the minute books, let's inform them that if I do it, they'll only be billed a fraction of what you will bill them. That way, they'll begin to automatically ask for me."

With a Mixed Messenger, you may have to clarify not just once, but two or three times, exactly what is expected until the Mixed Messenger learns where you will take responsibility and where you won't. Each time you receive a mixed message, speak up:

> "I seem to be getting crossed signals. Would you like me to ____ or
> _____? Thanks, now, I understand what you want is for me to _____."

This gives the Mixed Messenger a chance to sort out in his or her own mind what is really wanted.

The Promotion Teaser: This person is always promising you some sort of promotion or advance. The problem is, this promise is always made about events in the vague, distant future, and always has a hitch to it, such as "must get firm approval, of course." The Promotion Teaser probably doesn't have the authority to get you that promotion anyway. Handling this person involves utilizing the power of the written word. The next time you hear about this vague and wonderful promotion, capture the conversation in a memo:

> "Confirming our conversation of this morning where you indicated your desire to upgrade my assignments by having me attend various arbitrations: the ACME case is scheduled before Judge Harrison next week. I'll clear my calendar in order to attend. Thanks for this opportunity."

The Critic: Law firms are notorious for handing out criticism. The Critic never has anything nice to say about you. You never have an assignment completed on the first try with the Critic. It usually takes two or three tries before they are satisfied. Critics try to hide the fact that the person they are most critical of is themselves. They are hard on you because of their own insecurities.

What works with the Critic is to put the relationship on a more equal footing: "Thanks for showing me exactly what you wanted on that pleading.

It was very helpful." Or, when you hear a snide or unpleasant remark, compliment the Critic:

> "If what you are trying to say is that you are displeased with my drafting ability, I can't think of a better person to show me the right way of doing it." Compliments can help diffuse the anger.

Managing Attorneys to Get What You Need

Standing up to authority figures without fighting or creating aggressive confrontations is not an easy task. You certainly don't want to risk your job. But you can start practicing getting what you need from authority figures by managing them in low-risk situations. Try offering the attorneys you work with lists of optional answers, instead of asking open-ended questions in which the attorney must supply the answers.

Managing attorneys **isn't** a revolutionary idea. All we're really talking about is managing your career in such a way that everyone around you has confidence in your abilities to get things done and to help move the organization in a positive direction.

We are all creators of our own futures: here's to happy **and** successful careers!

On the Road Again

I was *supposed* to be driving down Pacific Coast Highway headed toward Malibu at this very moment. Sunroof open, stereo blasting, basking in the sunshine, and singing at the top of my lungs to the latest Michael Crawford tape.

Instead, I was huddled on a bench in the middle of the worst snowstorm in Minneapolis in 15 years. I tried desperately to warm myself with California's version of a winter coat, tossing my handkerchief-sized muffler over my reddened and semi-frostbitten nose. I felt like crying, only my glasses had iced over and I was afraid I'd make things worse.

> *. . .you also need to know that if you carry candy bars (instead of low-fat healthy food), dark chocolate doesn't melt as easily as milk chocolate. When you have flown 3,000 miles in a hailstorm, landed at 2:00 in the morning at the wrong airport, or find that all flight attendants are on strike in the midst of a holiday week when you absolutely have to travel, you have no idea how important this tidbit of information can be.*

Why, you may ask, was I subjecting myself to such abject misery? Well, it certainly wasn't by *choice*. I was literally stranded at the airport. Of course, it was only the middle of the trip and frankly, this unbearable element was infinitely better than how the trip started out.

The travel agent booked me on the wrong flight, at the wrong hotel, and on the wrong day. During takeoff, I was sitting in a window seat over the wing when a fireball about the size of Cincinnati exploded out of the engine. As we taxied back to the gate, the pilot announced we were going to "wait on the plane while the ground crew takes a look-see to find the problem, then we'll try taking off again."

Excuse me? A "look-see"? To find the problem? Let me get this straight: Take off again on *this* plane? AREYOUSERIOUS?????

Finally arriving at the hotel hours and hours late, the clerk insists on sending me back out into the cold because I don't have a reservation. Of course, I DO have a reservation, only it's at the downtown hotel instead. Miraculously, a room becomes available on the first floor. (It must have been my whining that worked.) So far, so good.

But wait a minute. "You mean the room that can be easily broken into through the sliding glass doors? No, I don't think so. How about a few floors up?" Giving me a nasty look, one that clearly indicates *I'm* the problem here, the room clerk throws a key toward me, which I grab as a drowning person would a lifeline.

I find myself on a deserted floor. Entering the room, I notice the wallpaper peeling off the wall. I sit down on the bed. It flips up on both sides of me. Groaning, but grateful to even be here, I get up and attempt to lock the door. It won't lock. I call down to the front desk.

"I'll send an engineer up to try and fix the lock," says the clerk. By now, patience is but a mere memory. I am *not* waiting another half an hour in the dead of the night for someone to fix what should have been working in the first place. I'm exhausted, hungry and in no mood.

"No," I said. "*Don't* send me a locksmith. I would like another room."

"No," the clerk replied, "I'll send up the engineer."

"*Get me the manager immediately*," I respond through gritted teeth.

Finally resettled into a much nicer room, one obviously set aside for someone else—the plate full of chocolate covered strawberries "For Betty, from your travel agent" was a dead giveaway—I crawled into bed. Sorry, Betty. Right now, it's survival of the most aggressive. I set my alarm for 6:00 a.m. (which is 4:00 a.m. my time), and try to get some sleep out of what's left of the night so I can be graceful, glamorous and agreeable for a 7:00 a.m. meeting in the morning.

My staff seriously razzed me about doing this article on traveling. "You're not serious," they said. "This is a *career advice* column. Surely, you're not going to give out little helpful travel hints, and become the 'Helpful Heloise' of the paralegal travel industry?"

Oh yes, I am. I have found that unless you get this down to a science, your trips out of town can be miserable. Very little work is accomplished because you are spending your time trying to fix what could have been prevented. You end up wasting time and money, maybe getting the job done, but inefficiently, and you're unwilling to go on the road again. So here are ten tips for enjoying a smoother business trip.

1. Get a Good Business Travel Agent

A no-brainer, you say? Believe me, any agent who is only used to booking cruises and resorts is not as likely to scrounge around getting corporate rates and cheap direct flights. Business agents also know how to cater to the woman traveller, the frequent traveller, the inexperienced, and the fun-seeker.

It is *infuriating* to stay in a hotel that cannot meet your individual needs. When you are stressed from travel, jet-lagged or befuddled about your unfamiliar surroundings, the suitability of the place you will call "home" for the next few hours or days becomes **very** important. Suit hangers but no skirt hangers, pants pressers but no irons or ironing boards, an easy-to-get-to location, and a friendly and helpful concierge—all take on new meaning.

2. Choose a Hotel that Caters to Business Travelers

Faxes, business centers, personal computers, cellular phones, air express drops, are now part of many hotel's standard operating procedures. I like to stay in one hotel in Minneapolis that offers an exercycle in the room for $10.00 more per night. I should only use the one I have at home.

3. Stay Away from Irate Taxicab Drivers

Most hotels offer free transportation to and from the airport. Save your firm money and spare yourself from angry taxicab drivers who want longer trips (and larger fares). Find out from your travel agent if hotel-sponsored transportation is available, and if so, whether it must be booked in advance of your arrival.

4. When Do We Eat?

While many of you will push Overeaters Anonymous membership on me for even addressing this problem, I can't tell you how many times I have booked connecting flights only to find out that there is no food on ANY of the flights. Okay, maybe for the first flight, but many are the times I have run through the airport, jumped on a connecting flight and made it to the hotel only to discover a real catastrophe: I'm in a different time zone!

When this happens, it's always after 10:00 p.m., room service has stopped serving, the restaurants and gift shop are closed, there's no mini-bar in the room, and NO ONE AROUND ME GIVES A DAMN. At this point, grouchy is a very *nice* way of describing my evolving personality.

In the event I end up food-less for eight hours, I now carry either a couple of granola bars or cans of Slim-Fast. I then tell myself how great this is for my weight-loss program.

Oh yes, you also need to know that if you carry candy bars (instead of low-fat healthy food), dark chocolate *doesn't* melt as easily as milk chocolate. When you have flown 3,000 miles in a hailstorm, landed at 2:00 in the morning at the wrong airport, or find that all flight attendants are on strike in the midst of a holiday week when you absolutely have to travel, you have no idea how important this tidbit of information can be.

5. Will You Need a Bumpershoot?

It's not unusual to forget all about the weather at your final destination when travelling. Recently, I jumped on a plane for a 50-minute ride, only to arrive in a pouring rainstorm. Because "rain" is merely a concept where I live, not generally a reality, it never dawned on me that this unlikely event may be occurring elsewhere. There we were, my colleague and I, Droopy and Sneezy, at your service.

I have witnessed Californians arriving in New York in the winter without so much as a coat, and folks from the East Coast arriving in La-La Land in the middle of a heat wave, dressed for the North Pole. A friend of mine tossed this off by saying, "No problem. I'll just go and buy new clothes." Sure. Spoken like a true thin person.

6. Save on Air Fare and Hotel Costs

Remember that law firms and corporations are heavily into cost-cutting measures these days. Luckily, there are so many ways to save on air fare and accommodations. Here are just three:

Check Out Pleasure Packages. If you will be staying more than one night, you may find a lower-cost air fare intended for those pleasure travelers. On a flight just last week, I found a brochure on Delta's "dream vacations" and discovered that for only $679 I could get a round-trip ticket across the country to New York along with three nights at a very decent hotel. Further, they insisted that I leave mid-week. Perfect for business! (Other packages may insist on Saturday travel, but this may work for you also).

Be sure and check whether refunds are allowed in the event you need to cancel.

Get Off at the Hub. Many careful buyers have found that if they are traveling to an airline hub, such as Dallas or Minneapolis, it is actually cheaper to buy a ticket to a destination *beyond* the hub, for a flight that changes planes *at* the hub. For example, a direct ticket to Dallas could cost $500. However, if you purchase a ticket for a destination beyond Dallas but change planes in Dallas, you may get the ticket for $300. Just get off the plane in Dallas instead of continuing on. The airlines outsmarted themselves on this one.

Ask for the Corporate Rate. Most firms have set up corporate rates for hotels in the cities frequently visited by the firm on business. Sometimes, clients will make their corporate accounts available to you as well. However, if neither of these situations exist, you can always ask to be given the corporate rate yourself. Most hotels will let you set up an account during your first stay; I just did this on a trip to San Francisco.

Getting billed the corporate rate can save up to 15% off the daily room charge. Sometimes the hotel will make deluxe rooms available for the price of a standard one. Of course, whether a corporate rate will apply depends on several factors: the basic room cost, the season, and space availability.

7. You Said You Were Where?

Of course, you say, someone in the office always knows where you are. Yet, the reality is that many times they *don't* precisely know your location. They only know for sure when you call in. Make sure your secretary and all other pertinent people know your travel schedule. Advise them when you are expected to arrive, where they can call you, and at what times.

In this day and age, not having a telephone company calling card is like not having an answering machine. Calling your office collect is not a good idea, nor can you stand at a phone booth laden with change. I was surprised at the number of people I have spoken to recently about this issue that do not carry telephone calling cards when they travel.

Another important point involves the cost of keeping in touch. Be sure you understand your firm's policy on the reimbursement of phone calls while on a business trip. Are phone calls home reimbursed? Which charges, if any, should be passed through to the client?

8. Firm's Policy on Travel Time Billing

Every firm has its own policies governing business travel and detailed guidelines for billing travel time. If you are traveling for one client, yet during the flight you work on a different client's file, how do you bill your time? Billing for travel time as well as any worked performed during that time can result in 28-hour day, which becomes an automatic target for auditing. Find out your firm's policies for traveling on business:

- Does the firm offer a reduced billing rate to the client for flight time?
- Is travel to and from the airport billed at all?
- What about while you are in the hotel?
- What is the policy for reimbursement of meals?
- Is there a strict per diem allowance?

- Does the per diem include cab fare?
- What about miscellaneous expenses such as toiletries?

9. Obtain Vendor Recommendations from Local Paralegal Associations

I have seen paralegals land in far off places, all intent on doing battle, yet not having a clue where to get the warriors. Members of your local association can provide recommendations about local vendors:

- photocopying,
- microfilming,
- temporary services,
- stationery suppliers, and
- whatever (or whomever) else you may need to get the job done.

Don't wait until you get there, expecting the client (or the attorney) to know exactly what you will need. Yes, you could spend precious hours finding what you need in the local yellow pages, but you won't know in advance what kind of performance to expect.

10. Don't Ignore the Stress of Jet Lag

Certainly, enough has been said about combatting jet lag. I have read plenty of articles claiming that if you eat carbohydrates and drink plenty of water the day ahead of the trip, you won't suffer jet lag. About the only thing I have gotten out of those tips is an extra five pounds and bloated.

Something helpful that I can tell you to try, however, concerns trip planning. If you can, try *not* to plan such an action-packed day on your arrival date that you wear yourself out for the rest of the trip. Even if you want to, you can't totally ignore time differences; eventually the time change will catch up with you. It's just so beastly to fall asleep at the conference table in front of your client and everybody!

So, hopefully, fellow travelers, these helpful travel tips will guide you through a safe and pleasant journey. I have to sign off now. I just learned that an ice storm is expected in Minneapolis. And my flight leaves in an hour.

[1] "Getting a Grip on Your Career: Strategies For Empowering Your Position," was first published in the September/October 1994 issue of LEGAL ASSISTANT TODAY.

[2] "In Search of Success," was first published in the September/October 1992 issue of LEGAL ASSISTANT TODAY.

[3] "Climbing the Invisible Ladder," was first published in the September/October 1991 issue of LEGAL ASSISTANT TODAY.

[4] "Ten Easy Steps to Leveragng Your Career," was first published in the July/August 1989 issue of LEGAL ASSISTANT TODAY.

[5] "Managing Attorneys to Get What You Need to Succeed," was first published in the July/August 1992 issue of LEGAL ASSISTANT TODAY.

[6] "On the Road Again," was first published in the March/April 1994 issue of LEGAL ASSISTANT TODAY.

Part
4

Life in the
Law Firm

For some professionals, the law firm environment offers a very different atmosphere than what they may be used to. Understanding office expectations and relationships are essential to achieving personal success.

Negotiating is a technique that is very rarely performed better than by attorneys. Legal assistants will accomplish more by understanding what the obstacles are and how to get what they need when review time comes around.

Retreats, outsourcing and personnel issues also may be very different from one office environment to another. As law firms are governed by committee rather than one individual, it is helpful to understand how to get through the system.

How Attorneys Evaluate Paralegals

When I undertook the assignment to write this article, I was surprised at the wide range of emotions that the concept of "evaluation" or "review" still conjured up in my mind after all these years. I decided to call two friends who I knew had recently undergone the process.

"Annie" works in a chic Beverly Hills law firm, known for its structured, well-oiled paralegal program, liberal attitudes and retention of good employees.

I quickly realized, after talking with many paralegals, that too many had only a marginal idea as to how their raises were set.

"I'm very upset over the increase in salary," Annie told me. "The maximum raise anyone could have received was 6 1/2%. That's what I got. However, I really outdid myself this year in billables. I was expecting a minimum of 10%. After all, there are partners here who made over $1 million in partner compensation. The very least they could do was pass a better portion of the overall profit on to me."

"Phil" had a different story. His firm, a very large Los Angeles office with offices nationwide and in Europe, was known for its excellent paralegal career path.

"My review was great," he beamed. "Not only were the attorneys completely knowledgeable of what I accomplished this year, they agreed to upgrade my level of assignments, see to it that I received appropriate CEB courses and gave me a healthy increase in salary, about 6%. I got a great bonus as well."

Why the diversity in reviews, feelings, and reactions to the review? What was going on here? It seemed as though we all knew *what* attorneys evaluated paralegals on. To be sure, I conducted a quick, informal survey to determine the ten most common topics. They emerged as:

1. *Teamwork.* Does the paralegal work in a harmonious manner with all the players (i.e., attorneys, supervisors, staff, clients, and vendors)?

2. *Ability to marshal information.* Does the paralegal gather pertinent information? Does he recognize important information above and beyond the original request? Does the paralegal present the information in a concise, organized manner?

3. *Knowledge of specialty.* Is the paralegal familiar with the specific assignments he can perform within his specialty? Can she suggest alternatives? Are the assignments performed consistent with the level of experience?

4. *Crafting political solutions.* Does the paralegal solve problems practically? Or does he miss the real issues?

5. *Workload management.* What is the paralegal's ability to juggle caseload and assignments? Is she on time with assignments?

6. *Judgment.* How does the paralegal handle day-to-day decisions? What is the outcome? Does the paralegal exercise independent thinking within the scope of his responsibilities? Does she know when to ask questions?

7. *Writing and analysis ability.* Are the paralegal's written assignments clear, concise and accurate? Are they grammatically correct?

8. *Initiative.* Does the paralegal go the "extra mile?"

9. *Organizational skills.* Can anyone else locate the paralegal's assignments or documents at a moment's notice?

10. *Billable hours.* Does the paralegal meet the minimum billable requirement? Does the paralegal have minimal write-offs? Does the paralegal bill fairly to the client?

Still, some questions remained. How do attorneys evaluate paralegals? What goes through their minds when they pick up the evaluation form?

Evaluating Subjective Qualities

Many paralegals question how an attorney can evaluate qualities which seem totally subjective, such as judgment.

"By focusing on choices the paralegal has made within his responsibility," says Douglas Ditonto, attorney in the legal department of Southern California Edison Corporation and previous supervisor of the business and property litigation paralegals, "an attorney can effectively evaluate judgment."

Did the paralegal focus on real issues? What was his day-to-day decision-making ability? Does he think objectively? Judgment is made up of how well someone thinks independently, discerns information and exercises discretion. Did she handle sensitive information correctly? Did he discern the true problems, events and tactics?

"I start from the very beginning," says Ditonto, who has a good perspective since he was employed as a paralegal while working his way through law school. "Is the paralegal eager and interested? Does he understand what's going on? If the assignment is beyond the paralegal's experience, does he speak up? It doesn't hurt someone if they have never performed a particular assignment. There must be a willingness to tackle something."

"Often, attorneys do not know how to properly utilize paralegals," said Benjamin Seigal, senior partner with Katz, Holt, Seigal & Kapor in Los Angeles and an instructor for the paralegal program at the University of West Los Angeles. "If attorneys aren't adequately trained to work with paralegals, they cannot adequately evaluate paralegals."

He evaluates a paralegal based on how well the work product is thought out. He also looks to see how well the paralegal worked with the lawyers.

Using an Appropriate Basis for Comparison

Seigal feels that attorneys have a tendency to compare the paralegal's performance with an associate's. This leads to big disappointment.

"Once you start treating paralegals like attorneys, you make a huge mistake," he claims. "You can't expect a paralegal to do what a lawyer does. Most of the attorneys in my firm buy into the theory of continuously upgrading paralegal assignments because we are strong advocates of the paralegal profession."

"What happens is that we begin to believe that paralegals have much more ability than they are actually trained for. We expect the paralegal to progress as an attorney. For example, initially we give paralegals simple work such as summarizing (depositions), drafting requests for production, interrogatories and simple legal analysis. As we begin to receive great work product, we want to keep upgrading—a 'sky's the limit' mentality."

"At some point, it is possible to hit the areas where the paralegal is not trained (i.e., theory). The paralegal simply is not trained to do a lawyer's work. Now our confidence level plunges downward because we get work product back that doesn't look like an associate's. The paralegal gets criticized in the review."

"You can't really go back successfully to 'the way it was.' You get much better results for both attorney and paralegal by setting reasonable goals. You must also be sure the attorneys are trained on the fine line of where the practice of law begins and the paralegal function ends."

Quantity and Quality of Work

Productivity was another criteria which emerged as a strong evaluation factor. A classic example came from Michael La Panta, vice president for Aspen Systems, one of the largest litigation support companies in Rockville, Maryland. Paralegals in this corporation are project managers. Aspen reviews the project managers' level of quality on the job. How well they have hired and trained their staff is a key factor. Do they maintain productivity and achieve their goals?

"Our paralegals are given tremendous responsibility," states La Panta. "Our profit is tied to how well they do. We treat them like business people."

"Paralegals are invaluable," states Barry Friedman, senior partner at Friedman and Phillips in Los Angeles. "I subscribe to the principles we read over and over that paralegals are in the firm for three reasons:

- to save the client fees,

- to save the attorney time, and

- to act as a profit center.

"Good billable time is an indication not only that the paralegal is working 'smart' but that (he has) become the right arm of the attorney and friend to the client. If I have to write off time because the work product is not up to par or the paralegal took too much time, I lose confidence in the paralegal. Often, it's not so much if the paralegal has the most hours, but whether those hours are good. I look to see if the paralegal's work product closely matches mine and when I combine their work product with my work if it comes across as one consistent product."

Economic Factors

I quickly realized, after talking with many paralegals, that too many had only a marginal idea as to how their raises were set.

Paul Bramell, director of administration at the 65-attorney firm of Dunells, Duvall & Porter in Washington, D.C. said, "The overall control is the budget limitation. Before we even set the individual increase, we determine how much of a percentage of increase to overhead the firm can afford. Say for example, we determine the firm can afford a seven percent increase to overhead. That means that when we give each and every raise, the total amount of increase to the firm's overhead is no more than seven percent."

To determine the individual increase, Bramell goes through surveys to determine the marketplace. "No one wants to believe that they are over market and no one wants to receive less than they received last year." The Consumer Price Index, general growth of the firm, and competing salaries are all factored in.

Bramell believes that people confuse the issues of salary and bonus. Salary increases are related to the marketplace and a bonus is a reward for specific caseload performance. A firm interested in rewarding through salary should keep their paralegals at the top end or slightly over market.

Bramell offered the following scenario as an example of the hazards of using salary increase as a reward for case-intense work: Someone working on a "mega-case" is recommended for a large salary increase by the attorney on the case and the raise is approved. However, after the case ends, the paralegal only has 1,000 hours billed during the following year.

The firm now has to pay the salary which is not commensurate with the market and ends up losing money on that paralegal. The paralegal becomes unfairly penalized the following year because the low hours billed do not justify the high salary paid. If, instead, the paralegal had received a bonus for the work performed on the "mega-case" the problem would have been avoided.

Debra Greenberg, paralegal administrator for the Boston firm of Hale and Dorr said paralegals should understand that phenomenal salaries for partners don't necessarily translate into big increases for paralegals. "It's the partnership that has taken the risk, not the paralegal. In lean years, the partners still keep paying the salaries while the attorneys take a decrease in their draws and profits. Partners are rewarded for the risk involved."

"People draw all kinds of conclusions based on lack of information, rumor, what they perceive their neighbor to be getting, and their opinion of the economics of the firm. Your neighbors will always tell you they got bigger raises than you and they really don't have to prove it. Your natural reaction is to buy whatever they tell you."

Personal Conflicts

Since office politics plays an important part in how one is perceived, paralegals often worry that one attorney's negative opinion of them will unduly influence the other attorneys.

"Phil" says, "It bothers me when you get an attorney you did one assignment for and it didn't go well. They hold that over your head and it can really affect your review and the opinion of other attorneys. Frankly, I try not to work for that attorney again."

Unfortunately, many paralegals are not in the same situation as "Phil," and will be unable to avoid future assignments with that attorney. A way to handle an uncomfortable situation is to confront the attorney in a nonconfrontational manner. Remember, attorneys are trained to confront adversaries, and if you approach the attorney in a hostile, angry or emotional state, his instincts will rise to the challenge.

A more practical solution is to wait until the storm calms and meet with the attorney when you can both be more objective. Take the assignment in to the attorney and ask him to go over it with you. Ask him to point out the areas that he feels you could have handled differently and take notes.

View this as a learning experience and ask that the attorney do the same. Don't be afraid to point out to the attorney what you need from him in order to more adequately perform the assignment. Ask for more specific directions on future assignments. Tell the attorney that, "Instead of telling me to work up the file, please tell me you need witnesses, medical providers and test results."

"Overhearing what other attorneys think of the paralegals is inevitable," observes Ditonto, "however, I consider whether the opinion is based on personality differences or is a valid criticism. Then I consider my own experience with that paralegal."

"For instance, if the attorney complains that the paralegal is always late with an assignment, I will look to my own experience and see if my assignments arrived late. There may be mitigating circumstances regarding the other attorney. Did that attorney give the assignment to the paralegal in time for the paralegal to complete it?"

Is there any way to keep personal feelings out of evaluating the paralegal? Ditonto felt that attorneys need to focus on the work product. "See if the work product stands up. Sometimes, however, your intuitiveness tells you a lot. It tells you if a person is fitting in with the group which is very important for the paralegal. Paralegals should be in the firm to solve problems and not create problems and stir everyone up. They are there to get things done."

Diana Musciannisi, paralegal administrator at the firm of Crowe and Day in Los Angeles felt that part of the reason attorneys may feel that they don't want a difficult time from paralegals is that it is hard for many attorneys to confront or give constructive criticism to employees they manage.

Debra Greenberg added that in her experience, "Attorneys don't like to give bad reviews or say bad things about paralegals for a number of reasons. First, of course, is the litigious nature of today's society. Secondly, however, is that lawyers are trained to practice law, not to handle people problems."

Even when attorneys are told to "be honest" in the written review, both Greenberg and Musciannisi felt that the single most important reason some attorneys may not want to be honest with criticism is that they simply may not be liked.

Ditonto agreed, with a second provision, "If you are not liked, then it is difficult to get a paralegal to work for you. No one wants to be the kid on the block no one else will play with."

One corporate attorney who chose not to be identified came forth with unsettling news about how some corporate attorneys can use the review. "There is fear in some corporations about putting a bad review in writing. If the paralegal is really terrible, the only way that an attorney can get the paralegal transferred out of the department is by writing a good review. No one will take a transferee who has screwed up in another department."

Many times the attorney who works directly with the paralegal does not have the authority to:

- hire,
- fire,
- promote,
- set the actual salary increase or bonus,
- conduct disciplinary actions, or
- approve additional benefits such as education, etc.

The most they can do is verbally give the paralegal significant praise for a job well done, or complain to the supervisor when a paralegal does an inadequate job. When these attorneys write the paralegal's evaluation, they can only hope that their comments will be taken seriously. The review becomes the only tool by which the attorney most familiar with the paralegal's performance can have any impact on the paralegal's evaluation.

Improving the Review Process

Both attorneys and paralegals can work to improve the process starting with the minute there is a hint of an assignment.

"Attorneys should prepare the work plan," advises Ditonto. "Don't stop the paralegal supervisor in the hallway and tell him you need a paralegal. Take fifteen minutes to define the plan in writing."

"If the attorney doesn't prepare the plan, then as the paralegal receives the assignment, it is the paralegal's responsibility to write it up," offers Greenberg.

Many times it's up to the paralegals to train the attorney on how to utilize them. Putting the assignment in writing will avoid misunderstandings. The work plan or assignment form is then kept by the paralegal and the paralegal supervisor to refresh memories at review time. The plan can also be used as an effective means of tracking growth.

Bramell recommends a two-step review process. The performance portion should be conducted by the person most familiar with the work product. The salary and bonus portion should be conducted by the administrator or the person directly responsible for setting the increases. Otherwise, the paralegal will sit in on the performance portion not hearing either praise or areas for improvement, wanting to get to the bottom line. Conversely, someone who did not set the increase cannot be expected to know all the factors that went into the determination.

Paralegals and attorneys alike need to work together as a team on the evaluation process. "There's nothing I like better," stated Ditonto, "than to celebrate with the paralegal on-his or her successful evaluation. Together we can conquer anything."

Tips for the Attorney/Evaluator

1. *Be a good counselor.* How well an evaluation is received depends a great deal on how you deliver the news. Make sure the paralegal hears and recognizes the praise. You can be sure that your criticism will be heard—acknowledging hard work will go a long way.

2. *Consider the paralegal's individual background.* How long has the paralegal been with the firm? Do you know anything about his training? What level of assignments correspond to her experience level? Have the assignments been appropriate?

3. *Determine whether you have provided your paralegals with the proper tools.* Do paralegals in your firm have to spend billable time hunting for research materials, office supplies, secretaries, messengers and the like? Are you penalizing them for things over which they have no control? Are paralegals given training or instructions necessary to complete the assignments?

4. *Keep assignments and performance in perspective.* Review the paralegal's assignments to track his growth as the assignments get more sophisticated. Be sure you know where practicing law comes in and the paralegal job ends. While paralegals deserve more sophisticated assignments, don't expect them to carry the same responsibilities as associate attorneys.

5. *Encourage individual growth.* If a paralegal has good organizational skills but is weak in legal procedures, spend a little more time with him instead of automatically routing that assignment to someone else.

6. *Get directly involved.* Don't hand down the responsibility of your paralegal problem to the newest associate. Find out for yourself what your paralegals need. Attend a meeting, speak at a seminar, or write an article. The people who know best what your firm's paralegals need are your own paralegals.

7. *Get feedback on the evaluation.* The purpose of the evaluation is to improve weak areas and reinforce strengths. Find out areas the firm could improve on from the paralegal's point of view. You may be surprised at the astute business people you have on your staff.

How Paralegals Can Insure a Mutually Beneficial Review

1. *Have realistic expectations.* Before your review, research competitive salaries and bonuses. Know the marketplace and what your position is worth. Firms

interested in retaining good employees will keep their paralegals in the top 10–25 percentile.

2. *Conduct an objective self-examination before your review.* Know your own strengths and weaknesses and don't let anything come as a surprise.

3. *Prepare a history of the assignments you performed over the course of the review period.* A copy of this list should be kept by both you and the paralegal administrator. Without it, evaluators tend to recall only the last two months or so.

4. *Set your own goals.* Use the review process to set goals. Write them down. When it's time for your next review, take out the list and prepare an assessment of what goals you met and what still needs work. Share this information.

5. *Get specific information on areas that need improvement.* Don't accept non-specific comments on areas in which you are expected to improve. "Needs to be more organized" is too vague and is not a directive to improve. "Needs to prepare more comprehensive lists of witnesses, files and documents with a copy on the attorney's desk" tells you exactly what is expected.

6. *If you don't already know, find out exactly what is expected of you.* How many billable hours are expected of you? Does that mean you are expected to go a certain percentage beyond that in order to be thought of as exceptional? When are your assignments due? Did you clear this with the attorney or is your opinion of "ASAP" somewhat different than his?

7. *Don't let constructive criticisms cancel out positive feedback.* Although it is human nature to focus on bad news, you need to remember your strengths in order to build on them.

8. *Be prepared to negotiate.* If you are not satisfied with your salary increase now is the time to discuss such things as title changes, continuing education, a better office or a bonus.

9. *Maintain a professional attitude.* If you feel as though you are going to "lose it" at any point during your review, ask to continue the discussion another time. Don't argue. Remember to calmly present your case if you feel you have been unfairly compensated.

10. *Keep your review confidential.* Don't discuss the details of your review or raise with your peers. It's no one's business how much you received and the information may cause problems among your peers.

Negotiating Salaries: The Undeclared War

Salary negotiations are tough. There's no way around it. Even in those rare instances when you get what you want right off the bat, you're left feeling uneasy—did I ask for too little?

The key to successful salary negotiation is preparation. You must know:

- How much salary you reasonably want?

- What salaries are paid to similarly prepared legal assistants? In your office, in the region, in the nation?

- What are the underlying issues of your employment and what other, nonmonetary concessions could you seek in lieu of money?

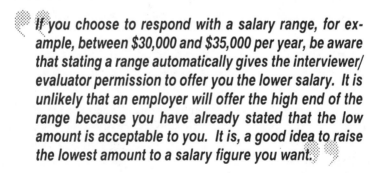

If you choose to respond with a salary range, for example, between $30,000 and $35,000 per year, be aware that stating a range automatically gives the interviewer/ evaluator permission to offer you the lower salary. It is unlikely that an employer will offer the high end of the range because you have already stated that the low amount is acceptable to you. It is, a good idea to raise the lowest amount to a salary figure you want.

The first step is to take a close look at yourself.

- What qualities have you brought to this position that justify an increase in salary, or a higher starting salary?

- How would you be more satisfied with the work—and therefore, in all likelihood, more valuable to your firm?

If you have a full understanding and confidence in your strengths, and a keen awareness of how you could make your job better, you have a full array of information with which to negotiate your salary.

According to William Ury in **Getting Past No: Negotiating with Difficult People** (Bantam Books), you must identify your position. For example: "I want a 10% increase in salary this year." Underlying your position, claims Ury, are your interests which are your motivations that lead you to that position. For example, what are your needs, desires, concerns and fears? It may not always be possible to obtain your position but it is possible to satisfy your interests. You may not get a 10% increase, but you may be able to get an 8% raise, with a review in six months if the firm is doing better.

Lawyers and law firm management depend on research, facts and investigation in order to prove and justify any decisions or actions they must take. This is particularly true for salaries, especially in this day and age of downturned economy.

Historically, law firms were known for increasing salaries at a very rapid pace, which was evidenced most likely in the early stages of your career. This is because **the steep learning curve** is recognized and rewarded. In the past, these same firms awarded legal assistants with cost-of-living increases well above the average. In recessionary times, this practice has changed. Convincing management today of the necessity of a substantial increase or higher starting salary takes on a whole new meaning.

Doing Your Homework

Before you walk into to any negotiation, do your homework.

1) List your accomplishments and talents.

2) List how you could make your job more meaningful.

3) Research what level of salary is usually paid for your level of work.

Your homework on salary information starts with your local paralegal association. You should investigate salary surveys such as:

National Association for Legal Assistants.
National Federation of Paralegal Associations
Paralegal school alumni surveys
Price Waterhouse survey
Legal Assistant Management Association Survey
National Survey Center (Washington, D.C.)
Legal Assistant Today Magazine Annual Survey

Be aware, however, that some national salary surveys do not break down the information gathered by region of the country. Looking at just national averages can give you a skewed picture of prevailing regional averages. For instance, if most of the national survey's respondents work in large cities, you will ordinarily find a higher salary average than normally prevails in smaller towns. To obtain the most accurate picture, you should also spend time reviewing both regional and local surveys.

When to Discuss Salary

If you have been interviewing for a new position, the salary discussion is generally timed by an experienced interviewer to occur at the end of the first interview or sometime during the second interview. If you are being reviewed by a savvy evaluator (and not handed your increase in your paycheck without explanation), the conversation about your increase will occur at the end of the review.

Allow the interviewer/evaluator to bring up the subject first. Be careful not to jump the gun. You should appear most interested in the work, review, level of assignments, firm or corporation. Keep your emphasis on how your skills, abilities and determination to succeed in this environment will benefit the company.

Going the Distance

You already know that law firms are populated with master negotiators. Attorneys spend years in law school mastering the latest techniques. Nonattorney staff members also learn to be just as sharp. If you haven't had previous negotiating experience, you can still play this game skillfully by understanding your "opponent" and knowing:

- what you want,
- where you will compromise,
- the job potential,
- what transferable skills you bring to the table,
- the history of the corporation regarding promotion of the field (how many vice-presidents came up through the legal department?),
- the history of the law firm regarding its use and career path of legal assistants,
- who you are negotiating with and what kind of power does this person have to get you what you want,
- if the firm or company pays a year-end bonus,
- when the next raises are scheduled, and
- whether the position pays overtime.

The overtime issue is critical to your negotiations. While the field is still split on this issue, if you are now getting overtime pay, you know that you can easily earn an extra $2,000 to $10,000 or more per year. On the other hand, if the firm is known for generous end-of-the-year bonuses, this might outweigh getting paid overtime.

Understand, negotiating is a two-way street. The goal is a win-win situation where both parties get what they want. Understand going in, you may not get the salary you seek. But because you have also conceptualized other criteria for getting you what you want, you are possessing information that may still make this negotiation win-win.

Skilled interviewers will place the ball in your court first. Be very careful to listen to the question. "What kind of salary are you looking for?" is much different than, "What kind of salary will you accept?" The first can be interpreted more ambiguously, the second is more firm.

By conducting your prenegotiating research, you will already have a general idea about the position. There is a natural tendency to throw the ball back in the interviewer's court by asking, "What does the position pay?" Most skilled interviewers will indicate that you response is required first.

Let's say that you have conducted your research and determined that a good salary in your region is between $35,000 and $37,000 per year. Now is the time to tap into your network, school, or placement agency to gain inside information. You must first determine whether:

- This salary holds true for the firm/corporation with whom you are interviewing or employed;
- You can accept this salary;
- You can be flexible in the exact amount of dollars you will accept;
- You can gain more dollars than the norm due to your transferable skills.

You can respond to the question in several ways.

- "I am looking to be compensated at market rate."
- "My salary requirements are in the mid 30's."
- "I understand through the blankblank surveys that the going rate for this position is $_____."

If you choose to respond with a salary range, for example, between $30,000 and $35,000 per year, be aware that stating a range automatically gives the interviewer/evaluator permission to offer you the lower salary. It is unlikely that an employer will offer the high end of the range because you have already stated that the low amount is acceptable to you. It is, therefore, a good idea to raise the lowest amount to a salary figure you want. If you really are looking for $33,000 per year, then indicate your salary range as between $33,000 and $35,000 annually, not between $30,000 and 35,000. Never set a single specific dollar amount because you then leave no room for negotiation.

If You are Offered Something Less than Desired

Never react if you are handed a less than victorious number. Remember, for every action, there is a reaction. If you are given a lower than expected salary offer, it is simply information for you to deal with. If you are in a review and find that you are getting emotional (" ...after all, I did bill 2,000 hours last year"), call for a time-out. You do not have to ask that the review be postponed until you calm yourself.

You can simply excuse yourself for a few moments by saying, "We've been talking for a while now. How about a quick cup of coffee before we continue?" If you cannot leave the room, Ury suggests diverting the situation with a story or joke. When negotiations resume, the tension has been broken.

Be sure you acknowledge your opponents feelings. It may be that the person giving you the increase or salary offer would like to give you more but feels that would be impossible. You may say something like, "I understand how you feel. If I were in your shoes..." You can effectively diffuse any upcoming tension by acknowledging feelings.

Look for a way to agree with your opponent. For example, you may say that you agree that the firm hasn't done well this year. The key word here is the word **and** not but. You may respond with, "I agree the firm hasn't done well this year **and** I have billed 2,000 hours." While not conceding to your opponent's point, you have further reduced any tension.

A few effective answers to lower-than-expected salary offers are:

- "Thanks, however, this offer is substantially less than I had in mind. The figure I had in mind is between \$_____and \$_____." (Remember your lowest figure is what the interviewer will probably use to play ball.)
- "I am worth more because of my education and prior experience. I believe that figure to be \$_____."
- "My background directly relates to this position. Therefore, it will not cost the company as much to train me."

Negotiating for Perquisites

You may be able to negotiate additional benefits and "perks", which can translate into more dollars. In attempting to do so, you must sell the interviewer or reviewer the value to the company of bestowing these items upon you. Some of the perks, include:

- Continuing education
- Law school or graduate school tuition
- Early salary review
- Bonus
- Hiring bonus (a one-time hiring bonus which is often used to attract associates).
- Association dues

Overcoming Objections

Objections to hiring you or giving you the increase you desire are bound to occur. Don't let it throw you. Objections will most likely be raised regarding your lack of expertise, salary expectations, prior work experience, or because of the firm's current financial situation. Some effective key phrases you can use to counter are:

- "Let's look at a different perspective to that....."
- "One alternate solution may be....."
- "It's certainly understandable how you have reached that conclusion. A different interpretation of that data may be..."
- "I am open to any suggestions you may have to overcome that problem."
- "What if....."

Whatever phrase you choose to use, do not issue ultimatums. If you do, you will immediately be designated as an adversary. An ultimatum may be perceived as "I have another job offer" or "If I don't get what I want I may have to leave the firm." You want your approach to be that of a team player, a quality most employers seek.

Attorneys do well when given alternatives. They are trained to review all options. If you hit what you perceive is a wall in the negotiations, offer an alternative. For example, you may say, "One alternate solution may be to give me an 8% increase instead of 10% now, with a salary review in 3 months. Or, we can do the 8% increase now, with a bonus based on a 20% increase in billable hours over the next six months." Chances are your opponent will pick between a or b rather than a yes or no situation.

What Not to Use as Negotiating Techniques

Even though you may have many years in the work force, it's good to have a refresher course on what not to say, even though most of it is common sense. We all get nervous and end up regretting having said what we said. Here are some sure-fire ways to guarantee an **unfavorable** end to your salary negotiations.

- "I cannot live on this amount."
- "My friend got $_____and that's what I want."
- "I have two children at home and need more."
- "I live an hour and a half away and am entitled to more."
- "I want more because I just know that I'll do a better job than anyone else."

Deadlines for Negotiation

According to Herb Cohen, author of **You Can Negotiate Anything**, conclusions to negotiations will occur as close to the decision deadline as possible. Therefore, you must establish a date for resolution of the issue. Ask the interviewer or evaluator when a decision is expected. Don't hesitate to follow up on that date to find out how the decision-making process is proceeding. Ask if you can offer any more information about yourself or if anyone else at the firm/company would like to see you again.

If the employer tells you that the decision is between you and one or two other candidates, let them know that you would appreciate knowing by a certain date, as you must move on in your job search process. Don't however, push yourself out the door by being overbearing or insisting the employer react to your deadlines. Be flexible and accommodating. Since most firms and some corporations make decisions on a committee basis, this is not always a quick process.

Your overall strategy is to make an adversary, not opponent, out of management when negotiating your salary. You have the power to win your most difficult negotiations. Go slow, be well informed and above all, have fun with the process.

In this undeclared war between management and staff you win when you "bring them to their senses, not their knees." Good luck. I wish you outrageous success.

Outsourcing: Cutting Costs and Adding Profits

Have you heard the one about the administrator who's been doing more with less for so long that now she can do everything with nothing? While this may bring a smile to your otherwise difficult day, it really isn't so far from the truth. And, in the right circumstances, outsourcing is a great way to get more done with less.

> **Business is now driven by quality control, cost containment, client satisfaction, value-added services, and staying just one step ahead of the competition. . . .the '90s have brought a realization that profits are harder to achieve and as a result, any person or function not "earning their keep" must be jettisoned.**

"Outsourcing," which originally described the practice of purchasing parts or services from nonunion or foreign suppliers, now also refers to the reassignment of certain tasks to services or individuals outside the firm.

Making the Most of Firm and Outside Resources

"One law firm I know initially contracted out their marketing efforts," states Tony Polk, president of Polk Communications, a law firm marketing organization based in Los Angeles. After the firm learned more about the marketing process, they brought those strategies in-house and saved a considerable amount of money.

Polk advises that "tasks such as telephone work, research, mailing list preparation, media placement and direct mail must be taught by an expert. It's always better to tap the brain of someone who knows what they are doing before you waste your money on ill-thought out strategies."

Cindy Daly, marketing director for the Los Angeles office of Pettit & Martin, a 27-attorney branch office of an international law firm believes firms ought to do both. "I like to take advantage of utilizing both outside *and* inside talent."

> The first thing a firm must do is seriously evaluate its available resources. Take the task of placing a newspaper story. You can delegate a portion of media placement to a company such as Business Wire, because they can rapidly cover every publication in the country. But inside the firm, someone can target a publication by personalizing the letter. Response rates to your press release may be significantly higher because of the personal touch.

Daly likes to give newspapers "a tidbit of information which causes them to call you directly. I then gain more control over whether the story can get published."

Combining outside and inside firm resources may not always work well, however. Lisa Burbick, human resource manager of the 90-attorney, Los Angeles-based firm of Jeffer, Mangels, Butler & Marmaro, is not in favor of hiring temporary secretaries. "We have found that attorneys prefer floaters to fill in for absent secretaries as opposed to temporary secretaries."

> As good as the temp may be, there is a learning curve, and it can take a floater a couple of weeks to get up to speed. But usually, secretaries must be able to handle the job very quickly. There simply isn't enough time for the temp to be cost efficient. By putting a floater secretary on permanent salary with benefits, we end up saving money.

Of course, confidentiality is always an important issue. Patricia O'Neill, administrator for the 6-attorney Los Angeles branch office of the 60-year-old San Francisco firm of Bishop, Barry, Howe, Haney & Ryder, prefers to keep MIS duties in-house. "MIS functions should be handled by someone familiar with the firm", she states, "someone who is accountable to you."

Ensuring confidentiality is the deciding factor: "Computers contain the firm's most confidential information—billings, cases and personnel data. The person in charge of these systems should not be consulting with other firms at the same time they are handling your data."

Maybe the best advice about when you should reassign firm functions to outside services comes from Paul Bramell, chief executive officer for the Seniors Coalition and former director of finance at two major Washington, D.C. law firms. "Farm out only those tasks that you can't do better in-house. If you have the horses to do the job, use 'em!"

Recognizing the Impact of Change

The business world is changing. We hear and read about trends in the global economy, the American way of doing business and the need to rethink our own understanding about how organizations are run. We read about the "just-in-time" work force, hired just when production demands of a company increase, and "disposed of" when no longer needed.

We read about organizations becoming restructured in ways that we had never before thought possible. The pyramid model with the CEO at the peak, managers in the middle and technical workers at the bottom is beginning to disappear. Middle management is being told to do more (with less) or eliminated altogether. Very large organizations are considered "dinosaurs" that may fall from their own weight. We read about highly mobile, flexible teams that can quickly move into organizations, complete a project and then move on to the next, using the expertise and skills unique to their profession.

Business is now driven by quality control, cost containment, client satisfaction, value-added services, and staying just one step ahead of the competition. During the "go-go" '80s, firms could afford to carry a certain amount of dead weight. But the '90s have brought a realization that profits are harder to achieve and as a result, any person or function not "earning their keep" must be jettisoned. This restructuring has occurred not only within company organizational charts, but in virtually every policy, procedure and protocol governing the functioning of the business. Companies are "downsizing" and eliminating their "unproductive resources."

Experts report that this is not a short-term situation. Restructuring efforts will endure long after the currently weak national economy has recovered. In other words, the work force of the future will look very different than it does today.

Evaluating Functions that Can Be Profitably Reassigned

Before you start identifying the core functions of your own firm, look at how other firms have used the technique of outsourcing. Several function areas that firms have profitably reassigned—general law firm operations, accounting, human resources and marketing—are discussed in turn below.

Operations

• *Photocopy Services/Facilities Management.* Facilities management is a good example of the most effective way to make do with less. In assigning the important function of the copy department to an outside service, many firms have both reduced overall costs and achieved greater service.

The facilities management company runs the entire copy service operation: supplying the copiers, personnel, paper and all other required items. This may also include establishing an effective tracking system to account for every copy made.   Many firms can bill clients more for photocopies than the facilities management service costs.

- *Mail Room/Fax Distribution.* In most cases, this service can be included as part of the facilities management function. It is typically paid for as part of the per-copy cost paid to the facilities management company. And, there is no need for the firm to deal with payroll, temporary employees, benefits, and related overhead costs.

- *Messenger Service.* Depending on frequency of usage, some firms have discovered that outside services can provide the necessary messenger function at a much lower cost than having in-house employee messengers.

- *Management Information Systems.* Because of the proliferation and growing complexity of personal computer systems, many smaller or medium size firms have found that outside computer specialists can provide for the maintenance of computer networks and data processing systems for less money than they would otherwise pay for a full-time MIS director.

- *Library/Information Services.* Because many firms cannot afford—or do not need—the services of a full-time librarian, they hire library filing services or freelance librarians to keep their libraries current. In such cases, the management of the library itself is handled by a committee of lawyers within the firm.

- *Records Management.* Some firms are also now experimenting with using outside services for their record management function. As precious and important as files are to lawyers, having specialists in legal file-keeping manage this function can not only reduce costs, it can definitely result in better service.

"We look at records management as yet another area in which we can save money and improve our services by outsourcing," said John Bullard, Jr., executive director of the 58-attorney San Diego firm of Jennings Engstrand & Henrikson (*Law Office Management & Administrative Report*, April 1992). Before reaching this decision, the firm had already reassigned its mailroom, photocopying, messenger services and office supplies maintenance to a facilities management company.

Human Resources

The past few years have seen agencies springing up all over the place, offering temporary personnel (sometimes called "project" or "contract" staff) to fill short-term needs on a very cost-effective basis.

- *Project Lawyers.* When cases or matters get hot, or the firm must gear up to handle unexpected workloads, hiring project attorneys is a very simple solution.

You bill the project lawyer's time at a rate higher than the agency charges. Not only are labor costs controlled, but the 30% to 40% add-on to cover benefits for full-time employees is eliminated. And, when the project is completed, the project lawyer is gone.

- *Temporary Document Analysts, Paralegals & Case Managers.* Clearly, hiring temporary legal assistants can be an added value—one that creates profits—for litigation firms. A large case may require a substantial number of people to code documents, enter pertinent information into litigation support databases, and work with the firm's attorneys to provide needed support.

  But as everyone knows, most cases settle, and the firm will no longer need these people. By using temporary staff, this situation is easily handled with a minimum amount of pain. The temporary staff members know they are only there to handle a specific project. When it's over, they will move on to the next case.

- *Deposition Summarizing.* Sending numerous depositions to an outside service for summarizing has proven to be very cost-effective for many firms. It can also result in having a superior product available for use by the attorneys. Almost always, a firm's investment in its existing paralegal staff can be better utilized in "thinking" projects rather than routine summarization. The individuals who specialize in summarizing depositions can frequently perform this task much more efficiently than even some of your best paralegal staff.

- *Administrators.* Some law firms have also successfully experimented with temporary administrators. This approach provides necessary staffing in the following situations:

  1) the firm is growing and needs the benefit of a full-time administrator but can't afford one yet,
  2) the firm is currently in between administrators—the former administrator has yet to be replaced but the need for full-time management still exists, or
  3) a temporary administrator is necessary to organize a particular project that cannot be handled by the current staff because of time constraints.

- *Employee Benefit Plan Administration.* Because of the complexity of federal (and state) recordkeeping requirements, managing this function typically requires a large clerical staff. While a number of firms now have formal human resources departments, they have also found that certain related tasks—processing all the necessary benefits paperwork—does not require on-site staff. This is especially true when the firm's "core" human resources staff is needed to handle more important functions.

- *Accounting Services.* While accounting appears to be an area that could not easily be assigned to an outside service, some firms are experimenting with it. In one case, the firm's internal accounting department was completely replaced by an outside accounting service. In other situations, certain functions of the accounting department have been reassigned, including management of accounts receivable and client billing.

* *Marketing Services.* Marketing is usually delegated to an outside company because the rainmakers in the firm are too busy bringing in new clients to spend the necessary amount of time in training, coaching and counseling future rainmakers. In addition, not all law firms have great marketing abilities, and need to bring in experts to help put together firm marketing plans and client development databases, along with typical marketing tools such as firm brochures, seminars, client newsletters.

By reassigning this function, the firm's rainmakers can have the benefit of giving their input to the process, while the people who are responsible for training, implementing and following up on marketing programs are on site only as long as necessary. This also saves the cost of a full-time marketing director.

Determining the "Core" Functions of Your Firm

Now you can start examining whether outsourcing is an appropriate tool for your firm. The first step requires a thorough examination of the functions performed by the firm. You must determine whether each function is a "core" or key function of the firm. Those functions that are not so classified must be considered logical candidates for outsourcing.

Whether a particular function should be reassigned to an outside service is, of course, a question that each firm must answer for itself. Clearly, the effective delivery of quality legal services produced by lawyers for clients cannot be performed by persons outside the firm. Without key lawyers, there is no business. Clients must be able to trust their law firms and know that the confidentiality of information being shared will not be divulged to anyone other than the individuals working on the case.

However, almost any other function of the firm can be assigned outside the firm. To succeed, these changes must be well thought out, and you must show that the benefits will be greater than the cost.

After establishing that a particular function is a good candidate for outsourcing, review the field of vendors available to handle such tasks. Prepare a request for proposal (RFP), asking each selected vendor to set forth how the function would be handled. Include in your RFP everything and anything you want done, fired, addressed or solved.

While there will always be ongoing refinements required to adjust to the new way of accomplishing certain functions, the time you spend researching and preparing in the beginning will yield great rewards once the change has occurred.

Now — Do It!

The opportunities for reassigning functions to companies outside the firm are truly limited only by your imagination and creativity. Outsourcing experiments can take place at all levels in many different firms. Of course, what may work for one firm may not work for another.

Successfully using the technique of outsourcing requires a thorough understanding of each function being considered for reassignment. You must also evaluate the costs of making such a significant change in the functions of the firm. Consider not only the direct cost, but all indirect costs—both monetary and the effect of the proposed change on people. The goal is not to relinquish management control but to add value and create profits for the firm.

When we become "magicians" in mastering and manipulating resources, we will be better prepared for what's happening now in the **business** of practicing law.

The Weekend Retreat: A New Benefit for Paralegals

Ten years ago, paralegals at major firms would not have dreamed of receiving benefits beyond the standard two-week paid vacation, paid holidays and medical insurance. Today, firms in general are treating their paralegals more professionally and are rewarding them with additional perquisites. Following are examples of firms which currently offer a weekend retreat as part of their paralegal benefit package.

> *Typically, the retreat begins with an icebreaker cocktail party on Tuesday evening. During the icebreaker, all attendees introduce themselves and speak briefly about their practice area and current projects. The next two days are comprised of educational courses and social events.*

Howard, Rice, Nemerovski, Canady, Robertson & Falk

The San Francisco firm of Howard, Rice, Nemerovski, Canady, Robertson & Falk held its first retreat in September 1988. Faced with implementing a three-tiered paralegal program with paralegals at various experience levels, the firm felt that it needed to reward its senior paralegals with something more than just a title. "We had a low-key approach," said Holly MacPherson, one of the firm's two paralegal administrators. "We weren't sure if the retreat idea was going to work. We did want to convey that it would involve both work and fun."

The firm employs 40 paralegals and 82 attorneys. Eight paralegals have the title "senior paralegal." The seniors are responsible for administrative duties such as recruiting, litigation support, training and workflow, all in addition to their caseload. Because the retreat concept was so new, the firm felt the seniors should have significant input into their own program.

Seniors Take Charge. The seniors rented a house for two nights on Stinson Beach, a remote and beautiful beach near the city of San Francisco. They chose the same weekend as the lawyers' retreat, thinking it would be easier to sell the paralegal retreat idea and thus have a weekend designated as the "firm's retreat weekend." On Friday night there was a social dinner to break the ice and set the tone, while Saturday was designated as a workshop day. Some of the topics on the retreat agenda included:

- growth and development of the senior program,
- job categories and descriptions,
- litigation support—how to establish in-house training,
- networking inside and outside the firm, and
- stress management.

"The interesting thing in stress management," states MacPherson, "was that we chose the wrong setting. Here we were having intense discussions while sitting on the beach where a gentle breeze was blowing. We had a difficult time relating to stress."

MacPherson cites two objectives for their first retreat: an increase in morale and setting goals for the paralegals. After the retreat, both MacPherson and Julie Barley, the corporate paralegal administrator, saw an increase in paralegal productivity and a clearer picture in the seniors' minds of the expectations of the firm's paralegals.

The entire weekend cost the Howard, Rice firm less than $1,000. The rental of the beach house was $400. The seniors did most of the cooking themselves. Discussions about the firm were held during meals as well as during the workshop. Free time was spent horseback riding, playing tennis and hiking.

MacPherson reflects, "If we had rented a conference room in a hotel somewhere, the cost of the rooms, meals and hotel could have been much, much more. Any firm can justify this kind of nominal expense when the results are so outstanding."

The Attorney General

The attorney general's office, headquartered in Sacramento, holds its annual three-day paralegal retreat in the month of May at Asilomar, a rustic conference center on the Monterey Peninsula. Barbara Clements, associate management analyst, and Steve White, chief of the criminal law division and an advocate of paralegals, put their heads together in 1986 to arrive at their retreat idea. This past May the group held their third annual conference, attended by 72 people including paralegals, attorneys and guest speakers.

The paralegals in attendance represented all four offices and the three major divisions of the attorney general's office: criminal, civil and public rights.

Barbara Clements, ultimately responsible for planning the event, appoints a committee each year to work on the details.

Typically, the retreat begins with an icebreaker cocktail party on Tuesday evening. During the icebreaker, all attendees introduce themselves and speak briefly about their practice area and current projects. The next two days are comprised of educational courses and social events. Some topics of discussion at past retreats have been rules of evidence, cite checking, the criminal trial process, and the new discovery act.

Additionally, the various resources available within the attorney general's office are discussed, such as computer software programs and the division of law enforcement, which is responsible for forensics and investigations. In the evenings, small groups are usually formed and paralegals network among themselves and become acquainted socially.

Asilomar provides an informal setting which lends itself well to relaxation, as well as to the educational process. The conference center is located near the beach in Pacific Grove, adjacent to Carmel. Asilomar is a unit of the California State Park System. Its surroundings include the Pacific Ocean and lush forests, including 105 acres of a natural ecological environment. Conference meals are served semicafeteria style, and rates are reasonable. A full range of services are available, similar to any resort hotel.

Future Plans. According to Barbara Clements, next May's retreat agenda will include an advanced evidence class, a session on digesting depositions (including an actual workshop), a mock trial, and a session on burnout/job enhancement. In this latter session, an outside facilitator will discuss the aspects of recognizing burnout and preventing it by enhancing the job before the negative aspects take over. The mock trial will be prepared in advance of the retreat, with paralegals from the four offices working in teams, each team working with the same set of facts. Each office will be responsible for one of four sections of the trial: discovery, prosecution, defense and outside players (judge, jury and witnesses). It is expected that the mock trial will successfully and educationally unite all paralegals from the four offices.

At the close of each retreat, Clements presents the chiefs of the three divisions of the attorney general's office with a report which outlines the details of the retreat, the attendees, the workshops, and a summary on the success of the event. According to Clements, the paralegals "love it" and "fight for the time to attend."

Popham, Haik, Schnobrich, Kaufman & Doty, Ltd.

The Minneapolis firm of Popham, Haik, Schnobrich, Kaufman & Doty, Ltd. held its first paralegal retreat three years ago. The retreat idea was conceived by a paralegal committee, including Nancy Husnik, coordinator of the administrative law and business departments and a working paralegal.

The retreat typically has been a one day event, beginning on Friday morning, with an outside speaker lecturing on a topic such as stress management or interpersonal communications within the law office. During lunch, the managing partner speaks in general about the firm, and in the afternoon, lawyers from the firm address legal issues such as ethics, legal writing, conflicts of interest and arbitration. At this year's retreat, the director of human resources gave a presentation describing her job and her newly created department, which gave the paralegals better insight into their firm. On Friday night, the paralegals met for dinner aboard a yacht which toured beautiful Lake Minnetonka.

Popham's retreat was initially attended only by the paralegals from its Minneapolis office. This year, paralegals from the Denver and Washington, D.C., offices joined in, and Husnick reports that the committee appointed for the 1989 retreat plans to seek approval for a further expansion of the retreat to one-and-a-half or two days.

The concept of a paralegal retreat is innovative. In its infancy, the idea has proved to be a good investment of firm revenue. The four firms highlighted here share common results:

- their retreats boost morale,
- they assist in recruiting new paralegals,
- they provide a valuable forum for uniting paralegals, and
- continuing their education.

These progressive firms have undoubtedly provided the groundwork for a positive trend, and one which we believe will expand to other firms in the 1990's.

SIDEBAR

A Perfect Retreat: Selling the Concept

Because the concept of weekend retreats is so new, some firms have a problem justifying the expense. Retreat costs usually are not built into the firm's budget, so its essential to know how to present the idea to senior management.

Plan Ahead

Think through and write down the who, what, where, when, why, how and how much of what you're envisioning. It can be done sketchily at first, just so you have an idea of the basics before you start asking questions. Then fine-tune all of the elements of your plan as you go along, with a final polish before you make a formal presentation to management. The retreat basics are

- *description of the retreat:* Include proposed length (one or two-day), site, dates, as well as how often they're to be held
- *purpose of retreat:* Establish realistic goals and objectives, the tasks that will be performed to reach your objectives, and a mechanism by which to measure your success.

- *activities:* What will occur? Workshops, seminars, speakers, networking, program planning, leisure activities, etc.
- *attendees:* Will all paralegals attend ... senior paralegals ... paralegal clerks?
- *responsibilities:* Who pays for the retreat, who plans it, who will speak, who will mind the store if everyone leaves on a Friday? Also, who will do follow-up in three, six or nine months to see if the objectives were accomplished?
- *costs and materials:* Include lodging, transportation, food, seminar materials, speaker fees and extracurricular activities (tennis, golf), etc.
- *benefits:* Spell out the time or money objectives, the increase in morale and improvement in working relationships, etc., as specifically as possible.

Find an Ally

Once you have a feel for what you'd like to propose, discuss your plan with your mentor, ally, paralegal associate, partner, supervisor or administrator. You can use the feedback these individuals give you about your idea to gauge what it will take to get approval. Authority figures who like your idea will be most likely to back you when it comes time to make a presentation. Because most firms and organizations move by consensus of opinion, it will be easier to gain support for your plan by going through the proper channels.

You can also invite key firm members to speak at the retreat. Not only do they become part of the retreat, but teaching each other is an effective learning device.

You'll also want to keep the tone of the proposal positive and professional. Nothing will kill the idea faster than to appear rebellious or frivolous, or to present the retreat as a possible gripe session. However, don't be reluctant to use peer pressure to your benefit. If you can find firms in your area who hold retreats, use this information to help you get commitment from the top.

Make Conformity Key

The design, tone, scope and cost of your retreat should reflect the specialty, nature and tone set forth by your firm. Anticipate the growth and future plans of the firm and set your goals to accommodate them. For example, if your firm expects an increase in the number of deposition summaries needed over the next six to twelve months, an appropriate retreat goal might be to address increased turnaround on deposition summaries in the firm. The corresponding tasks at the retreat might be to teach:

1) the paralegals what can/cannot be eliminated in summarizing,
2) quicker editing techniques,
3) how to look for 'smoking gun" testimony, and
4) how to increase word processing turnaround.

The objective here is very measurable. If the plan is to increase average deposition summary turnaround from 10 pages per hour to 15 pages per hour, with a margin of two pages either way, the firm could realize an increase of three to four deposition summaries a week.

Stress the Benefits

Be as thorough, specific and realistic as possible when presenting the overall benefits of your retreat plan. Don't promise the impossible, or you may kill the idea from the start. Although some goals may make measuring success difficult, they still provide valuable results. The most common benefits include:

- cost-effective billing time increased,
- quality of work increased,
- paralegal assignments upgraded,
- increased office morale, and
- an increase in effective communications.

Last, but not least, be honest in indicating the importance of including free time for activities.

Bay Area Paralegal Administrators Speak Up About Personnel Issues

The San Francisco legal community is very proactive in terms of professional legal assistant use. Salaries are competitive and the length of time a legal assistant stays in the profession is high. The city's paralegal administrators seem particularly satisfied in their careers.

> *I've done a number of seminars, starting out with the basics, for everyone who's new to our firm. I also asked for input from the legal assistants in the program and they all want to learn more about computerized litigation support. So we've started that. I also stress our in-house training when I'm interviewing. Candidates love to hear we have it.*

LEGAL PROFESSIONAL interviewed paralegal administrator representatives from some of the Bay area's most prestigious law firms for their viewpoints on issues like recruiting and hiring, certification, training, and career development:

- Mary Lou Peterson — Shartsis, Friese and Ginsburg
- Meg Charnley — Littler, Mendelson, Fastiff and Tichy
- Michelle Egan — Brobeck, Phleger and Harrison
- Claire McAuliffe — formerly with Coblentz, Cahen, McCabe and Breyer; now with Estrin and Assoc.
- Ann Kemp — Landels, Ripley and Diamond
- Karen Zammitti — Lempres and Wulfsburg

- Barbara Grajski — Pettit and Martin
- Naved Khan — Thelen, Marrin, Johnson and Bridges
- Wilma Horwitz — Pillsbury, Madison and Sutro

Here's what they had to say to and about legal assistants and the key issues affecting them today.

Recruiting and Hiring

Q: In some firms and corporations, a demand is made for the B.A. degree and a certificate. Why do San Francisco firms appear to request only a B.A. degree?

A: Many of San Francisco's high level colleges produce intelligent, motivated graduates who want to break into this field and want to remain in the Bay area. San Francisco may be a little unique in that respect. I think some firms would prefer to have these trainable people as opposed to someone without the higher level of education.

- I think most firms want a B.A. or B.S. degree. A certificate is secondary, unless the in-house training program is superb. A B.A. plus certification is ideal. A B.A. plus experience is second best. Most of the large firms want well-honed research and writing skills... skills of the scholar. They want candidates who can organize material, analyze it, make good judgments and write clearly and concisely.

- For me, when a candidate has a certificate, I'm more secure that they'll stay in the field. I don't want to hire people who are passing through on their way somewhere else. Especially when you're trying to develop a legal assistant program.

Q: And yet in hiring, some of you feel San Francisco emphasizes a B.A., but not certification. True? And if so, why?

A: It leaves the options open. If you see a star candidate without a certificate, you want to have the option of hiring him or her.

Q: But you would still prefer a certificate?

A: Yes, or experience.

- I prefer to hire a paralegal who has just a B.A. — no certificate, no experience — for case clerk positions.

- That's what we do. Actually, we don't even require a B.A. for case clerks; we require it later if they're to be promoted to legal assistant.

- That's why we require the B.A. up front. It puts you in a bind if you have to require the B.A. later.

- Sometimes a firm will purposely look for a very bright, motivated person who they know may not remain an assistant for more than two years, because they're going on to law school or grad school.

Q: Do you feel that there's a significant difference in that type of hiring as opposed to hiring a career legal assistant?

A: It depends on the position, the cases and the attorneys. I think a combination of career and transient legal assistants is best for us.

Experience

Q: What does your firm or organization mean when it specifies experience?

A: We ideally look for experience the candidate can put to use in the specific job opening, as well as related experience.

Q: How much experience?

A: It depends on the specific job. Hiring requirements for nonlitigation positions are quite different. There we do look for both certification and experience.

- We mostly look for discovery and trial preparation background. We don't necessarily expect legal research experience, because research assignments are rarely given to legal assistants.

- At a recent practicing Law Institute seminar on legal writing for paralegals, well over 50 percent responded that they did legal research. And over 50 percent of the attendees were from smaller firms. At the smaller firm, the legal assistant seems to be more versatile, less specialized.

Salaries

Q: The Bay area offers some good salaries. When comparing L.A. with San Francisco, San Francisco is very close, maybe slightly less. What's interesting is the diversity of salaries in the area. What's happening, and how does it affect your hiring?

A: I'm often not familiar with area salaries until I see something printed on it. We have a problem in that we need to pay attention to the entry-to-third-year level, to adjust the salaries up enough to keep people to the third year.

Q: I see some corporate legal assistants getting up to $40,000 with only two to three years of experience. This is often where there are no experienced people available, though.

A: That's important, and we do tell legal assistants that corporate and specialty positions pay more.

Q: How does the $40,000 per year affect your hiring, though? Do you pay that for only two years of experience?

A: Sometimes you turn people away... and give someone else more pay to stay. You can't put your whole organization's salary scales out of balance. You've got to be equitable to the whole staff.

- You can't always set a ceiling on it though. You have to see what's available and how badly you need the person.

- Some of the branch firms are paying very well now for litigation people — it's hard to find experienced litigation people. Santa Clara College is starting to produce very good candidates. However, San Jose firms are luring people away. One firm is now offering close to $50,000 for high-level corporate securities legal assistants.

Training

Q: If you could give a message to paralegal schools in the area, what would it be?

A: To provide more practical experience. They provide theory, but no actual hands-on with deposition summarizing, for example.

- I think several schools in the Bay area do a very good job, but they don't require their students to have B.A.s, and it seems to me that's where the trend is in education. The firms are requiring entry-level legal assistants to have B.A.s, but the schools are not. The ABA approved schools only require 54 or 60 semester hours. This leads to difficulty finding a position for the entry-level person.

Q: So there's no real uniformity in terms of credentials or qualification of the graduates of the Bay area paralegal schools?

A: Some of the schools just emphasize the speed of getting a new career.

- There is an inconsistency and a wide range in the basic abilities of the students.

Q: Do you feel there's a discrepancy between what some of the schools are saying and what the firms are saying in terms of qualifications?

A: Well, there are other firms, smaller ones not represented here, who look for someone with paralegal school skills and who don't require a B.A.

Q: You were telling me earlier that in-house training seems to be hot this year, and that more firms are getting on the bandwagon in one way or another. What are some of your firms doing?

A: I've done a number of seminars, starting out with the basics, for everyone who's new to our firm. I also asked for input from the legal assistants in the program and they all want to learn more about computerized litigation support. So we've started that. I also stress our in-house training when I'm interviewing. Candidates love to hear we have it.

- I noticed that too. The job candidates I interview often say they want to go with a firm that has in-house training. They want to gain new skills.

- We also videotape the training session, to keep a library for new hires. You develop a vast resource library before long.

- The larger the firm, the more important training is. We have a combination of seminars on things like discovery (which the attorneys get involved in also), on document production and on computer support.

- We also have a mentor program for new hires and it's evolving into a formalized apprentice-type training.

- Another aspect of in-house training is the development of standardized practice manuals. We've done one on document production—what has to be done at either end of production, step by step. Everyone gets one—all the attorneys, litigation, etc. We'll have a follow-up seminar on it as well. We've done the same thing with standardized pleadings.

- I think senior legal assistants like to be involved in the standardization process through a manual. I think it's one way of rewarding senior level people. They can put on their resume that they've written the computerized litigation in- house support manual. It creates the potential for management, the next step for senior assistants.

Q: So you see in-house training as a way of rewarding longevity and superior performance?

A: Yes, but in-house training ought to be for everyone. It's a responsibility as well as a reward.

- You can also send senior people outside the firm to attend training in related fields, such as environmental seminars, and these individuals can then come back and lead several in-house seminars.

- We have in-house early morning programs for incoming attorneys, and one of the programs is on working with legal assistants. It's brand new for us and I don't know if anyone else is doing it.

- Yes, ours is similar—we call it new associate orientation.

- In our firm, the legal assistants and the associates are going to be trained together for a year. We're finding that the majority of time write-offs are with new associates who don't know how to make the best use of legal assistants' time. Our partnership won't commit to form standardization, though. For example, a deposition digest may be perfect for one associate, while another hates it. We're hoping the joint training will help.

Q: How do you measure tangible results of in-house training?

A: The attrition rate drops. We had really high attrition about 4 years ago when 80 percent of our assistants were brand new out of Berkeley or Stanford. Now we have more experienced people and attrition is low.

- We have a three-day training session where our attorneys talk about their expertise in labor law. The associates and legal assistants take part, and it includes practical hands-on for the firm's day-to-day operations. It's very valuable. Our productivity is high, and so is the billing rate.

Q: How many firms represented here have legal assistant committees?

A: We have one comprised of myself, the office administrator and three attorneys. We meet once a month, and I report on the meeting.

Q: What does the report contain?

A: Personnel matters, education topics, planning, coordination work I've done on cases, and goals for the firm. We meet with the entire legal assistant group once a quarter.

- I have a committee that's grown with the firm. We discuss policy, and our membership is at ten right now. There's a designated coordinating attorney from each practice group. That attorney's function is to balance in-group workload.

Career

Q: What would you say to legal assistants to better prepare them for their careers today?

A: To shore up their communication skills, both written and verbal. And in terms of a legal assistant being intimidated by an attorney, I look for more aggressive candidates. With some attorneys, you can feel you may be eaten alive.

Q: Would you recommend an assertiveness class?

A: Yes, that's a great idea. Perhaps taught by an attorney.

- Also important is to learn to take the initiative. Don't always expect to be asked everything. I think the best legal assistants are the assertive ones who are not afraid to ask questions.

Q: How do you determine assertiveness in an interview?

A: Ask about past experience and the type of work they did. Did they do anything in management? What functions did   they perform, or, how would they handle a certain situation?

- And if it's a recent graduate, you look at the activities - management lists, volunteer programs, legislative aide work.

- References can also give that information, if you're tapped into a network to get straight answers from a reference.

Trends

Q: Where are things headed for the next five years?

A: There will be more career legal assistants. I also see more professional organizations and networking power for legal assistants.

Q: Do you think there will be a glut of legal assistants on the market?

A: Some people say so, but I don't think so. I think the opportunities are expanding as fast as the number of legal assistants. I see legal assistants moving more into management of case work—supervisory work.

Q: What about other kinds of administrative positions in a firm? For example, marketing the firm, more client contact, or specialized divisions for legal assistants that will help profitability for the firm without necessarily paying an attorney's salary? In other words, nontraditional roles?

A: I think a lot of firms are just beginning to establish these roles—marketing, training coordinator, MIS coordinator or director, conflict of interest specialists, computer programmer.

Q: Is there life after legal assistant manager?

A: Firm management. Or legal assistant recruiter. Consulting services are another option. Opening your own business, such as a deposition summarizing service. And there's a lot of free lance work... especially computerized.

Q: Are you satisfied in your careers? Do you want to stay in the field several more years?

A: My job is such an evolving one. I have so many challenges, I can see myself enjoying this position for a long time. It's kind of like running a mini-law firm. I have a lot of the issues an office manager would have without having to deal with partnership lists, or collections.

- I'm always called on to teach or give a seminar at a local school, so I'm always out in the middle of things... always learning. I like that.

- Sometimes you feel like you're hitting your head up against a wall. On the other hand, you're encouraged to be creative and participate. I think job satisfaction can depend on how much of a contribution the partners and administration feel you are making. We find our partners are really encouraging seniors to participate from the very beginning in large cases... and the seniors love it.

Q: In talking to legal assistants and legal assistant managers across the country, we notice something interesting. We see a lot of job satisfaction from the management faction—not so from the legal assistants themselves. Care to comment?

A: Maybe we should pay more attention, as a group, to getting our legal assistants involved in program development. I think that might increase overall job satisfaction and give them a sense of increased participation in their career development.

Q: Since most of you started out as legal assistants, what do you think separated you from others who did not become administrators, coordinators or management?

A: I think it was the Girl Scout leader in me. A fellow legal assistant had lost her job because of poor communications. She thought she was doing a great job. The attorneys didn't think so and they thought they'd communicated that. Everyone was upset. So I took the initiative afterwards to make a proposal to establish the position I have now.

- I had a teaching background and our training program at the time did not include associate interaction. I suppose I exerted some confidence and some ability to get along with the attorneys.

Q: As a manager, do you feel you walk a thin line sometimes... not part of the legal assistant staff and not part of the attorneys? Do you feel alienated?

A: We have about 65 attorneys. I'm involved on a daily basis... hands-on in some of the cases, and I think I feel closer to the assistants when they see me as a legal assistant, doing a lot of what they're doing.

- I think the camaraderie and the talking in our monthly management meetings helps to alleviate the alienation when it exists.

Q: It seems that the San Francisco legal assistant management community is one of the tightest knit groups I've found in a long time.

A: We have a very committed chapter. We were involved in supportive activities ten years before we got involved with LAMA.

Q: For those of you with legal assistant responsibilities, how do you juggle those with being a manager?

A: It's really hard.... difficult to wear two hats.

 • Also, if your exempt status ends up with overtime, you go back to nonexempt status wishing they would pay for that overtime.

 • Some of us have a double pay standard. My job is 50 percent exempt and 50 percent nonexempt. My position is recognized as two different positions. I wouldn't be there all weekend getting ready for trial if I wasn't getting paid for it, frankly.

 • In separating out my time, there's a special category for legal assistant administration. As far as billing, I'm expected to bill half the normal billing time. The attorneys have made it clear that they want me to be the coordinator and judge on the use of my time, but billing is secondary to coordinating.

 • My administrative hours vary extremely month to month. I report on it monthly. Emphasis is on legal work under time constraints. The trial is a go whether you're there or not.

 • I do my best to make sure a case is staffed by other people. If we need temporary help, I get it. I don't like to plan on myself as a major legal assistant arbitrator.

Q: A topic of concern to you is the hiring of staff attorneys who, with intention, will never be made partners. They're very profitable and they may come in to stay for three or four years, working on a particular case, or they stay forever, taking those cases the other attorneys don't want. I think this is something managers should be aware of in terms of a ceiling on or competition for legal assistant profitability.

A: I think that may depend on the commitment of the firm and the specific kind of people they want to hire. Sometimes attorneys are a lot of trouble to hire in terms of intense interviewing and firm suitability. A firm will then often hire contract people to fill the gap.

 • I think there's a difference, though, between contract and staff attorneys. I don't think a staff attorney would replace a legal assistant. Staff attorneys typically have six-plus years of experience, and most legal assistants aren't working at that level. Where a legal assistant could make inroads is at the first, second and third year levels, if you could convince firms to be more moderate in creating entry-level attorney positions.

Q: Do you see firms abandoning the hiring of more experienced legal assistants in favor of using younger associates working with case clerks?

A: I see more of that, if there's an opening they want experience. Because they've come to rely upon it. They don't want to go back to doing things the old way, delegating to younger associates. I don't think firms could have grown at the rate they have without legal assistants' support.

- Plus, you can adjust legal assistants' fees more flexibly than you can attorney's fees. And you can hire temps and case clerks as needed.

- In the last five to ten years, attorneys have come to a better understanding of who legal assistants are and what they can do. It's okay for a legal assistant to hire five case clerks to get the job done. Just do it!

Well, your excitement for new opportunities is evident. You've shared a wealth of information with us, and given us some food for thought. Thanks so much for your time.

[1]   "How Attorneys Evaluate Paralegals," was first published in the January/February 1991 issue of LEGAL ASSISTANT TODAY.

[2]   "Negotiating Salaries: The Undeclared War," was first published in the May/June 1992 issue of LEGAL ASSISTANT TODAY.

[3]   "Outsourcing: Cutting Costs & Adding Profits," was first published in the June/July 1993 issue of THE LAW FIRM PROFIT REPORT.

[4]   "The Weekend Retreat: A New Benefit for Paralegals," was first published in the March/April 1989 issue of LEGAL ASSISTANT TODAY.
By Chere Estrin and Marci Raybould. Marci Raybould previously worked as a recruiting coordinator for C.B. Estrin & Associates. Also was the paralegal manager at Lyon & Lyon and member of the Paralegal Administration Committee at Latham & Watkins, she holds a B.S. from the University of Illinois.

[5]   "Bay Area Paralegal Administrators Speak Up About Personal Issues," was first published in the September/October 1989 issue of LEGAL ASSISTANT TODAY.

Part

5

Overcoming Pitfalls and Problems

What? My career may have pitfalls and problems? Are you serious?

Yes, it's true. However, just as with any career there are solutions to any problem. Probably the solution lies within the problem itself.

Square Pegs in Round Holes

"Where all think alike, no one thinks very much."

— attributed to Walter Lippmann

When we went to school, no one, to my knowledge, took a course on how you were supposed to behave or who you were supposed to be when you landed a job. There were, naturally, courses on the skills, techniques and functional knowledge, but no one ever sat me down and told me the role I was supposed to act out on the job. I naively assumed that my employers would accept me just the way I was.

> *Remember, discrimination should be dealt with appropriately. You do not need to ignore the issue. . .the general rule of thumb is as follows: If the criteria does not relate to whether you can successfully complete the job, it is none of the employer's business.*

I guess my first indication that all was not going according to plan was three weeks after starting a new position as paralegal administrator with a major firm, when the director of administration took me to lunch. I was somewhat flattered that the DOA was treating me with such equality. During the bonding process over corned beef sandwiches—being freshly attuned to all the recent management books—I pressed to establish our long-term working relationship. Then, after telling me all the usual hype about my impending success, the administrator told me that if I wanted to fit in with the firm's yuppie image and succeed, I was going to have to lose weight.

Well, I guess I knew right then and there that I was going to be moseying on down the road pretty soon. That firm quickly became a mere memory.

My good friend, Joyce, who is the paralegal coordinator for a national law firm, was once asked in an interview how she would feel about working in a place where the partners were younger than she. Her response was that she hoped they weren't as handicapped in their litigating as they were in their thinking. Needless to say, she neither wanted nor was offered that job.

A person attending a seminar I was conducting recently described some difficulties of being a male paralegal in an otherwise female-dominated field. "Attorneys have asked me 'What's a nice guy like you doing in a female job? Why don't you go to law school?'"

Another friend of mine was once asked, in a telephone interview by an employment agency for a multi-office law firm whether she had children, who took care of them, and "oh, by the way," was she white or black? When my friend called the home office of the firm to report these illegal questions, she was left with the impression that her complaints were just going to be brushed off.

Were these stirrings of discrimination? In the field of law no less? Impossible. Surely people in this field know better, right? Certainly, we've all been taught the no-no's and the yes-yes's of proper business conduct. Who better to know these rules than those in the legal field?

Yet these kinds of subtle—and some **not** so subtle—discriminations continue. And in the same way that many women have endured sexual harassment on the job, falsely believing that it's simply a part of the scene, many legal assistants have faced discrimination in one form or another. Discrimination in violation of the law—or simply not quite fitting in—can be equally damaging to your self-esteem and your own estimation of self-worth to your company.

Let's talk about this "not quite fitting in" stigma that haunts many of us. In an intellectual arena where the primary widget sold is how well you can outwit your opponent, tremendous emphasis is placed on the bonding and melding of the corporate team. The "outsider," the soldier who marches to a different drummer, can be viewed as a threat to those who run in the mainstream, those who "belong."

In a small firm, a family-like atmosphere is usually prevalent. Generally, there is no caste system, co-workers treat each other like "family" and the managing partner can wear many hats. As the firm grows in size and stature, different dynamics take place. People start jockeying for "favoritism" from the boss. One-up, one-down relationships occur. The managing partner now delegates many of the duties she once had. Those closer to the boss are seen as favored. Where your office is, how close it is to the supervising attorney, what floor it's on, window vs. cubicle—all these factors indicate status, favoritism and positioning.

Small groups will band together, combining certain likenesses. For example, phrases such as "Well, you know those guys in probate" can be heard. You can even identify the groups by the criteria:

- hiring ("must come from certain schools");
- a particular look ("they all have the 'Westside' look");
- age category ("this is a 'young' firm, the average age of partners is 40"); and

- attitudes ("most people here belong to the Republican/Democratic party," "are so and so activists," or "we're proud of the number of women partners," etc.);

Even the use of the phrase "we encourage individualism and nonconformity" is itself a criteria for belonging to the group. A distinct culture begins to form.

The criteria for "belonging" filters all the way through the firm. If you run contradictory to that culture, the group begins to circle the wagons. If the firm is set on its culture and closed to new ideas, catalysts for change or front runners, your chances of success in the firm begin to minimize.

Lately, I've noticed a few articles in paralegal association newsletters describing how in some firms, legal assistants don't eat with attorneys. There seems to be a lot of concern about who lunches where. Some of that has to do with acceptance of the legal assistant position, your status and the belonging issue. As head of my own company—and an employer—I am acutely aware of this power structure. (Fortunately, we're all on diets.)

When are you discriminated against, and when is it simply a matter of not fitting into the culture? Probably only a labor law attorney can delineate the situations for you. However, it is important to understand what your rights are. Remember, discrimination should be dealt with appropriately. You do **not** need to ignore the issue. While I am not an attorney and cannot advise you, the general rule of thumb is as follows: If the criteria does not relate to whether you can successfully complete the job, it is none of the employer's business. For example:

- Where you live is not important. You can live three hours away from the position. An employer can only be concerned with whether or not you can arrive on time to the job.

- Whether you have children, who takes care of them and what kind of day care you have is irrelevant. Your employer is entitled to know whether you can or cannot work overtime.

- How old you are should not be discussed on the job or during an interview. Can you do the job and do you have the required experience and schooling are the only necessary topics to discuss.

- Discussion of gender is inappropriate to the legal assistant position. Yes, this is a female-dominated position. However, the implication that something may be wrong with you because you are a man in this profession is discriminatory. Further, if you are appointed a team leader or put in charge solely because you are the only male, the females in your firm need to speak up.

- Your physical appearance, such as how much you weigh, has nothing to do with whether you have the skills to complete an assignment. If you are expected to perform physical labor, there may be some restrictions. You may be required to live up to a dress code. However, that dress code must be in effect for everyone.

- Whether you are married, heterosexual, asexual, gay, single, divorced or still interviewing is unimportant to whether you can do the job. Neither is your significant other's attitude toward your working overtime. Nor is what that person does for a living of value to anyone but you.

- Your religion or political affiliation does not relate to whether you can do the job. You may have certain preferences, such as working in a liberal vs. conservative atmosphere. However, these are **your** personal preferences and should not be imposed by the firm.

If you are asked questions about any of the above matters, or are expected to conform in any way, you may want to handle it this way:

If asked questions such as whether your husband supports you, whether you have proper child care, etc., you may respond: "Everything in my home life is supportive of my position." You do not have to give specifics.

If asked questions about such matters as your religious or political affiliation, how old you are, or comments about your gender, race or nationality, you may respond: "If what you are asking (saying) is whether I can do this job, the answer is yes."

If you feel as though you do not fit in because of the firm's culture or that are unsure of the reason why, you may want to examine another set of questions:

- Do I feel inferior because of the firm's lack of acceptance of legal assistants?

- Do I have a problem with authority figures, no matter who they are?

- Do I have trouble relating because of differences in value systems, moral judgments or politics?

- Do I have a problem with the kind of law this firm practices?

- Am I insecure on the job because of my educational background?

- Do I feel I don't fit in because I am insecure about my socioeconomic background? Would I feel this way anywhere I worked? Or is it primarily in atmospheres where the authority figures earn large dollars?

- Is it true that people in this firm have a certain "look" that I don't feel I have? Do I really not have it? Does it really matter? Would I feel this way anywhere I went?

- Do I have trouble making friends in general? Am I expecting to find a "family" in my work environment?

- Am I heard? Is anyone listening?

If you are career oriented, it follows that how you feel about yourself on the job is of utmost importance. If you dread coming to work in the morning, you must recognize the problem. If you decide that you do not fit into the culture and are not being discriminated against, then this is not the firm's problem. It is your problem.

The firm will probably not change because you want it to. In all probability, you do not have that kind of power. Don't misunderstand. You **can** initiate changes to create a better work environment. However, you probably cannot change culture. Therefore, the problem becomes yours.

Analysis of the problem through the help of a career counselor, a therapist, good friends or even by yourself can help you pinpoint the problem. You may decide that you are uncomfortable with your skill level, the firm's attitude toward legal assistants, upward mobility, the type of assignments, salary level or a whole host of other legitimate situations. You may also come up with the belonging issue, and that there is simply a difference of opinion, philosophy or value judgment between you and the firm. It is then up to you to decide whether you want to stay in such an environment.

Working in the legal field can be thrilling, rewarding and challenging. The time we spend dedicated to our careers takes up the majority of our day, our week, our lives. Being in the right environment for you—with people you enjoy—is crucial to your success. It's not always about the money. It's about happiness and your right to have it.

Expectations for Women on the Job Are Different

With all of the hullabaloo lately about "Nanny-gate" (you know, the nomination of Aetna General Counsel Zoe Baird and the troublesome search for attorney general), I have taken another look at the role women play on the job. To me, the real horror of the Baird incident was not whether Baird hired an illegal alien or paid Social Security taxes, but that she was asked a special and separate set of questions than any of the male nominees for Cabinet positions. The child care question came about *only* because she is a woman. Ron Brown, the new Secretary of Commerce, states he was *never* asked questions about *his* child care arrangements.

> *...disparities in the working worlds of men and women continue. I recently visited a client, the head of an in-house legal department, who insisted on calling me "dear." I knew as I sat there, that income to income, I probably made more than three times what this fellow earned. I had created, bought and sold more businesses than he would ever experience, and knew that I would be heading home in a car he could only dream of.*

Even though, by the time you read this, the nomination for Attorney General will have been settled, I wonder just how settled the larger issue of equal treatment on the job will be. Will the issue just have quieted down, with everything returned to "normal"? Or will women on the job continue to face the widely different expectations and standards that have been set for a woman to achieve.

I had thought that, over the years, circumstances had changed, and much for the better, for women. Now, I am beginning to wonder whether all the apparent changes are real.

A few months ago, I presented a seminar on finding a job in a tough market to the St. Louis Legal Assistant Association. The other speaker at this seminar was a labor attorney whose addressed the topic of discrimination. She brought me sharply back from the future when she asked the crowd how many women recalled, years ago, being asked during an interview what kind of birth control they used. Several people, including myself, raised their hands.

We do have a new set of laws that supposedly protect women from this kind of discrimination. But the reality is that the interrogation women face today seems no less discriminatory than the questions that were asked twenty years ago. And even though recent statistics point to a 95% increase of women filling management positions between 1980 and 1990, I firmly believe that these are the women who understand and play to a different set of rules than their male counterparts.

While women in other fields face similar problems, it seems to me that paralegals experience a sort of "double jeopardy." The fact of the matter is that people working as paralegals are primarily women, while attorneys are primarily men. And paralegals report to attorneys—women reporting to men.

Do paralegals automatically experience more limited success by the very nature of this reporting structure and gender dominance? Whenever you have a large group of women reporting, for the most part, to a large group of men, I believe that the impact on the success of women cannot be overlooked.

Recently, I became the "E" word, an "employee." I was recruited for, and accepted, the presidency of a new division for an established company. Top management of the parent company was excited, in part, because I would be their first woman executive. I too was excited about this event, for a whole host of reasons, none of which had to do with my being a woman.

I quickly found that I was faced with a dilemma. Some of the people I worked with did not know how to react. In fact, one person, who was much further down the organizational chart than I, started calling me "kid" and "honey," in an apparent attempt to "equalize" the situation. I could not, no matter how hard I tried, envision her calling the CFO, the CEO, or the president of the parent company (all men), any of those endearing terms.

I also faced another perception problem. Here I was, a woman executive on a very rapid track, in charge of steering a multimillion dollar ship. I found that my requests to others in the company for assistance, along with my working style, were labeled "demanding." Naturally, this kind of label disturbed me.

I asked the president of the parent company how I would be perceived within the company if I were a man. Would I be labeled "tough," which is viewed more positively, instead? Fortunately, starting up this new division has opened up more opportunities than closed them. I have found myself working with what I consider the greatest group of people. In fact, they're teaching me just as I am teaching them.

But disparities in the working worlds of men and women continue. I recently visited a client, the head of an in-house legal department, who insisted on calling me "dear." I knew as I sat there, that income to income, I probably made more than three times what this fellow earned. I had created, bought and sold more businesses than he would ever experience, and knew that I would be heading home in a car he could only dream of.

Yet, as I sat there across from his desk, I realized that in his eyes, I would never be an equal. All my achievements, which were evident through dollar recognition, would *not* automatically give me the equality that I deserved. I knew I could never "fix" this situation; I could only learn to influence the outcome. My first reaction then, was to give this guy what he wanted—a *man* to deal with. When I approached the president of the parent corporation (a very progressive person) for assistance, he pointed out the fallacy of my thinking: "Go back in there and deal with it. You're not going to change this guy—but you can still get the job done. Don't knuckle under."

That has to be the approach adopted by paralegals. Sure, you have to be practical enough to realize that there will be situations you simply cannot change. Yet, it is critical to always turn and face the tiger.

As women, we cannot single-handedly change years of ingrained double standards, but perhaps we can raise awareness. Our success comes, in part, from the extra energy and effort we have to exercise in order to succeed. Not only do we need to learn the rules of the game, we need to learn the game plan.

I had lunch with a legal administrator the other day who told me that she recently was not offered a position with another firm because the other candidate was considered more "aggressive." The apparent thinking was that the other candidate, a man, could probably relate better to the attorneys in the firm, which had *no* female partners. I found this curious, because the administrator I was lunching with currently worked for a major firm, and had been there for fourteen years. Her tenacity and triumphant climb to the top was due in no small part to her ability to deal with very particular and authoritative attorneys, who, let's face it, only know "hard ball" tactics, and play to win every time. The only real difference between her and the other candidate seemed to be gender. Was there something happening here?

I have noticed that men are not the only deterrents to women's success. Women have also been known to impede other women through put-downs. Calling one another "girl" is a classic example. I once heard a female paralegal recruiting coordinator stand before 200 seminar attendees and say, "I found a girl a paralegal administrator position in a major firm in New York." I wondered at the time exactly *what* a 12-year-old was doing in a $75,000 a year position. Any person using the term "girl" to describe a wage-earning female adult only serves to ensure that this person will be categorized as subservient.

Another true story illustrates this point very well. An administrator at a top firm was having one of those crazy kind of days. The phones were ringing off the hook. Her secretary was nowhere to be found. As the administrator dashed from her office en route to a meeting, she stopped at her secretary's desk to answer a phone. Her secretary, who happened to be a man, was dashing back to his work station, and ran into the administrator's office to pick up yet another ringing line. At the same time, an attorney new to the firm walked into the administrator's office and told the secretary, "I need this now. I can't wait for your girl to get off the phone."

Important men used to say stuff like this all the time to other important men. Unfortunately, some of them still do, and sad to say, some women insist on promoting this abuse by referring to themselves as "girls." I have never heard the phrase, "I can't wait for your boy to get off the phone," from either men or women. The discrimination suits that would be filed (and won) over the use of *that* comment not only would pay for the national deficit, we would have change left over.

How women are perceived on the job relates, to some extent, to the differences in what men and women look for in their careers. I have, for example, never had a male candidate tell me he was looking for "job satisfaction." I have also never had a male candidate state that what he really wanted was a "people" job. Because traditionally women have been more harshly judged than men, this "softer" approach from women is often misconstrued as weakness.

While I am convinced that many women have healthier attitudes toward their jobs, I am also convinced that men, in general, are more willing to take greater financial risks. Take for example, my experience in interviewing paralegals for alternative careers. I have found that for sales and marketing positions, most women tell me they want a straight salary with a small incentive, while most men tell me they want a "sky's the limit" commission and a small base salary. I firmly believe that women somehow know that the price they have to pay when they make a mistake on the job is much greater than the price men will have to pay.

From experience and from listening to other women, I have learned that the rules for women in a male-dominated business society are not exactly nice. We can't do much about that in the short term. However, we *can* continue to positively influence the way business is conducted in order to accomplish real change. And we can positively influence and change some people's thinking.

As women continue to achieve higher positions in the work force, the more we speak out, the more we say "no" to discrimination, and the more we learn the game in order to *change* the game plan, the better for *all* involved.

Maybe I'll burn my bra.

Office Politics: In-House "Kissing"

To hear people talk, you would think office politics is a game of love—involving a certain amount of kissing. You kiss various parts of the anatomy, you kiss up, or you say phooey with the whole thing and kiss off.

Of course, most people really do not think of office politics as love. This discourse, in fact, suggests the opposite—that they see it as a Machiavellian game in which affection is used as a weapon.

> *I want to discuss one of the saddest aspects of paralegal office politics—fighting between other paralegals. Many paralegals who have worked in large organizations acknowledge that they sometimes engage in office political struggles with other paralegals. It's ironic that people in similarly uncertain class strata in an organization should fight among themselves but it is typical of this difficult position.*

I hold a slightly different view. While it is clear at times that office politics are dangerous and counterproductive, it is also dangerous and counterproductive to take the view that you're above them and ignore what's going on.

In the same way that everyone is political—even nonvoters are political by not voting—every employee in an office large enough for office politics is a player in that political drama, even if only as a pawn.

I believe office politics are no more than a broader version of interpersonal relationships. You will notice that in small offices of two or three persons, there are seldom office politics. Instead, everyone has relationships with everyone else and those personal relationships usually determine the dynamics in the office.

However, the larger the office, the more prevalent the politics. When the power dynamics of interpersonal relationships evolve into the power dynamics between groups, then politics comes into play.

Paralegals, both as individuals and as a group, are in a difficult and unusual position in office politics. Their political status is loosely defined by comparison. Purportedly above other staff, like secretaries and clerical people, they are never on a par with even the lowliest of associates.

This makes for extremely difficult dynamics, both on a personal and political level. For any person, it is difficult to function in a stratified world when your own place and status is unclear and unequal. In relationships between men and women or among friends, unequal status almost always leads to trouble.

Think about unequal relationships you know between men and women. When one's work is "more important" than the other's, problems almost always develop.

In the same way, the very nature of the attorney-paralegal relationship is problematic. It's like that of doctors and nurses—two groups of trained, specialized professionals, one with high status, the other with less status.

How each paralegal and attorney works out this disparity in their personal relationship determines whether or not the relationship is going to be professionally successful. Attorneys who treat paralegals like dogs sometimes get bitten. Paralegals who view everything as a personal affront to their status become office pariahs to be avoided at all costs.

Personal and professional relationships built on mutual respect and awareness of strengths and weaknesses usually work out best. That's true of the personal relationships between paralegals and attorneys and other staff. It is also true in political relationships between paralegals as a group and other groups.

Paralegal Infighting

I want to discuss one of the saddest aspects of paralegal office politics—fighting between other paralegals. Many paralegals who have worked in large organizations acknowledge that they sometimes engage in office political struggles with other paralegals. It's ironic that people in similarly uncertain class strata in an organization should fight among themselves but it is typical of this difficult position. Even nurses don't usually openly fight doctors, they often fight among themselves!

The reason for this, I think, is that paralegals struggle for status against each other because they cannot obtain it from attorneys (who themselves barely give it to each other).

Now, what does all this mean in terms of how to participate in office politics? Simply this: If office politics are a broader application of interpersonal relationships, then groups need to treat each other as they would want to be treated as individuals.

Say a paralegal named "Polly" is ensconced in a warehouse 1,000 miles away from the office. She is overseeing a massive document production operation. One day she climbs a 20-foot ladder and finds a box of documents hidden in the rafters. In the box is the "smoking gun" of the case.

Polly phones the office and describes her find to Doug, the associate overseeing the case. You are another paralegal working with Doug on the case and you hear him claim credit for Polly's find. What do you do?

Is it to your political advantage to remain silent and let Doug perpetuate his deceit? Why, you may ask, should I jeopardize myself by challenging Doug to enhance Polly's position?

The key here is that Doug's behavior probably has little to do with Polly and much to do with the group dynamics between paralegal and attorneys. You may think Polly will get ahead if she gets all the praise for her find and that may somehow lessen your position. But my reading of the situation is that not only will your status not go down as Polly's goes up but by remaining silent to Doug's deception you will diminish the status of paralegals in your office as a whole—which could ultimately have a negative impact on you.

Going back to the notion that politics are just a broader application of interpersonal relationships, think of how you personally would react if you were in Polly's position and discovered Doug's deceit. You'd want to tell him off.

If you were sophisticated in handling interpersonal relationships, you (as Polly) would assertively—not aggressively—let it be known that the find was your own in front of Doug and a partner, you might say something like, "Doug was so thrilled when I called him to say what we'd found. I was so pleased to be able to make such a contribution to the case."

It's easy to see how to behave interpersonally and I submit that those lessons also apply to politics. In this case, when you spot Doug taking credit for something he didn't do, it's to your overall interest to clearly—but not aggressively—let him know that you know the truth and won't permit any adulteration of it. In front of a partner, you might say, "Doug was so thrilled when Polly called him to tell him what she'd found."

Office politics often accomplish unstated organizational goals. They're used to:

• spur competition between individuals and groups,
• isolate outsiders and newcomers,
• gather and disseminate information via the "grapevine,"
• quash individual initiative, and
• make sure that everything is accomplished "the way we've always done it here."

The message is that if you can view office politics as you would interpersonal relationships, you have a guide as to how to cut through the nonsense and behave in ways that are interpersonally and professionally appropriate to your own interests.

If an attorney tries to instill competition with another paralegal by telling you that a paralegal is billing 40 hours a month more than you, the answer isn't to downgrade the other paralegal. The more appropriate answer is to ask the attorney directly what is expected of you and how you can best meet those expectations.

If you feel you deserve a raise when you hear via the grapevine that another paralegal doing similar work is being paid more than you, it is appropriate to argue that you deserve more money based on your own high level of performance rather than to complain that the other paralegal makes more.

One final note about office politics: Whether you consciously play or not, citing office politics as an explanation for anything is entirely counterproductive.

Once a paralegal came to me seeking another job. When I asked her why she wanted to leave her firm she cited "office politics."

"What don't you like about the firm's office politics?" I asked.

"I don't like the way some people get promoted and others don't," she said.

"What is it you don't like about it?"

"I don't like how some people get to manage cases and others don't."

"Were you passed over for promotion?"

"Yes," she said.

This paralegal had told me things she never intended to tell me. I knew that she felt victimized and powerless to do anything about it. I knew she was a person who looked away from herself when determining the source of her problems. I knew she wasn't assertive in handling herself.

How different my reaction would have been if she had explained her desire to leave her firm like this:

"I was passed over for a promotion which I believe I deserved. Whatever the reason for that, I want to move to a job where I can more easily display my talents and where they'll be more easily recognized."

That's an explanation I like. It tells me she is self aware, assertive and a clear thinker—my kind of paralegal.

Personal Problems on the Job: The Ultimate Conflict of Interest

Success doesn't mean you won't have one. Money can't always fix it. And even the most unexpected people, from Princess Di to Woody Allen, have them.

We're talking about personal problems. Unfortunately, everyone, at one time or another, experiences personal situations that ultimately make their way onto the job scene. Whether the problem is in the form of an illness, a heartbreak, financial woes or even a bad hair day, personal problems can interfere with your career—if you allow them to.

> *Personal problems are changeable, elusive and hard to adhere to the "solve on your own time" slots. They follow us onto the job. Our minds inexplicably wander to the problem when we least expect it. And because paralegals are diligent problem solvers and dedicated professionals, this presents a dual challenge: solve the problem instantly but don't think about it while on the job. Above all, don't let it interfere with billable hours.*

What exactly is a personal problem? The bottom-line definition is: a difficulty in your life outside of your job which allegedly should have no bearing as to how you perform your duties. Most employers expect you to take care of your "outside life", (particularly during a crisis) with little or no disruption to your job performance. Impossible? You bet.

I once had an assistant who, when told about a colleague's baby-sitting problems, promptly replied, "Oh, that's a P-squared." "Pardon, me?" I said. "A P-squared—you know, personal problem." The term immediately became a euphemism around our office for any situation we simply did not want to deal with. It was a way of separating out what we could control on the job with what we couldn't control in our personal lives.

Sometimes there are situations which are so devastating to us that we cannot help but bring the problem to the job. These kind of situations are chronic. They are ongoing and can last a significant period of time. These problems can include a serious illness, a divorce, relationship stresses, financial problems, problems with the kids, an addiction, or other similar difficulties. These heavy stressors do not simply "go away" from nine-to-five while you are at work.

Other personal problems are temporary, or short-term and can affect us if only for the day or the week. They are likely to include such situations as car problems, not getting to the bank in time, a baby-sitter who didn't show up, or backed up plumbing at the house. While the problem can be short-lived, it is sometimes necessary to deal with it while we are on the job. Too many of these "short-term" problems and employers start raiding your personnel files.

Even good situations are sometimes thrown in the category of personal problems. A wedding, a weekend away with someone new, remodeling your living room, planning a long awaited vacation, a diet, a new roommate, a new relationship—all can affect your performance on the job. These situations are distracting and take energy and time that employers feel belong to them.

Personal problems are changeable, elusive and hard to adhere to the "solve on your own time" slots. They follow us onto the job. Our minds inexplicably wander to the problem when we least expect it. And because paralegals are diligent problem solvers and dedicated professionals, this presents a dual challenge: solve the problem instantly but don't think about it while on the job. Above all, don't let it interfere with billable hours.

Bouts with personal problems are part of life. With time, most personal problems are solved. However, without maintaining control or making a conscious effort to solve the problem, a situation can get out of hand. A person suffering from an addiction refuses to seek help. Someone else who isn't ready to leave a bad relationship carries the problem onto the job. In some instances, the employee has no control over what is happening to them: a serious illness requires time for recovery. For some people personal problems snowball. An illness in the family leads to a care-taking position which leads to financial problems which leads to divorce.

While many employers are sympathetic, very few want employees to bring their personal problems into the job scene. Many employees armed with this knowledge and fearful of losing their jobs, are reluctant to alert their employers to their situation.

Take the case of Lois Schaetzle, a senior legal assistant with the Sumter, South Carolina firm of Bryan Bahnmuller, King, Goldman and McElveen. Discovering that she had breast cancer, Lois was prepared to walk out of her job. She struggled with approaching her firm about the problem. When she finally made the decision to ask the firm for help, her boss, Charles L. Griffin, III, was totally supportive of the treatments she was about to undergo.

> "Everyone in the firm was so helpful," Lois says. "They kept in touch by phone, they wrote to me—it was a total support group. I was willing to turn in my resignation and they held the job open for me. I never lost a

> lick in income. I met other people who lost their employment in similar circumstances. I didn't have all that much to worry about. This was an aid to my survival."

After eight months of intensive chemotherapy, Lois kicked the cancer. She returned home to a wave of acceptance. "Coming back, my office was festooned with balloons and cards. It was incredible. I wish anyone in any field could have that kind of support."

Sometimes we are not even aware that what is going on at home is affecting our job performance. Let's examine a few of the sure signs and patterns that indicate your problem has crossed over into your job life:

- You start arriving late for work (if only 10 minutes) and continue to blame the traffic. Or, you leave early several times a week.
- You miss meetings or deadlines. You're sure that your supervisor gave you different dates.
- You've lost or gained weight.
- You don't seem to dress as carefully or meticulously as in the past.
- Your office or your car is messier than it has ever been.
- Your billables are down but the amount of work is the same.
- You can't seem to focus on any conversation.
- You keep repeating yourself.
- You snap at coworkers or worse, *clients.*
- You find yourself crying in the shower in the morning or in your office later. This seems to be happening on a regular basis.
- You've lost interest in the job.

So how then, do we cope with the realities and pressures of our personal lives and balance the time and dedication that we are expected to give to our employers?

First, identify the real problem. This may sound simple, however, there may be many layers to the problem. Be specific about what has happened. For example, "Trish", a senior-level paralegal looked forward to entering law school. However, each time she was about to start, her husband "lost" his job, throwing them into dire financial straits and hindering her progress. A good counselor finally showed her their pattern—he needed to sabotage her success and she needed to care of him.

Confide in a friend. Even the worst secrets are not so bad when you can tell an understanding friend your problem. Good friends won't make value judgments.

Stop blaming yourself and stop beating yourself up. You're human. Whether the problem is not so serious such as forgetting to pay the phone bill or very traumatic such as a breakup of a serious relationship, remember that we are not perfect at all our roles. You haven't failed as a human being. This was a specific experience, not something that defines your very being. Isolate the experience.

You can view the situation as something unfortunate that happened to you, one experience out of many. Or, you may regard it as an error in judgment—an experience that is part, but not all of you.

Get the appropriate help. One paralegal I knew was consistently out "sick" on Mondays. When I brought this to her attention, she stopped immediately. What I didn't know then was she suffered from an eating disorder. She only binged on weekends, causing her to be sick on Mondays. Instead of getting help, she tried to cover the problem which manifested itself in other ways. Thankfully, she eventually sought the appropriate help and is on her way to recovery.

You may have to confide in a supervisor. This is an individual decision that must be based on each separate situation. Alerting your supervisor and asking to keep the situation confidential may help you in a bonafied crisis. Many firms and corporations now have employee assistant programs, therapists they can recommend, agencies that can help, flex time to get over the crisis or just be able to lend a shoulder. On the other hand, use your judgment. If this is the fourth boyfriend you've broken up with in the same amount of months, you will get little, if any, understanding or sympathy.

Take an early vacation. Now may be the time. While it may not cure the problem, you may be able to relax and get a different perspective as to what is happening to you.

Exercise and stay healthy. In a personal crisis, it is important to have a feeling of some control over your life. Exercise can help you feel better and give you a sense of control.

Take appropriate action. This sounds much simpler than it is. When you are in the middle of a problem, it is sometimes difficult to separate your emotions from practicalities. However, taking action for the problem is empowering. Remain positive, be realistic. Confront the problem and process it.

It may be okay to obsess on the problem. Sometimes it is better to obsess on the problem, even if it is a lost love, rather than try to minimize or deny what is happening to you. In a way, it's like chocolate. The minute you know you can't have it, you want it. Again, if the problem gets out of hand, you may need to seek help.

Personal problems are a fact of life. We all have them. We all dread them. Dealing with your problems in a mature and capable manner is your responsibility. If you can handle it yourself, handle it. If you need help, acknowledge the fact and get help. Whatever the scene, remember you and you alone are in charge. Above all, take care of yourself first. The rest will follow.

[1] "Square Pegs in Round Holes," was first published in the March/April 1992 issue of LEGAL ASSISTANT TODAY.

[2] "Expectations for Women on the Job Are Different," was first published in the May/June 1993 issue of LEGAL ASSISTANT TODAY.

[3] "Office Politics: In-House 'Kissing'," was first published in the November/December 1991 issue of LEGAL ASSISTANT TODAY.

[4] "Personal Problems on the Job: The Ultimate Conflict of Interest," was first published in the March/April 1993 issue of LEGAL ASSISTANT TODAY.

Part

6 '90's 2000

Dealing with the Changes of the '90s

Historically, law firms have been very slow to change. But the '90s brought about a very different style law firm. Leaner and meaner, these firms are about **business**.

No longer are attorneys made partner automatically. No longer are employees given life-long opportunities. New careerpaths abound. New technology has been implemented. Budgets are taken seriously.

There are tough choices to be made. And the great news is, yes, there is life *after* the law firm!

Seniority Does Not Equal Security

Y ou're pounding the pavement for the first time in a very long time. You're totally panicked. This wasn't exactly what you had in mind when you reached your tenth anniversary with the firm. Instead of a healthy raise in your review, you were handed a pink slip with your name engraved on it. How could this have happened?

> *You need to continue to be assertive, go after continuing education and look at business opportunities for the firm. Show that you are viable not only from a cost center but you can bring in fresh ideas to run that case.*

In this day and age of downsizing or rightsizing, firms and in-house legal departments no longer give extra Brownie points for seniority. No longer does status as the most senior employee guarantee exemption when the axe is about to fall. If this has happened—or you know it is about to happen to you—your survival instincts have probably kicked in. But if it comes as a surprise, it's probably because you have ignored or refused to read all the warning signs. Ask yourself the following questions:

- Are there rumors circulating about the firm's financial stability that I don't believe apply to me because I am a paralegal or part of the support staff?
- Do I think the minimum billable hours requirement doesn't *really* apply to me?
- Am I the sacred cow? Have I been with the firm so long and feel so secure that I don't believe the firm requires *me* to put in 110%? (Don't they remember how hard I've worked in the past?)
- Am I at risk to be laid off because the firm really no longer needs my specialty? Am I doing anything to garner new skills in the areas the firm **does** have work?

- Have I ignored the fact that my technology skills are not up to par?
- Am I a senior level professional performing assignments at the mid or entry level?

Long entrenched employees may not recognize that they, too, must adapt to the lean and mean approach of the today's law firm. The problem, career advisers say, is that too many people delude themselves for too long. Familiarity can breed a false sense of security for many senior level employees.

"There's not that much difference in billing rates between a mid-level and senior-level paralegal. But the difference in salary is considerable," says Joyce Wilson, paralegal administrator of the Los Angeles office of Fried, Frank, Harris, Shriver & Jacobson. "Law firms no longer want to pay higher salaries if they can get the same thing for less dollars."

Firms are carefully scrutinizing the performance level of assignments of senior paralegals and how that corresponds to bill rates and salary levels. For example, senior level litigation paralegals billed out at top rates whose duties include summarizing depositions, indexing documents and basic mid level and entry-level work, may find themselves out in the cold. Firms are finding it is more cost effective to hire a junior paralegal who can competently complete the same assignment—at lower billing rates and less overhead. The argument that it takes a senior level paralegal less time to complete the assignment doesn't always hold true. Following are just a few recent examples.

The short sightedness of a firm was evident when a paralegal administrator was recently laid off. This senior level professional contributed over 15 years experience to the firm and found herself out the door. This administrator had contributed significantly to the firm's paralegal program, designing, structuring and implementing professional growth for all members of the program, including training attorneys on proper utilization and profit centers.

Another paralegal with over 13 years experience was told she was through even though her work was quite good and highly valued. She was working too slowly to satisfy the firm. The lawyers felt all of her time could not be billed. Instead of a raise, she was notified she was no longer needed. Even though they told her to "take her time", the message was clear: the sooner you leave, the better.

A firm looking critically at annual costs instead of contributions resulted in another layoff. A paralegal with over seven years at the same firm was let go unceremoniously in favor of a two year paralegal. However, when asked what her skill level was this senior paralegal could neither claim expert computer skills, trial skills, or anything beyond the mid level to justify a senior-level salary.

"What happens, is you get too comfortable and stop trying to impress your employers," states Cynthia L. Nader, president of the Orange County Paralegal Association and senior paralegal. "You need to continue to be assertive, go after continuing education and look at business opportunities for the firm. Show that you are viable not only from a cost center but you can bring in fresh ideas to run that case. The best thing that has happened to me recently was to become president of the association because it made me more active. I have newer ideas and more relevant information."

Senior paralegals can earn anywhere from $45,000 to $80,000 which includes overtime and bonus, exclusive of benefits. At that salary, the billables the senior paralegal achieves and the rate billed to the client must be in line in order for the firm to see the senior paralegal as a profit center.

Barbara Grajski, South Bay legal division manager of Certified Personnel emphasizes the value of senior paralegals: "There is a lot of demand for senior paralegals to have specializations in areas like corporate or intellectual property. These are practice areas where seniors can perform the level of work that justifies a billing rate high enough to support that salary."

What makes someone truly invaluable? "When they do an associate's work for paralegals salary," claims Ralph O. Williams, managing partner at King & Williams in Century City. "A senior paralegal can be as effective as a third year associate. The key to success is specialization on part of the paralegal and training and supervision on part of the firm."

Wilson, who has been in the paralegal field over 12 years, offers solid advice to senior paralegals who may be targets for layoffs. "One way to make yourself a little more secure is to take on duties that the mid-level person can't do such as high level administrative work. Another avenue is to develop a particular expertise no one else in the office has. For example, if they do a lot of environmental or land slide work, develop an expertise in that arena. The operative word is to pay attention".

Honey, They Shrunk the Firm: Surviving in Today's Law Firm

The Way it Used to Be

In the olden days, in a far off place called LawLaw land, long before buzzwords such as "cost containment" and "downsizing" were even invented, paralegals had the rule of the land. In the culture of the day, getting the job done quickly and well always came first—the issue of price was secondary. In those golden times, paralegals had tremendous buying power.

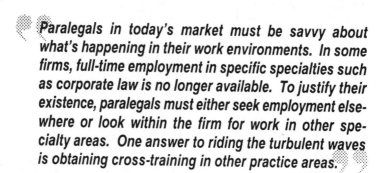

Paralegals in today's market must be savvy about what's happening in their work environments. In some firms, full-time employment in specific specialties such as corporate law is no longer available. To justify their existence, paralegals must either seek employment elsewhere or look within the firm for work in other specialty areas. One answer to riding the turbulent waves is obtaining cross-training in other practice areas.

Need photocopying for a large case sent out of house? No problem. And while you're at it, make an extra set "just in case."

Need temporary paralegals to staff a case? Ask for rush staffing—only people with top backgrounds—and *then* ask about the fee schedule. Oh, and by the way, send along an extra person "just in case."

Need to digest a deposition? Take as long as necessary—depending on the complexity of the case—to create a readable, yet succinct summary. Just make sure the attorney's needs are met.

In those days, price was never the primary issue. And, after 30 years of establishing just what it was a paralegal could do, the profession now had carved out certain assignments that were specifically classified and *understood* as "paralegal duties." Associates would rather be hogtied than tackle what had previously been considered appropriate first or second-year attorney assignments, tasks that were now officially deemed "beneath them." To enhance that belief, clients were educated about which assignments were best delegated to the "lowest competent level" of staff.

In those days, management consultants touted leveraging the partner/associate/paralegal pyramid to one paralegal assigned to three associates, who were assigned to two partners, as the optimum ratio. Raises averaged 8% to 10% and even higher. Many large and mid-sized firms paid bonuses upwards of $10,000 to $20,000.

Paralegals fought for—and sometimes won—window offices as recognition of their status. Firms allowed employees to choose from a variety of employment benefits, including profit-sharing and 401K plans. Many paralegals wouldn't even consider a new job unless the firm paid for continuing education, paralegal association dues, the full cost of parking, and medical insurance with a mere $250.00 deductible.

Such were the riches of the firms that summer associates—many with pimples still on their faces—were wined, dined and signed at starting salaries their parents worked all their lives to achieve.

Ah, yes, it was divine decadence at its best.

The New Reality

But, in today's market, now that the seemingly never-ending flow of legal business no longer exists:

- pay raises average only 3% to 4%, if they are given at all;
- required minimum billables can be 1800 hours or more;
- year-end bonuses are marginal to nonexistent;
- benefits have been cut to the bone; and
- the summer associate programs in many places have all but disappeared.

Most corporate clients are now dictating exactly what costs and legal fees they are willing to pay. Many frequently specify who should perform their assignments. Clients are more informed about the business of providing legal services, they are more knowledgeable about their power as the customer, and they're definitely flexing their new control.

In some firms, associates are performing work that had finally come to be considered paralegal tasks. Many of those paralegals who had garnered a window office are still there now simply because there's no one else to take up the space.

What on earth is going on here? Honey, they've shrunk the firm.

What's a Paralegal to Do?

Paralegals in today's market must be savvy about what's happening in their work environments. In some firms, full-time employment in specific specialties such as corporate law is no longer available. To justify their existence, paralegals must either seek employment elsewhere or look within the firm for work in other specialty areas. One answer to riding the turbulent waves is obtaining cross-training in other practice areas.

Consider the plight of a corporate paralegal in a firm that is no longer getting merger and acquisition work, a real estate litigation paralegal whose firm has experienced a decrease in cases, and a real estate transactional paralegal in a firm that is no longer doing any development deals. These paralegals are prime candidates for cross-training into other specialties. Being proficient in more than one practice area, particularly one that is vulnerable to work slowdowns, is a good way to ride out the peaks and valleys.

Savvy paralegals working in firms that are experiencing slower work should consider this avenue for achieving job security. Even those extremely busy legal assistants working in currently "hot" practice areas like environmental law, health care, insurance defense and bankruptcy, may want to protect themselves from future demise by getting cross-trained in other areas in which their firms may be doing business.

Unfortunately, too many paralegals believe that responsibility for training lies in the firm's hands, and they ultimately lose out when the firm inevitably fails to respond. In order to succeed, you *must* take matters into your own hands. Seek the training you need!

What Areas Should You Target?

If you want to expand your areas of expertise within your current organization, you need to determine in which direction the firm is headed. Perhaps the firm is looking to increase its business by seeking new practice specialties. Are the partners trying to increase the firm's business in patent and trademark? intellectual property? Business litigation? Bankruptcy?

If you cannot directly ask members of the executive committee, get information from others in the know. Great resources for the gleaning the firm's long-term strategy include the following people:

- your firm's recruiting administrator (if the firm still has one),

- the hiring partner or hiring committee, and

- the director of administration or office manager.

Find out if the firm is recruiting, what level of attorneys they are seeking—partners or associates, and in what practice specialties. New associates are hired to support the firm's current workload. But, hiring new partners means new business. Firms generally recruit partners with at least $500,000 in "portable business" (clients they bring with them). This increase in business or switch in directions for the firm can mean work for you.

Once you pinpoint a new area in the firm that can utilize paralegal support, you may need to actually create a position for yourself. Since the new areas may not need you on a full-time basis yet, you'll probably stand a better chance of convincing the firm to try using a paralegal. There is less of an investment and risk on the part of the firm for part-time involvement.

Use Support Memos

One of the best ways to inform a firm of how to cross train you is the Support Memo. This tool for expanding your horizons lists new areas in which paralegals can be utilized. It requires a response (and attention) from the attorneys in the areas requiring assistance. Let's say that the firm has a new matter in patent and trademark and has never used paralegals in this arena. You may list the areas the attorney can use paralegal support by saying:

> The renewal is due on the ABC Engineering patent. We need a response **no later than June 23rd** in order to file a timely renewal. Please indicate the areas in which I may be of assistance.
>
> _____ Prepare patent summary report
>
> _____ Draft response to trademark registration application
>
> _____ Review patent filings with engineers
>
> _____ Draft power of attorney
>
> _____ Conduct on-line information search

Of course, you must be prepared to handle these tasks if the answer is yes! Take outside courses, seek out an experienced associate who can train you, find a paralegal in another firm to show you how to get done what you need, order the proper materials and texts on the subject, and go for it! Don't assume that the firm has a duty to train you.

Associates Performing Paralegal Assignments

It's sad, but true. In some firms, associates have either been instructed to perform paralegal duties rather than be laid off, or are desperately trying to keep their billables up by tackling paralegal assignments.

In this particular case, about all the paralegal can do is wait. You cannot demand that firms stop assigning work in this fashion. But, time *is* on your side.

Associates simply are not trained to do paralegal work. Further, either the client will eventually demand that this work be billed at paralegal rates, or the associate will leave because he or she has gotten frustrated with the lower level of assignments. Firms will eventually wise up to the cost of turnover in associates and client aggravation, and hopefully reassign the work according to the appropriate level.

Learning Cost-Effective Measures

Paralegals must learn how to survive within strict budget constraints and get the most for the firm's dollar. One positive aspect of this tough market is that vendors will do just about anything to get your business. They'll send flowers, they'll send cookies, they'll buy you lunch, they'll sing you songs. But most importantly, they will competitively price their products and services.

Here's one way to adapt to the current market and shine in your firm's eyes. Negotiate *all* prices, don't just accept the first price stated. Very little today that's available from a vendor is nonnegotiable. From office supplies to photocopying to microfilming, imaging and scanning, litigation support services, expert witnesses, placement services, computers, office space, and equipment, very little today cannot be negotiated for a lower price.

However, *be careful* that you do not compromise quality for those low, low, prices. You may end up with the lowest price in town, but with more headaches than you ever bargained for.

Make sure to iron out ahead of time exactly what you need. For example, you know that you will be attending a large document production the following week. Send a memo to the supervising attorney to get approval ahead of time for all anticipated costs. Don't let anything come as a surprise. Your memo should include questions such as:

- How many sets of copies are required?

- Is microfilming preferred?

- On-site or off-site copying preferred?

- Are temporary paralegals authorized?

- Should the documents be numbered by Bates stamping or sequential computer labels?

- Is paid overtime authorized?

- Will imaging or scanning be necessary?

Be sure you memorialize your negotiations and let the firm know exactly what you are doing. You are the information gatherer and you could also be the decision maker. You should:

- document the file, showing with whom you've spoken;

- what services, products, and prices were offered; and

- how long that bid or quote is valid.

Sometimes, by the time you get back to the vendor, so much time has passed that the original bid is no longer good.

Make Yourself Invaluable

Over lunch the other day, the paralegal administrator of a major firm told me that four years ago, her firm had 130 paralegals and 140 attorneys on staff. Today, that firm employs only 17 paralegals and 85 attorneys. I wanted to know what it was that made those 17 paralegals stand out from all the rest.

"We run lean and mean today," she said. "Those paralegals that withstood the test knew the system inside and out, maintained quality, had high billables and knew how to be cost-effective. That's what firms are looking for in today's paralegals."

Congratulations, You've Been Laid Off!

lthough you probably may not agree with me right off the bat, if you have been merged, scourged or otherwise purged, it may be the best thing that has ever happened to you. Getting fired or laid off from your job can have devastating effects on your life—if you let it. You can, however, not only recover from this traumatic event, you can turn it around into a meaningful and motivational experience.

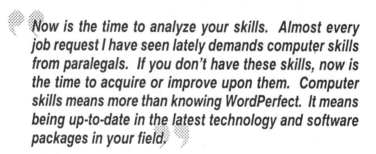

Now is the time to analyze your skills. Almost every job request I have seen lately demands computer skills from paralegals. If you don't have these skills, now is the time to acquire or improve upon them. Computer skills means more than knowing WordPerfect. It means being up-to-date in the latest technology and software packages in your field.

In this recessionary market where law firms are here at 5:00 p.m. and gone by 9:00 a.m. the next morning, the last thing you want is to get fired or laid off. If it happens or is about to happen to you, your survival instincts have probably kicked into play. However, don't get caught because you were in denial and refused to read all the signs. Ask yourself the following questions:

1. Were there rumors circulating about the firm's financial stability that I ignored?
2. Did I think that the minimum billable requirement didn't apply to me? Or that I was excused from filling out prompt time reports?
3. Did I hate coming in on Monday mornings?
4. Was I capped out, but stayed because, after all, paralegals aren't ever going to make partner?
5. Did I truly believe it was the firm's duty to train me? Did I seek out the training I needed on my own?

6. Was I the sacred cow? Was I there so long and felt so secure that I didn't feel putting in 110% was necessary any longer?
7. Was I so highly compensated for the work I was doing that I was overcompensated?
8. Was I a victim of a layoff because the firm really no longer needed my specialty? Was I doing anything to garner new skills in the areas the firm did have work?

While these questions were not designed to point a finger at or blame yourself for losing your job, it is incumbent upon you to practice safe careering. By refusing to grow, you may have set yourself up to become the victim of a firing or layoff.

A good example can be found right in the paralegal field. In the late eighties, corporate and securities paralegals were among the highest paid paralegals. While there were fewer corporate positions than litigation, firms were willing to pay higher salaries for transactional paralegals. As we entered the nineties, there were fewer and fewer mergers and acquisitions. Those corporate paralegals in firms with diminishing M&A business who refused to cross-train into other specialties, suddenly found themselves out of work. A similar situation existed with transactional real estate paralegals. Salaries plummeted and these paralegals who not so long ago were highly sought after, now had problems finding jobs. Someone wasn't minding the store.

A wonderful book, written a few years go by Emily Koltnow and Lynne S. Dumas called *Congratulations! You've Been Fired* gives powerful advice to anyone who has lost their jobs either through layoffs or firing. In it, Koltnow and Dumas stress reassessing your goals and redirecting your energies to achieve the position you really want. They emphasize that "getting kicked out of a company can be just the kick you need." Structuring your approach to getting a new position is the only way to attack the situation. Interestingly, they quote the four main reasons of getting fired as:

1. New management
2. Office politics
3. Economics
4. Personality conflicts

Poor performance is only a very small percentage of why people lose their jobs. In today's legal market, economics may very well rate as the number one cause of job loss.

What Do I Do? What Do I Do?

The first thing is *not* to panic. All of your emotions will be raw at this point. You may be in shock and your coping skills not quite up to par. Your self-esteem may be low, you may experience extreme anxiety over your finances and you may feel anger and depression over your situation—particularly in today's market when jobs are not that easy to find. Get in touch with your support mechanism immediately.

Next, make sure your story coincides with the firm's. If, for example, you were laid off because of financial reasons, make sure the firm knows this is the story you will tell on interviews. Unbeknownst to you, they may be singing a different tune because they do not want it public knowledge that the firm is in trouble. They may be telling prospective employers something that will not help you get the job.

Your resume and cover letter must be put together immediately. Pay particular attention to the look of the resume. So many bad resumes have crossed my desk lately that I am not surprised when a candidate tells me she or he has been unable to locate a position. If the firm has offered you an office and phone to use while you are looking for a position, take advantage of this offer. It is much easier to find a job while you are employed than not.

If your financial situation is in crisis, sign up as a temporary employee. There are many agencies now that handle paralegals. Don't think that since you have received severance pay that you will most certainly find a position before that pay runs out. You might, but there is no certainty as to how long the search may take. You will also be employed, which makes a stronger resume. Be sure your COBRA is in place because many agencies cannot offer benefits.

Sometimes temporary positions can turn into permanent situations. This also gives you an advantage to view a firm before taking a permanent position. You'll know most of the pros and cons *before* you accept, not after. It can also help your self-esteem. Work with the agency and let them know you are seeking full-time employment and may have to take time off for interviews. If they're good, they'll know how to work with you.

Understand today's job market. If you haven't interviewed in awhile, brush up on your technique. In today's market, there may be as many as 100-200 people applying for the same position. Employers are interviewing more candidates than ever before and taking much longer to make up their minds as to who they want. Don't get discouraged. Just put on the table that it may take longer, and that you may need to send out more resumes and encounter more interviews than in past years. You will find a job. It just may not be within your desired time frame, however.

Now is the time to analyze your skills. Almost every job request I have seen lately demands computer skills from paralegals. If you don't have these skills, now is the time to acquire or improve upon them. Computer skills means more than knowing WordPerfect. It means being up-to-date in the latest technology and software packages in your field. Knowing spreadsheets also seems to help.

Make sure you can offer more than just your specialty. Having ancillary skills such as recruiting, management, writing skills, teaching abilities, foreign languages, interpersonal skills, human resources background, technical, medical, marketing, and organizational skills can put you in a more powerful position as a candidate.

The hot areas these days for legal assistants are in:

- environment,
- bankruptcy,
- health care,
- computerized litigation support,
- banking, and
- in the corporations.

If you have any of the skills or backgrounds, now is the time to take advantage of them.

If You're No Longer with a Firm

There was something validating about being able to whip out your business card and hand it to someone. Now, since you don't have one, you may feel a little awkward about a lack of ability to identify yourself. Have business cards made up with your name, address and phone number on it and simply the title "Legal Assistant". This tool will help give you a professional appearance. You never know when you may meet someone. And as long as we're on the topic, never go anywhere without your resume. You just don't know who you're going to meet.

Organize Your Job Search Plan

Put together a job search plan. If you are off the job, plan on spending eight hours every day looking for a new position. It is a full-time job to look for a full-time job. The plan should include an organized approach for each day. Be sure to:

1. Call prospective employers each day.
2. Know which agencies to sign up with.
3. Send resumes out.
4. Read newspapers (not only the legal paper, try other industries and the local news). There may be stories about cases or other events. One entry-level paralegal I knew of in St. Louis had an innovative approach. When she read about a paralegal who won $18 million in the lottery, she sent a letter to the firm stating, "I understand you will soon have an opening. Chances of my winning the lottery are slim to none, so I will be able to guarantee long-term employment if you hire me."
5. After sending out resumes make follow-up calls with the firms check on interview possibilities.
6. Send thank you letters after interviews. Be sure they are typewritten.

7. Try to network. Your best source of job information is and always will be, other paralegals. If you don't belong to an association, join now and attend the meetings and get the newsletter. Job opportunities are surely to be found here.

You May Not Know It, But You're in the Drivers Seat

You've been handed a chance to change your life around for the better. Never before have you had to act so quickly, decisively and positively. If there was any doubt at all in your mind about your skills, growth or ability to start something new, here is the break of a lifetime.

Getting fired or laid off can push you out of a job you have outgrown, hated, or stagnated in and can launch you into a world of new opportunities. It's a tough scene, and at times you're sure the bottom has fallen out of your world. Remember that to exist in a law firm or legal department takes a survivor, a person with above average intelligence and stamina. You've proven that, no matter what happened.

Now you've been handed an important opportunity to position yourself for the job or career you've always wanted. Take advantage of it, revel in it and rejoice. And above all, have faith. The best is yet to come.

Tough Choices!

Staying in a job you once loved is a little like staying in a bad marriage. What once filled you with hope, dreams, and promises now finds you tolerating a situation—hoping it will somehow magically get better. You try desperately to change things but are faced with the reality, in this situation, that personal happiness may not be yours to claim. The decision to risk leaving can be excruciatingly painful.

> *The best way to decide. . .is to make three lists. The first should list everything you like about your current job. . .*
>
> *The next list should reflect everything you don't like, not just about your current position, but the role of a paralegal generally.*
>
> *The final list you prepare should contain thoughts on what you really want in a job, whether it's in the legal field or not. . .*

Generally, shortly after the beginning of a new year, law firms often experience a mass exodus of paralegals. The exits usually involve money. Many paralegals have waited for their yearly increase and are unhappy with the figures. Others, dissatisfied with their roles, have waited for their year-end bonuses. After receiving the anticipated gifts, not wanting to appear ungrateful, they wait an acceptable grace period and then start sending out resumes. Recruiting coordinators and agencies brace themselves, and the gates to the recruiting season are officially open.

Leaving on the basis of money or job dissatisfaction is *reactive* rather than *proactive*; these paralegals feel they have no control so they quit. Either of these reasons is sufficient to leave the firm—or the field entirely. But the proactive paralegal:

- will have a career plan,
- will know what he or she does want, and

- the decision to leave or stay will be based on whether the current position fulfills the plan's objectives.

(Such approaches take into consideration that even the most carefully thought-out plans may not materialize on schedule and contain contingency programs for obtaining goals.)

Proactive paralegals are clear in their goals. They can, for example, tell you where they would like to be in their careers one, two, and five years from now. They leave a position only after all possibilities have been exhausted or they realize that the firm does not now, and never will, meet their game plan. This well-prepared legal assistant believes that personal happiness is a right and an entitlement. A well-oiled career is like a happy marriage: you enjoy going to work in the morning much like the happily married person enjoys going home at night.

The seven primary reasons for leaving a job are:

1. Salary
2. Lack of recognition or respect
3. Location of job
4. Stress
5. Personality conflict
6. Lack of career path
7. Lack of power

Sometimes it's easier to quit than to "fight it out" or make necessary changes. On the other hand, when do you come to the realization that no matter what you do in your current situation, it's not going to change and you need to move on?

"Scott" was a litigation paralegal who enjoyed the family atmosphere and entrepreneurial spirit of his firm. During the late '80s, the firm grew, spiraling from 15 attorneys to 65. The family atmosphere evaporated as a more corporate environment took hold. Structured departments emerged, systems took place and the firm was now governed by committees instead of one or two partners. Scott felt he had lost his identity, assignments took on a more compartmentalized approach, and the informal, easygoing attitude of the firm changed into a more structured environment.

Could Scott change his needs to fit those of the firm? In his heart, he knew he wanted the smaller firm atmosphere. There was nothing really wrong with the current firm, everyone there was great. But the firm simply no longer met his needs and more importantly, there was nothing within Scott's power that could change that. Scott made the decision to leave and today works for a smaller firm where he feels in full control of his own destiny.

I believe there is a fundamental conflict in the role of the paralegal that prompts so many to decide to leave their positions. After working with, talking to and speaking before literally thousands of paralegals, I know that this is a field that attracts people of high intelligence. But by the ABA's own definition, paralegals often perform "routine and repetitious" tasks. After an incoming paralegal has paid his or her dues, the contradiction between the level of tasks and intelligence of the people in the field often surfaces with a vengeance. It is at this point that many paralegals feel they must make changes—either by finding a new position, creating a new role for themselves with their present employer or exiting the field altogether.

Recently, my colleague, Andrea Wagner, and I have been conducting workshops for legal assistants called "Changing Fields for Paralegals." We have taught several hundred professionals, who are in the process of deciding whether they should change specialties, take a position in another capacity in the field, or leave the field entirely. Legal assistants in this workshop have cited several conflicting reasons for leaving:

- overwork,
- salary capping/lack of advancement,
- impossible deadlines and repetitive work,
- no authority/subservience/lack of power,
- impossible billing requirements,
- working below their capabilities, and
- female dominated.

On the other hand, workshop participants also cited positive factors in their jobs:

- autonomy,
- respect from others outside the field,
- interesting and challenging issues and transactions,
- acceptable salaries and bonuses,
- the "buck doesn't stop with you,"
- growth, and
- travel.

Before considering whether you should leave your job or even the field, focus on why you feel the way you do. Some questions to ask yourself are:

1. Am I leaving because I didn't get the salary increase I expected?
2. Was that salary increase realistic given the economic conditions of the firm/ legal field at this time?
3. Am I leaving because of one incident or situation that I can't seem to overcome?
4. Is it possible the same situation could occur again at another firm?
5. Am I leaving because of one particular person? Does this one person impact my feelings about the entire firm or position?
6. Does this position offer the vertical or horizontal career path I seek?
7. Am I very clear on what that career path is? Do I have an action plan that will help me succeed?
8. Is the reason for leaving one that has been repeated in my employment history?
9. Am I doing what I need to do to correct a possibly inappropriate "flight pattern?"

10. Do I fantasize that I am in another career altogether?
11. Is it time to seek out another career?

You also need to ask yourself whether you are in a negative or positive reinforcement firm. In a negative reinforcement situation:

- You are only as good as your last time sheet.
- You have the feeling that you will never be fully respected or accepted for who you are.
- You feel that what you do goes unappreciated.
- You are always bracing yourself, consciously or unconsciously, for a battle.
- Feedback is only received when you've done something "wrong."
- You feel as though you are working below your capabilities.

In a positive reinforcement firm, you are encouraged to go beyond your comfort zone to reach for assignments in which you can grow:

- Feedback is both positive and constructive.
- You are recognized not only as part of the team but on your own merits as a worthwhile professional.
- You feel good about yourself and those around you.

Those of you who have experienced both situations and know the difference are very fortunate. Those of you who have only experienced a negative reinforcement firm may not realize that another kind of environment does exist and that you can be a part of it! No one is a slave to *any* situation. There are always healthy alternatives where everyone wins.

When contemplating leaving a job, most people are very clear on what they don't want in another position. Mostly, this arises from anger over how they **were** treated or what went wrong. For example, you may hear a candidate say:

- "I will never again work for a large firm; small firm; solo practitioner; or corporation..."
- "I will never take another job on the westside."
- "I will never again summarize another deposition."

It is important to concentrate on what you *do* want. Remember that all jobs have aspects that you will not like, not now, not ever. We're just going to have to put that on the table and live with it. However, you are entitled to personal happiness and you can go after what you do want. We are not part of our parents' generation. We are no longer expected to stay in the same job if we're unsatisfied and realize that it will not get us what we want.

However, before you even consider leaving, you must be clear on what you really want and whether that goal is attainable. We asked our seminar attendees to create their ideal job. In doing so, they listed, in preferential order, what features were of the utmost importance to them. Topics included:

- working environment and conditions,
- salary and bonus,

- assignment level,
- location of job,
- career path,
- overtime,
- training,
- client and people contact,
- authority and power,
- autonomy,
- firm culture,
- cooperative employer,
- recognition,
- low stress,
- and others.

Then they rated the features by:

- Must Have
- Will Compromise
- Can Do Without
- Will Not Compromise
- Not Important

One legal assistant who was considering leaving the field altogether discovered that what she really disliked about her current position was the working environment. Her preferences showed her to be a strong "people" person who loved to interact. But she was a litigation legal assistant who had been stationed in a basement collating documents for most of her career. Based on this experience, she believed she faced an entire career in the basement. It did not occur to her that there might be a better life within the field.

She switched specialties and ended up investigating immigration and personal injury cases rather than getting out of the field. Returning to our comparison of career and marriage (and certainly not making light of either institution), in a way this legal assistant enjoyed the idea of marriage, but simply had the wrong mate.

Another legal assistant discovered that what she was craving was recognition, feedback and a more lively environment than she currently had. She loved her firm but the department she was in was rather stuffy, lacking team players. In short, she wasn't having any fun. Her distress with her position carried over into her personal and family life. Was there another practice specialty or department within her mid-sized firm that she could join? Apparently not.

However, she ended up creating a position for herself with attorneys in another department by enlisting the support of one overworked associate who utilized her as an "extra" paralegal for one huge deal. Gradually, she went from an "on call" entertainment paralegal to full-time. Today, she feels she has a better life for herself and her family, having finally created both the work and environment she wanted and deserved.

- *You* need to decide what's important to you.
- *You* need to determine if these needs are at all negotiable.
- And *you* need to decide whether your nonnegotiable needs can be met where you're currently working.

The best way to decide these issues is to make three lists. The first should list everything you like about your current job (yes, there are probably a few things), such as:

- Do you like the people?
- The location?
- Your office?
- Your secretary?

The next list should reflect everything you don't like, not just about your current position, but the role of a paralegal generally. You may discover that you like the job of a legal assistant, just not at your current firm, like Scott. You may also find that a paralegal position simply doesn't meet your needs.

The final list you prepare should contain thoughts on what you really want in a job, whether it's in the legal field or not:

- Do you like working with people?
- Do you want to get away from paperwork?
- Do you like being a manager?
- Do you like to work with computers?
- Do you enjoy teaching?
- Do you like to write?

After you've completed these lists, you will have a better idea about what's important to you. Armed with this information, you can make an **informed, proactive choice** about your working environment, career growth and plan for the **future.**

I'm not encouraging anyone to go right out and quit his job. What's important to understand, however, is that you have a right to *choose* how you will live your life. By the very nature of the job, paralegals can be told what work to do, how to do it, and what time constraints exist. The very existence of the position depends on another source, the attorney. What some legal assistants must learn is that you have a right to choose what the quality of your life will be, and that quality of life extends to your career.

Is There Life After the Law Firm?

Several weeks ago, I was asked to be a speaker before a major metropolitan paralegal association on whether a vertical career path for paralegals actually exists.

Some attendees argued that since paralegals often have to go outside the law firm environment to advance their careers, there is no real vertical career path for them. It was almost as if they felt they had to betray their careers to advance them.

> *Every career has a cap. Every career has its own limitations. The trick is not to get stuck, to keep moving in a way that fits with your needs, whether it's a move up, laterally or out—for more exciting adventures, more money, more prestige, stimulation, etc.*

In my view that is a terribly limiting notion. While nonfirm work for paralegals may fail outside the ABA's definition of "paralegal," it nevertheless capitalizes on valuable and transferrable skills that you possess and enables you to create the kind of life that you want for you and your family.

If you believe that your career as a law firm paralegal is at a dead-end, then it is imperative to use your skill and imagination to change that. The Department of Labor survey which claimed that paralegalism would be the fastest growing career of the 1990s probably did not take into account a recession or war... so if you're not satisfied with where you're going or how fast, there's a lot you can do about it.

When I talk to paralegals in the throes of debating what's the "right" thing to do, I am reminded of playing a board game with a new group of people. In rolling the dice for your next turn, one of your dice rolls off the board. "Do you count that as a legitimate turn or do you play that I have to take my turn over?" you ask your new friends.

While everyone present may have an opinion on the issue, the reality is that no one really knows, because even if it were written, the question remains—can you bend those rules and still be playing the game legitimately?

Who made those rules and why? While you may go along with the group on a board game—just to be friendly—your career and your life are far too important to let unwritten rules about what "real" paralegals do determine your behavior.

When I owned my own company, a national paralegal services corporation encompassing temporary and permanent placement and deposition summarization services, I was responsible for literally hundreds of paralegals on various projects all over the country. I was constantly on the road. I was responsible for the bottom line, payroll, hiring, advertising, new business development—all the tasks you do in business.

Yet I never considered myself outside the paralegal field. I lived and breathed paralegal careers. My background as a paralegal administrator and later as a speaker and author served only to enhance an exciting and financially rewarding career.

"Yes," my friends tell me, "but you are the exception. Few people will take the inherent risks involved to become an entrepreneur." True, but what about paralegal entrepreneurs who hire other paralegals? What about people who use their paralegal background to jump off into related legal fields? What about those careers with one die off the board?

I have always disliked the term "alternate careers" because it reinforces the idea that the only "real" paralegal career was in a law firm. I prefer the term "expanded careers" instead. I made a list of paralegals I know personally who have successful careers outside of law firms or have developed adjuncts to their careers inside firms. The list includes only people who are excited about their careers, financially successful and consider themselves within or related to the paralegal field.

I came up with 150 names, and these were only people I had met or had heard about. Surely there are hundreds, maybe thousands more. The variety and success of these new careers suggest just how valuable a paralegal background can be for advancing your career or creating a new one. Surely I was on to something. Here are a few of those people and what they do:

- Bill Gutman worked as a paralegal on a large litigation case regarding a hotel fire and spent 1-1/2 years in San Juan, Puerto Rico. He's now with Litigation Management and Training Services in Los Angeles.

- Lisa Montier, a litigation computer expert, is working for Denton, Hall et al., an American law firm in London, England as a project manager.

- Phillip Signey, litigation paralegal for Jones, Day, Reavis and Pogue wrote an excellent fast-selling book, *Litigation Paralegal* and is also an Associate Professor at California State University at Long Beach.

- Ann Kotsovolos-Roberts is an assistant to the head of the contracts department at MCA, the entertainment conglomerate, and is now working on movie deals.

- Teri Cannon, one of the most respected authorities in the paralegal field, went from paralegal to dean of Paralegal Studies for the prestigious University of West Los Angeles (earning a law degree in the process).

- Michele Shannon, litigation paralegal, opened a highly successful microfilming and scanning company, Shannon Micrographics in Los Angeles.

- Judi Bandel, a corporate paralegal, owns Paralegal Consultant Associates in New York, a legal management consulting company.

- Rick Kraemer works for Executive Presentations, a company that produces professionally designed trial exhibits.

- Leanne Cotham, a litigation paralegal, is an editor with James Publishing Company, and edits books for paralegals.

- Carolyn McKown, president of InCorp America, Inc., a corporate services company in Delaware, went from the attorney-general's office to a corporate services company to owning her own business.

The list goes on. What if these people said they couldn't take the risk? What if they felt that they were betraying the field or that leaving the law firm meant that the new career was not a paralegal career? And what about paralegals who became vendors—those people who now provide services or products to law firms and legal departments? Did their training and years in the law firm go to waste?

Of course not. Every career has a cap. Every career has its own limitations. The trick is not to get stuck, to keep moving in a way that fits with your needs, whether it's a move up, laterally or out—for more exciting adventures, more money, more prestige, stimulation, etc.

Take a look at the senior partner in a law firm. That partner is as far as she can go. Unless she branches out into other areas (i.e., owning a business, becoming an officer of a corporation), the only option she has is to keep bringing in more new clients, billing more hours, and of course, making more money. At some point, she caps.

There are many exciting and rewarding careers within the law firm or legal department of a corporation. But the career doesn't stop there. Here are a few suggestions if you are considering branching out from the law firm or legal department:

1. *Do you really know what your career "likes" and "dislikes" are?* If not, make a grid chart. Across the top put: highly competent, competent, somewhat competent, not at all competent. Along the side put: absolutely love, like, somewhat like, dislike entirely, hate. List your skills, environmental preferences, and people preferences. As you fill in the chart, you will begin to get an idea of:

   - what you are doing that you are good at but may dislike,
   - what you are terrible at but love (skills which you may be able to cultivate), and
   - what you love and are highly competent at but may not be doing.

If you need career counseling, Dick Knowdell of Career Research & Testing in San Jose, California, offers a copyrighted version of this skill test and for a fee may assist you. Dick, who specializes in career transitions in the legal field, can show you that certain skills in your grid are your burnout skills and how to avoid them. He can be reached at (415) 559–9454.

2. *Form an advisory committee or join a support group.* There are many, many paralegals out there who share the same dilemma—is there life after a law firm? You don't need to be alone in your search. Arrange to meet once a month in someone's home or have Sunday brunch. Discuss your ideas and concerns in a safe haven. It's best not to choose people from your own law firm. Get input from people who can bring a different perspective to the table.

3. *Conduct informational interviews.* Information gathering interviews are highly effective in determining where you would like to land. You do not need to get to the hiring authority. What you do need is to contact a paralegal in a field that attracts you.

   Are you really a good artist? Can you use those skills to produce professionally-designed exhibits? Are your talents in writing? Can you write a book? Have you secretly desired to be in the entertainment industry? Paralegals in positions outside the law firm are generally more than happy to share their experiences with you. You will also get an idea of whether you need further education—no, that is not a sign of failure, almost all careers require further education at one time or another. You'll also find out salary information which may pleasantly surprise you.

4. *Find out how many company vice presidents came up through the legal department.* If you are considering a position with a large corporation, find out how they treat members of the legal department. It may be the wrong department for your goals.

   For example, in one entertainment corporation, litigation paralegals did not appear to advance up the corporate ladder. Once a litigation paralegal, always a litigation paralegal. However, paralegals in the business affairs department became heads of departments and one paralegal recently became vice president. Find out the company's attitude before your accept the position.

5. *Working for a vendor does not always mean sales.* There are exciting and lucrative positions with the vendors. Don't be an elitist! If you knew the salaries some of the vendors made (along with travel to fun places, client contact, developing new ideas and promotion to higher positions), you might be less inclined to disregard working for such an organization. There are expanded careers for paralegals with expertise in:

- computers,
- teaching,
- social services,
- deposition summarizing,
- medical records,
- document management,
- corporate services,

- recruiting,
- writing, and
- foreign languages.

6. *The "S" word (sales) is not a nasty word.* I have witnessed paralegals in sales representative positions earning between $75,000 and $110,000 per year! Unless they were totally familiar with paralegal responsibilities, legal terminology, law firm procedure, etc., they might not have been able to advise the law firm as successfully regarding services and products the law firm depends upon.

   If higher salary is a motivation to you (to some people it is not), and you enjoy one-on-one contact with clients, sales can be a rewarding option for you. Regarding commissions, remember you are given an incentive to produce. The more you produce, the higher (usually) the incentive.

   In many ways, this is, unfortunately, much like the bonus in some law firms which is based strictly on how many hours you have billed. In those law firms, the more billable hours you produce, the higher the incentive.

7. *What kind of reputation does the company have and how long have they been in business?* A start-up situation may be fine in some instances, however, find out more about the person or persons responsible. A company in business for more than five years may be solid financially, but may not have the excellent reputation you may want to be associated with. Tap into your network.

8. *If you are considering opening your own business, go through all the necessary steps:*
   - research the market;
   - prepare a business plan;
   - obtain solid financing;
   - know and understand your product or service;
   - put together an advisory board; and
   - take courses in marketing, management and accounting.

   Many books have been written on the topic. Read as much as you can. A couple of good ones: *How to Succeed as an Independent Consultant* by Herman Holtz (Wiley), and *Competing for Clients* by Bruce W. Marcus (Probus).

9. *Keep your options open-stay flexible.* You just never know when an opportunity may come your way. Working in a law firm is a terrific experience. Sometimes it is just time to move ahead in a little different manner, like taking your turn with one die off the board.

[1] "Seniority Does Not Equal Security," was first published in the March 7, 1994 issue of the Los Angeles Daily Journal.

[2] "Honey, They Shrunk the Firm: Surviving in Today's Law Firm," was first published in the November/December 1993 issue of Legal Assistant Today.

[3] "Congratulations, You've Been Laid Off!" was first published in July/August 1993 issue of Legal Assistant Today.

[4] "Tough Choices!" was first published in the January/February 1992 issue of Legal Assistant Today.

[5] "Is There Life After The Law Firm?" was first published in the May/June 1991 issue of Legal Assistant Today.

Part

7

What It's Really Like

The professionals featured in the following interviews are veterans of the wars. They have seen action in the field, done combat in the trenches, run through the minefields and consistently come up winners. Above all, they made critical choices that would change the course of their careers.

Each individual has a unique story to tell. Each ventured down a different path. But the common bond they share is that they love what they do and how they do it.

Molly George

When Molly George set out to become a paralegal in 1971 she had no idea of the journey that lie before her. Little did she know that in 1992 she would be jetting to London. She never realized that she would be preparing presentations on litigation support for worldwide organizations like The International Association of Defense Counsel and The Society for Computer and Law. Nor would she have been able to predict that she would be responsible for putting together and executing a public relations program and media plan in the United Kingdom for one of the United State's most prestigious litigation support companies.

George travels extensively, attending legal technical conferences like the New York Legal Tech extravaganza, and meets interesting people throughout the world.

Today, as marketing manager for Quorum Litigation Services, Inc., George has made the most of a number of opportunities crucial to career growth. More importantly, her latest job move, has afforded her the opportunity to work with a much larger platform of resources. Quorum, with its well-established client base and national sales force, is the largest privately held litigation support company in the nation. It has offices in London, Los Angeles, Minneapolis, New York, Philadelphia, San Francisco and Washington D.C.

George travels extensively, attending legal technical conferences like the New York Legal Tech extravaganza, and meets interesting people throughout the world. Just after she started working at Quorum, Bruce Aho, President and CEO, was scheduled to give an address to the Society for Computers and Law in London. In no time, George took on the responsibility of preparing this presentation. Working with graphic artists, she put together an educational presentation that introduced all the steps involved in a litigation support project to a keenly interested but vastly inexperienced audience of solicitors, barristers and judges.

Since Quorum opened its London office on Trafalgar Square, George has worked with Quorum's UK consultant to develop and execute a public relations program and media plan. The goal is to build awareness of Quorum's services in the litigation support arena. This international work has provided George with a number of writing opportunities. She is currently working on an article for *International Corporate Law*, a magazine published by Euoromoney.

How does your everyday paralegal from the Midwest catapult into such a fascinating international spot? She began by working as a paralegal with the Hennepin County (Minneapolis) Attorney's office with the goal of going to law school. George left the County to begin a career as a freelance legal assistant. "I kept putting off law school for a number of reasons," says George.

> My husband and I had our daughter in 1976 and began building our
> house the next year. With all this going on, the time just never seemed
> right to commit to law school's rigorous demands. Instead, I began
> taking legal assistant courses at night from the University of Minne-
> sota, in order to enhance my freelance credentials.

Looking for new challenges in 1985, George decided to open even more avenues by beginning work on an M.B.A. in marketing at the University of St. Thomas in St. Paul, Minnesota. Around the same time, some freelance projects introduced her to the use of computerized litigation support. She recalls trying to convince a particular client to let her complete deposition summaries on her home personal computer.

Working with Associated Paralegal Consultants at a time when technical innovations were infiltrating law firms, she helped start one of the first computerized transcript summary services. George also offered consulting for law firms to help with in-house database design and document coding.

By 1989, George moved into a new position as Marketing Director for Access Management Corporation, a litigation support company in Minneapolis. Once again, George was challenged with building and diversifying the company's client base. In this capacity, she co-wrote an article, "Taking Automated Litigation Support In-House," for the 1991 ABA book, WINNING WITH COMPUTERS: TRIAL PRACTICE IN THE 21ST CENTURY.

Networking has played a crucial role in George's career growth. By 1992, after having established a high profile in marketing computerized litigation support services, George accepted the position of marketing manager with Quorum Litigation Services.

"I want to stress to all legal assistants the career opportunities available in the technical area," George says. She also pointed out the number of other former paralegals who have followed similar career paths.

> In August, Quorum held a client advisory panel of litigation support
> managers from major law firms and corporations throughout the na-
> tion. Half the panel members began their careers as legal assistants.
> Eventually, they actively began learning about computerized litigation
> support and applying this technology in their own firms and compa-
> nies. My legal and technical experience—combined with my love for
> the challenges of marketing—has given me an electrifying career path
> that is both enjoyable which provides continuing avenues for growth.

Jon Montgomery

Senior Legal Assistant specializing in real estate with over 11 years experience. Past President of the California Orange County Paralegal Association.

What made you get into the field?

I always had an interest in law, even in high school. I thought it was a good way to get into the field of law without getting into law school.

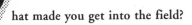

I enjoy title review more than anything else. Every one is different. Generally there are problems, and I like problem solving. You have to plan your strategy and execute your play. See how you come out. It's exciting.

Why didn't you go to law school?

I didn't want to. I also had a lot of family problems at that time.

Did you have another career?

I was in retail management for three years. I really liked it. I got out because of a recession in 1980.

How would you describe the job duties of your current position?

It's real estate focused. It requires a business law background. I work with various lending clients which involves loan workouts, dispositions, portfolio acquisitions. I assist with due diligence, drafting real estate documents including leases, assignments, amendments, loan modifications. I review title and environmental reports.

Whom do you report to?

I work with four regular attorneys locally. I also work with attorneys all over the country. Or, I could go out of town on assignment. When I do, it's usually to assist with due diligence or work on a closing on a transaction. We still have some big clients that are acquiring a great deal of real estate.

What are your favorite assignments?

I enjoy title review more than anything else. Every one is different. Generally there are problems, and I like problem solving. You have to plan your strategy and execute your play. See how you come out. It's exciting.

What was your worst experience as a paralegal?

Probably the worst experience I've had is when I worked on a huge transaction that went on for three months. I worked 18-plus hours a day, sometimes 6 days a week. My wife asked, "Why did we move so we could be closer to work? Just so you could work 18 hours a day?" The assignment was a business transaction and a sale of a multi-national company.

What was your best experience?

I spent three years working on an estate of a little old lady who came to us because her house was being foreclosed. She said that she and her husband used to be very well off. Only her husband didn't tell her anything about his transactions. She didn't have a clue as to what went on during her marriage. She just didn't know what to do. I found several million dollars in assets that contained records of her husband. It was wonderful to be able impact someone's life so positively. It was close up and personal. Sometimes when you work for large corporations, it's satisfying to save dollars for companies, but it isn't personal. This assignment had a dramatic impact on this woman's life. She was ready to lose it all.

What kind of attorneys do you like to work with?

Mellow. All of my attorneys are mellow and very nice people. They are very tuned into training. They are continually progressing in their career. There's always something new to learn and they treat you like a co-equal.

How do you get them to do that?

Always be enthusiastic about what you are doing. Show them you will take on the responsibility and do the best job. Always own up to your mistakes. If you make a mistake, say so.

What kind of attorneys don't you like to work with?

Disorganized, hyper, unethical.

What kind of colleagues do you like to have around you?

I don't work with others very often. It's a hard question. I'm not in litigation where you work closely together. I did assist in training a business law paralegal. She's great, very smart.

How do you establish your boundaries?

Usually, when I get into a transaction, I assess the work to be done and ask if I can do what should be done. If it's something I've never done before, I'll speak up and say I'd like to learn how to do it so that the next time I'll have experience in the area.

What don't you like?

I hate time sheets. I hate taking the time to figure them out. It's a nuisance because there are other things that need to get done. I have to write down each and every thing. Nowadays, each client has certain things they like to see. You have to stop and think: How am I billing this? Sometimes the clients are difficult.

How do you deal with a difficult client?

It's fear driven, believe me.

What do you say?

I get very calm. I try and not to let them know they ruffled my feathers and I convince them that whatever they need will be taken care of.

You have a very strong association background. Tell me about the importance of belonging to a paralegal association.

It's part of being a professional and taking the responsibility of the direction of your profession. It can also assist you in continuing education just because of what you learn from other paralegals. If you are looking for a new position, that's where you learn about it first.

How did it feel to be president of an association?

Different at different times. There were times when it felt like an achievement: something positive and that I accomplished a good deal. Other times, it didn't feel so great when problems were out of my control. It's frustrating because it's like having another job. It took a lot of time away from my family which was terrible. There's a tremendous struggle in our lives to keep things in balance. You try to do the best for family and work. There is a limited resource. You must realize where your resources are.

There's a lot of talk about this being a female dominated field. What are your feelings on the topic?

I just don't focus on it at all. It doesn't make a difference.

Do you get more respect being a male?

No.

Do you get more money?

No. I know lots of women who make plenty more than I do.

What do you think of the licensing issue?

I think that paralegals need to self-regulate. This doesn't mean licensure—that's government imposed. Certification controlled by the profession is better.

What are your goals as a senior paralegal?

What are anyone's goals when they reach the top. My focus is turn to ways to improve my profession.

What advice to you give brand new paralegals?

Be enthusiastic.

How?

Have a positive attitude—be hungry to learn. Be aggressive about getting new assignments working with attorneys you haven't been with before. Try to become invaluable. Become your attorneys' right hand. Always seek out a new avenue.

Where do you think this profession is headed in the next 10 years?

In California, it will stay the same with the exception that there will be self-regulation. I see a split from the legal technician field. I see that as a whole different area. Paralegals want more professional status than the current legislation is giving them.

How about nationally?

I think there are states where we would see licensure and where paralegals will need malpractice insurance. They will own pieces of law practices. We're seeing the signals now in Washington D.C. and a couple of other places. I think that will expand.

Do you think paralegals are well paid?

Some are and some are not. It just depends.

What about the current education criteria for paralegals?

Whose criteria? There is no standardization of education for paralegals nationally or statewide. It's horrible. It has the potential to ruin the profession.

Why?

Let me give you an example. A paralegal graduates from a program that requires basically 6 days of study. He somehow gets a job with a law practice who never has hired a paralegal. He's not capable of very much paralegal work and ends up Bates stamping or performing only clerical functions. That's the impression that lawyer has of a paralegal. To the extent that we as a profession do not demand high standards, the schools which are money driven, are certainly not going to push for it. This disaster can easily spread.

What kind of educational background is right for the profession?

A B.A. or A.A. is best. I think the paralegal certificate needs to be post-graduate and should be about an additional one year of work. Some students who are quite capable in their undergraduate studies may be able to take a shorter, accelerated program, but it's not for everyone. And, so much of what we do pertains to business. You should really have a business background—even for specialties such as family law.

Is there anything else you want to tell students?

Basically, always be proud of your profession. It's not second best to being an attorney. I could be an attorney if I wanted to. I'd rather be a paralegal and have the attorney as the ultimate client.

Patricia Eyres

L ittle that **Patricia Eyres** experienced as a civil litigation attorney prepared her for the extensive use of paralegals that she strongly advocates now. Currently Eyres is president of Litigation Management & Training Services (located in Long Beach, California). Eyres has learned first-hand the valuable role legal assistants can play in the management of documents, database building, and other aspects of trial preparation.

> *Eyres' alluring career has included speaking on a panel with Dan Quayle on tort reform—a group of just 30 people were selected to meet with the vice-president to discuss civil justice reform.*

Part of Patricia Eyres' consulting and training effort involving computerized litigation support is to educate lawyers on how to best utilize paralegals. (Yes, this is still necessary!) As a result of Eyres' international reputation in litigation support consulting, she was asked to recruit an American paralegal to fill the position of litigation support manager for an English law Firm.

Lisa Montier is now happily ensconced in this role at Denton, Hall, Burgin & Warrens in London. "In England, there is no paralegal category," says Eyres. "This was a unique experience for everyone." Eyres explained further:

> While England does have a category called the Legal Executive, it is very different from a Legal Assistant. The English legal system is about ten years behind us in computerized litigation support, an area that paralegals here have just about overtaken. We virtually had to teach the English about a whole new category of available nonattorney support.

Eyres was then faced with the task of educating the London office of an American firm on how to make the best use of the talents of paralegals. Part of this effort included helping the firm organize its litigation unit and develop a work product retrieval system. While consulting in England, Eyres also worked with representatives of the Chancery Courts regarding their automation needs.

She continues to teach attorneys in the States about the effectiveness of paralegals. Currently she is working with a firm in Phoenix, teaching paralegals how to train other paralegals. "The best person to train a paralegal is another paralegal," Eyres claims. "Just as I think I can do an effective job training other lawyers, paralegals have their own unique way of managing and their own frame of reference. A lawyer simply cannot speak the same language. It's definitely two separate and distinct positions."

Eyres also cites her success in filling the demanding position of litigation support project manager with an experienced paralegal. The manager's responsibilities included supervising document coders and other clerical staff as part of an effort to develop a database of information pulled from technical financial documents. Eyres described the challenge of selecting the right person for the job:

> The client first insisted that the work could only be accomplished by an attorney. I convinced the client that the best person for this job was a paralegal, not an attorney. The paralegal was able to develop a creative training vehicle for working with people who were responsible for abstracting financial data. It allowed the client to extract financial data without hiring expensive financial experts.

Eyres' alluring career has included speaking on a panel with Dan Quayle on tort reform—a group of just 30 people were selected to meet with the vice-president to discuss civil justice reform. Eyres has spoken at London conferences on developing support staff roles for in-house litigation support. For her own company, she uses paralegals extensively as litigation support project managers and intends to expand this use in future training seminars and workshops.

A Phi Beta Kappa graduate of Stanford University, Eyres also graduated with honors from Loyola University School of Law, where she served as chief note and comment editor on the *Loyola Law Review*. She was former president of Women Lawyers of Long Beach and a former board member of the American Society of Training and Development. Currently, Eyres is a member of the Associate for the Development of Computer Based Instructional Systems and an instructor on computerized litigation support at California State University.

Dixie Dunbar

Having a name identical to that of a former silent film star wasn't the only factor that lead **Dixie Dunbar** into the entertainment industry. A 20-year veteran of the paralegal wars, Dunbar frankly found probate and litigation too repetitious and routine for her interests. Rather than get out of the legal field entirely, Dunbar, determined to maximize this career, decided that she should seek out the most exciting and glamorous specialty she could find.

> *Every day, I am handed something new and different to do. For example, I may have to create documents to fit a brand new situation. Handling licensing agreements is something I've never done before. However, I don't feel uncomfortable because I've been in the business so long. I know I can either handle the project myself or ask the appropriate attorney for help.*

In her current position as senior entertainment paralegal for Ziffren, Brittenham & Branca, Dunbar works for one of the hottest entertainment law firms in the country. A particularly interesting feature of this firm is the fact that it has no associate attorneys. The firm instead relies on partners and paralegals to negotiate some of the deals. In this environment, Dunbar is involved with many of the major movie studios and well-known agents, directors, writers, producers, and TV and movie stars. Everyone in the know, in entertainment, knows Dixie Dunbar.

Dunbar negotiated on behalf of Jessica Tandy and Hume Cronyn for rights to make a movie based on the book, TO DANCE WITH THE WHITE DOG. She also worked on a deal to obtain the clothing licensing rights for the motion picture called "Indecent Proposal" starring Woody Harrelson. Dunbar's most fun client is "The Simpsons" television show, because she never quite knows what projects related to that show will involve.

Part of her responsibilities involve assisting with mergers and acquisitions of production companies and studios. She worked on the Interscope and

Polygram deal. (Interscope is the production company that produced "The Hand that Rocks the Cradle.") Dunbar recalls the excitement she felt in talking with Dr. Joyce Brothers about obtaining the rights to her book titled *Widowed.* Television's "Movie of the Week" (MOW) deals that Dunbar has participated in include an MC Hammer Special, an HBO Special with comedian Bob Nelson, and "Everybody's Baby: The Rescue of Jessica McClure."

For all of us who are so fascinated with Hollywood and the entertainment industry, Dunbar explains "working on deals":

> Initially, the client wants to acquire the rights to a book or life story. Sometimes they have done some of the negotiations and want me to close it or just handle the whole negotiation. I mostly work on TV deals but I expect that will change as a result of the Interscope/Polygram merger.
>
> Once the client sells the idea to a studio, I negotiate for how much they are willing to pay the writer. I go back and forth with the agent, the network and the client for terms of the deal. I prepare the writer's contract and deal with the writer's attorneys regarding comments to the contract.
>
> If the picture is actually made after the script is written, we get involved in the production work. This means I complete all the appropriate SAG [Screen Actors Guild] package of forms. The firm has a standard production package which includes location agreements, releases for people on the street caught up the filming and things like that. I complete the actors' contracts and all "above the line" contracts, those for directors, producers, etc.
>
> Often, I am asked to review contracts for the production company involving the city or for filming at a public building. After the movie is completed, I review the credits and conform them to Guild agreements. Then I copyright the motion picture.
>
> I also attend staff meetings with legal departments to go over the status of projects and answer any questions they might have concerning my involvement with the production.
>
> People always want to know if I am invited to Hollywood parties. Well, yes. I am invited to wrap parties and screenings. Some of our particularly pleased clients have sent me flowers, baskets of muffins and Mrs. Grace's Cakes.

Lest you get the impression that all this is just fun and games, Dunbar describes her most fear-inducing project. Shortly after the attorneys in her firm decided that paralegals should negotiate some of these contracts, she was handed her first project for a two-hour MOW on a Thursday, and the project had to be completed by the following Monday.

> The agent and I could not see eye to eye, and I really wasn't prepared for how skillful or high-powered the agent was. I felt like a

fish out of water. Two years later, I look back and laugh because I was
so scared. Now, thank goodness, this is all second nature—I can't
remember exactly why I was concerned in the first place.

Dunbar's enthusiasm for her job continues. It is the variety of challenges
that piques her interest:

Every day, I am handed something new and different to do. For
example, I may have to create documents to fit a brand new situation.
Handling licensing agreements is something I've never done before.
However, I don't feel uncomfortable because I've been in the business
so long. I know I can either handle the project myself or ask the
appropriate attorney for help.

Asked if she had any advice to give those interested in becoming entertainment paralegals, Dunbar added:

It's difficult to get into this field and there are no certificates for this
specialty. You can get into this through litigation or corporate. I got
my start by working in the corporate general counsel's office of 20th
Century Fox, handling litigation cases. I knew that I wanted to be in
the studio legal department where all the action was. I went after it, I
got it and I love it!

Andrea Wagner

"I'm a classic example of a paralegal with an alternative career path," states Andrea Wagner. "Not only do I find jobs for other paralegals, I can relate to the job search extremely well because I've been through the exact same process myself."

> *. . .Wagner is also a well-known seminar leader who frequently zips around the country, speaking to entry-level and experienced paralegals. She has spoken to groups in Pennsylvania, Los Angeles, San Francisco, Seattle, New York, New Hampshire, Costa Mesa and Chicago.*

A typical day for Wagner as a career counselor with the Jewish Vocational Service finds her conducting job search seminars; reviewing and revising resumes; counseling paralegals, attorneys and other legal professionals about how to find new positions; and advising corporate clients on outplacement services. This is all done as a service to the community.

Author of two books on the paralegal career, Wagner is also a well-known seminar leader who frequently zips around the country, speaking to entry-level and experienced paralegals. She has spoken to groups in Pennsylvania, Los Angeles, San Francisco, Seattle, New York, New Hampshire, Costa Mesa and Chicago. To entry-level paralegals, she teaches the basics of finding their first position. In seminars for more experienced paralegals, Wagner discusses how legal assistants can move up, laterally, or even out of the legal field all together.

> What many paralegals fail to recognize is how their legal skills translate into other positions. As a result, many people have the impression that they have to start all over again. But all they really must do is develop an understanding about how their current paralegal skills can translate into another position entirely.

193

Wagner's books and articles have lead to TV and national talk radio appearances. "I always get nervous when I'm on TV or the radio," she says.

> The interviewers usually start out by asking for a brief description of the paralegal career. Then the avalanche of questions starts: "How can someone get into the field?" and "Why isn't the consumer entitled to lawyerless representation?" I have to know the latest status of the paralegal licensing controversy, information about educational requirements and law firm hiring criteria, and any controversial issues that may affect this profession, such as the lowering of legal fees through the use of legal assistants.

Unhappy working as a litigation paralegal, Wagner found the job stress in a major firm overwhelming. But it wasn't because she didn't enjoy deadlines, challenging assignments or a crisis-driven mentality. The real problem was the lack of feedback, unrealistic expectations and negative reinforcement that she experienced. Her teaching and theater arts background had accustomed Wagner to a more positive atmosphere.

However, not willing to abandon the profession altogether, Wagner opted for a career as placement director for a prestigious paralegal school. She then moved into the position of National Placement Director for one of the largest permanent and temporary paralegal agencies in the country. In this role, Wagner helped place paralegals nationally from Alaska to Puerto Rico, and from California to New York.

She still provides employment guidance and assistance in her current position. "I recently helped a paralegal who had been out of work for almost two years," Wagner reported.

> He had been laid off and hadn't been able to find work in his specialty. We went over and over the interview process, restructured the cover letter and the resume and knocked on every door we could think of. I hung in there with him to assist with his very strenuous fight to stay in the paralegal field. Just last week, he was offered a terrific job. Now — **that's** what it's all about.

Andrea Wagner is author of two books: How to Land Your First Paralegal Job and Where Do I Go From Here? Career Choices for the Experienced Legal Assistant. She has written several articles about the paralegal job search process for *Legal Assistant Today*, the Los Angeles *Daily Journal* (a legal newspaper), and also for the Los Angeles Paralegal Association (LAPA) newsletter.

Rose Ors

"create jobs for paralegals," boldly claims Rose Ors, president of Project Professionals, a well-respected Los Angeles legal placement firm specializing in temporary attorneys and paralegals. "We have temporary paralegals placed all over the country. One client has over 100 temporary paralegals for one case alone." Ors, in business since 1987, has written many articles, including one for *The National Law Journal* which strongly urged attorneys to make better use of paralegals.

"Paralegals are dramatically underutilized," Ors says.

Ors trains law firms to evaluate and promote paralegals to handle legal research, factual analysis and how to work as a liaison between the client and the law firm.

These professionals are highly trained and in many instances can do a better job than an attorney. With one of our major clients, we are putting in paralegals in management roles. On one large case, we have a managing paralegal in charge of handling all human resource and personnel issues that are major aspects of large cases. We have also provided training for new technology and software programs for paralegals. We help them become experts in computer software and control and management of documents.

Ors views herself as a consultant on large projects. Her staff of paralegals sizes up projects and makes recommendations about staffing and how to most efficiently use paralegals. Believing that more widespread use of fixed fee arrangements by law firms will promote greater use of paralegals, Ors trains law firms to evaluate and promote paralegals to handle legal research, factual analysis and how to work as a liaison between the client and the law firm.

Frequently, Ors gives talks to paralegal schools as part of an ongoing effort to raise their consciousness about what law firms and in-house legal departments want from legal assistants. "It's a battle," she says. "We have schools that are behind the times in training, and at the same time everyone is short of money to implement new courses."

This is a very tight market. We recently put together a great class in computerized litigation support for paralegals at UCLA, but it didn't take off because law firms have cut back on paying for seminars. The economy is such that individuals can't afford to attend seminars and law firms won't pay. Law firms need to restructure so there are fewer people on the payroll. As a result, they can make better use of temporary resources.

In this recession, Ors has advocated that firms and corporate law departments take advantage of the abilities offered by experienced paralegals. She first notes, "Everyone deserves an opportunity to work," but then points out a more troubling problem:

I've just given a talk to a conference which included a discussion about discrimination toward paralegals. Where I find discrimination is not in ethnic backgrounds or age so much as in overqualification. Clients tell me they "don't want someone with that much experience." That is discrimination. Our clients lose valuable talent by not taking advantage of people who want to work, even if they are somewhat "overqualified" for some tasks.

Rose Ors is co-author of a forthcoming book, BREAKING TRADITIONS: WORK ALTERNATIVES FOR LAWYERS, which will be published by the ABA. She is also the author of several articles on the cost-effectiveness of paralegals, which have been published in the Legal Assistant Management Association's newsletters and in *The National Law Journal.*

Deanie Kramer

Independent Paralegal with over 10 years experience. Kramer now is president and founder of A Divorce Resource and provides paralegal services directly to the community.

ow did you arrive in the paralegal field?

"Basically, I was a burned out elementary school teacher. One more romp around the play yard, and I was ready to weave rope soled sandals in a sanitarium."

Many of the skills involved in being a legal administrator are transferable from the paralegal field. You must have people skills, be a team player, organized, detail oriented, a good negotiator, and able to deal well under pressure.

So I take it you have a B.A. degree, etc.

Of course. I also have a certificate from one of the top ABA approved schools in the country.

What was your most important discovery in your 10 years in the paralegal field?

Learning that being a paralegal in a law firm just wasn't the ticket for me. I rapidly became a legal administrator. Then I felt I was more in charge of what was going on. More like, "I'm in control here." Although, I did like the field of law very much.

How did your paralegal background help you in becoming a legal administrator?

Many of the skills involved in being a legal administrator are transferable from the paralegal field. You must have people skills, be a team player, organized, detail oriented, a good negotiator, and able to deal well under pressure. Understanding a crisis-driven environment was also helpful. Recruiting, interviewing and managing other paralegals and secretaries trained me as well as developing policy manuals and training guides. As a paralegal, I also negotiated vendor contracts. I was able to transfer all these skills to the legal administrator position.

How did you make the transition into opening your own business?

I discovered that the traits I exhibited were entrepreneurial. Wanting to be the leader, managing my own time, "being in control", were all character traits of the entrepreneur. I loved the legal field, didn't want to get out, but I really didn't want to work for anyone anymore. I wanted to run my own show.

What made you decide on paralegal services to the consumer rather than another business?

This is the wave of the future. The client no longer wants to pay exorbitant legal fees, particularly in those areas that are noncontested: divorces, wills, adoptions, bankruptcy. The consumer is speaking out. It isn't just the corporate client, either. Why would you pay anywhere from $2,500 to $20,000 or more for a divorce when both parties are in agreement as to what they want? It doesn't make economical sense anymore. The consumer no longer wants to be victim to the legal system.

I sensed a business opportunity as well as a commitment to provide quality services at fees that clients could afford.

Who should be in this kind of business?

I get very angry at some of the people who think they can enter this field without training, experience or the proper education. You should not enter the business of independent paralegal unless you have been properly trained and have extensive law firm background. This is an extension of the field and it is too difficult and risky for someone who doesn't know what they are doing.

What would you say the criteria should be?

I believe that the paralegal should have a B.A. degree and a certificate from a reputable school—no "matchbook" cover schools—schools that advertise on the backs of matchbook covers. You know, "be a paralegal, earn big bucks. Can you draw this picture? Then you too, can be a paralegal".

He or she should also have at least five years experience in the field before venturing out on their own. They should also take continuing education courses on a regular basis and be fully conversant in the codes and changes in the law. Further, they need to fully understand unauthorized practice of law and never, I repeat never, attempt to practice law or give advice unless they are a licensed attorney.

How do you feel about licensure or self-regulation for independent paralegals?

I definitely think there needs to be some. I think we should have guidelines and be held to as close a standard as attorneys are as far as education, licensing, ethics, confidentiality—everything.

How do you feel schools should prepare their students for the profession?

Since teaching and education is my former career, I have definite opinions on this topic. Schools should offer a comprehensive curriculum, not an overview. Schools should prepare the student with what they will be doing. They should involve the paralegal community and employers on their advisory board to make sure that they stay in touch with what is happening in the community.

Who are the teachers? Are they qualified to teach? Do they understand the dynamics of teaching? Just because you are a competent paralegal or attorney does not mean you are a good teacher.

Some theory of the law should be presented so that the student understands the entire picture. However, too many schools talk about the practice of law but leave out practical application or procedure. Too many students arrive on the job only to discover they don't know how to complete the assignment.

If the school isn't doing its job, and the paralegal is half-way through the course, either change schools or find out on your own what paralegal assignments in your region are like. You can find out through other paralegals. Ask them for sample assignments and find out if your school is teaching that.

Schools should also offer a lifetime placement center so the student can have placement services throughout the life of his or her career. Find out what firms utilize the school. Call former students and find out how they found their job and how long it took. Some schools will tell you they place at certain firms, but the firms don't seem to know anything about it!

I also like schools that take students on a field trip to a real law firm. Many students have never been inside of a firm before and the trip can be very valuable. They see for themselves what the "service center" is; how the file room works; how the litigation support center works; if the firm has a word processing center, how it relates to the rest of the firm; what a paralegal office can look like; and just get a general feel for the profession they are entering.

When I teach paralegals, I make it mandatory that my students complete a paralegal internship at a firm so that they understand what will be expected of them and get first hand experience with the entire procedure.

Can you make a lot of money at this?

It's all relative. What's a lot of money? Is it $40,000, $50,000, $100,000 per year? If you come from a government agency background and are making $22,000 per year, then $40,000 is a lot of money. Not skirting the issue, however, I know of independent paralegals who earn well over $50,000 per year.

What do you like most about this field?

I like being able to assist people through the court system with minimum costs. I am able to offer the best alternative available to traumatic court battles, high legal fees and emotional distress.

What do you like least?

Not having a regular source of income can get difficult. I have to continually market, market, market.

At the risk of prying, can you tell us how old you were when you decided to go into business for yourself?

When I started this business I was almost 50 years old.

Who are your clients?

They are 61% female, 39% male, from 18-80 (literally), most are middle class, working people. I have people with no assets and people who own 18 pieces of property but have agreed to work it out without attorneys. I refer to mediators, attorneys almost every day. I have a wide network of other professionals that I work with: psychologists, attorneys, mediators, financial planners. All of us are dedicated to helping middle income people. There is an incredible need in the community for people who cannot afford high legal costs. I work with people of like mind who are dedicated to helping those who might otherwise fall through the cracks.

There are resources for very low income people; people with a high income can go anywhere.

If you had it to do over, what would you do differently?

Start a little earlier. I would have liked to totally understand all of the aspects of starting your own business with out the trial and error.

What is your vision for your business?

Expand the services provided. Be able to take care of more and more people.

What pushes your panic button?

When the phone doesn't ring.

What is the future for paralegals?

I think the future is wide open. There are so many areas that paralegals can work. If they have first gotten really good areas and to take that out into the business world. All of the skills are transferable to other arenas.

What advice do you have for students just entering this field?

Learn as much as you can. Get as much experience and variety of firms: large, small, different specialties. Try to discover what you really enjoy and focus in on doing what you feel good about.

The following publications were written specifically for practicing paralegals. These books contain useful forms, detailed checklists and numerous practice tips.

Some publication dates are approximate. Check with the specific publisher listed for further information. (*See* publishers' information at the end of this section.)

Administrative Law

ADMINISTRATIVE LAW, by Daniel Hall (Delmar/LCP, 1994)

Bankruptcy

BANKRUPTCY: MANEUVERING THROUGH THE MAZE, by S. Suzanne Walsh (Clark Boardman Callaghan 1994)

BANKRUPTCY BASICS FOR SMALL BUSINESSES, by S. Suzanne Walsh (Clark Boardman Callaghan 1994)

Career Assistance

CALIFORNIA PARALEGAL CHECKLIST GUIDE, by Joyce Wilson (Butterworth Legal Publishers 1994)

HOW TO LAND YOUR FIRST PARALEGAL JOB, by Andrea Wagner (Estrin Publishing 1992)

HOW TO SURVIVE IN A LAW FIRM, by Dana L. Graves, Nancy Pulsifer & Jill Levin, Esq. (Wiley Law Publications 1993)

LEGAL ASSISTANT LETTER BOOK, by Sonia von Matt Stoddard (Prentice-Hall 1994)

PARALEGAL CAREER GUIDE, by Chere B. Estrin (Wiley Law Publications 1992)

Where Do I Go From Here? Career Choices for the Experienced Legal Assistant, by Chere B. Estrin & Andrea Wagner (Estrin Publishing 1992)

Worlds Apart: A Special Guide for Firms Serving Japanese Clients, by Paul D. Jordan (Estrin Publishing 1993)

Corporate

Corporate Formation: A Primer for Legal Assistants, by Patricia A. Dris (Wiley Law Publications 1994)

The Law of Corporations, Partnerships, and Sole Proprietorships, by Angela Schneeman (Delmar/LCP, 1993)

UCC Basics: Introduction to Secured Transactions, by Mark John Glancey (Wiley Law Publications 1995)

Environmental

Environmental Law Compliance Handbook (Clark Boardman Callaghan 1995)

Environmental Law Resource Guide, by Craig B. Simonsen (Clark Boardman Callaghan 1994)

The Environmental Law and Regulation Deskbook, by Raymond Takashi Swenson, J.D., LL.M. (Clark Boardman Callaghan 1995)

Employee Benefits

ERISA: A Practice Guide for Legal Assistants, by Garrison Lee (Wiley Law Publications 1994)

Family

Family Law, by Ransford Pyle (Delmar/LCP, 1994)

Long Distance Parents: A Child Support Handbook, by Gila Brownstein (Wiley Law Publications 1995)

Intellectual Property

INTELLECTUAL PROPERTY: PATENTS, TRADEMARKS, AND COPYRIGHTS, by Richard W. Stim (Delmar/LCP, 1994)

THE BUSINESS OF SHOW BUSINESS: *Copyright, Development, Production, Distribution & Licensing in the Entertainment Industry*, by Dixie Dunbar (Estrin Publishing 1995)

Legal Ethics

LEGAL ETHICS AND PROFESSIONAL RESPONSIBILITY, by Jonathan S. Lynton and Terri Mick Lyndall (Delmar/LCP, 1994)

Litigation

CIVIL LITIGATION FOR THE PARALEGAL, by Peggy N. Kerley, Paul Suyks, and Joanne Banker Hames (Delmar/LCP, 1992)

COMPUTERIZED LITIGATION SUPPORT, by Despina C. Kartson & Norman F. Strizek (Wiley Law Publications 1993)

DESIGNING LITIGATION SUPPORT DATABASES, by Despina C. Kartson (Wiley Law Publications 1995)

HOT DOCS & SMOKING GUNS: MANAGING DOCUMENT PRODUCTIONS & DOCUMENT ORGANIZATION, by Stacey Hunt & Rhonda Gregory (Clark Boardman Callaghan 1994)

LEGAL ASSISTANT'S GUIDE TO ALTERNATIVE DISPUTE RESOLUTION, by Judy Quan (Clark Boardman Callaghan 1994)

LITIGATION TEAM BUILDING & CASE MANAGEMENT (Clark Boardman Callaghan 1995)

THE NUTS & BOLTS OF CIVIL LITIGATION PRACTICE, by Jennifer Dwight (Clark Boardman Callaghan 1994)

THE PARALEGAL'S ROLE AT TRIAL, by Kerri W. Feeney (Wiley Law Publications 1993)

SMART LITIGATING WITH COMPUTERS: *The Step-by-Step Guide to Computer Applications in the Nineties and Beyond*, by Patricia S. Eyres, Esq. (Wiley Law Publications 1992)

USING MULTIMEDIA & ADVANCED TECHNOLOGY IN THE COURTROOM, by Patricia S. Eyres, Esq. (Estrin Publishing 1995)

WINNING METHODS FOR TRIAL PREPARATION, by Terry Noro & Barbara Heughins (Clark Boardman Callaghan 1995)

WRITE TO THE POINT: TECHNIQUES FOR CREATING FIRST-RATE DEPOSITION SUMMARIES, by Dana L. Graves & Ron Cogan (Estrin Publishing 1995)

Personal Injury

THE PLAINTIFF'S PERSONAL INJURY HANDBOOK, by Kathleen M. Reade (Clark Boardman Callaghan 1994)

PREMISES LIABILITY FOR LEGAL ASSISTANTS: FROM SLIP & FALL TO ATTRACTIVE NUISANCE, by Jodi McMaster, Esq. (Estrin Publishing 1995)

MANAGING PRODUCTS LIABILITY & OTHER COMPLEX TORT CASES (Clark Boardman Callaghan 1995)

MEDICAL MALPRACTICE GUIDE FOR PARALEGALS, by Stephanie Danelson (Wiley Law Publications 1993)

SUCCESSFULLY HANDLING THE AUTOMOBILE ACCIDENT CASE, by Jimmie W. Murvin (Wiley Law Publications 1994)

TORTS AND PERSONAL INJURY LAW, by William Burkley (Delmar/LCP, 1993)

Real Estate

THE LAW OF REAL PROPERTY, by Michael P. Kearns (Delmar/LCP, 1993)

REAL ESTATE TRANSACTIONS HANDBOOK (Wiley Law Publications 1995)

Accounting services, 117–18
Achievers, 64–65
Airline hubs, 92
Ancillary skills, 166–67
Assertiveness, 131–32
Assignments, 63–64
    upgrading, 75, 80–81
Associates
    comparing paralegals with, 99
    performing paralegal work, 159,
        161–62
Associations, 52–55
    benefits of, 53–54
    dues in, 54
    leadership skills in, 54–55
    officeholding and career boost, 54
    and politics, 53
    strategic bonding in, 52–53
Attitude, 61
Attorney General of California, 121–22
Attorney-paralegal relationship, 147
Attorneys, 59–60
    difficult, 85–88
    evaluation of paralegals by, 97–105
    managing, 82–88

B.A. degree, 127
Baird, Zoe, 142
Billing, 48, 100
    travel time, 93–94
Bonuses, 101
Boss, managing, 64–66
Brag letter, 22–23
Bramell, Paul, 100–101, 103, 114
Broker, Linda, 50
Brown, Ron, 142
Bullard, John Jr., 116
Burbick, Lisa, 114
Business travel, 89–94

Call, Kathleen, 50
Callegari, Charlotte, 7
Cannon, Therese, 51
Career
    advancement of, 62–63, 74–78
    leveraging, 79–81
    preparation for, 131–32
Career jobs, 4–6
Career marketing, 59–60
Caste systems, 65, 80
Certificate, 127
Changing jobs, 169–74
    deciding what you want in new job,
        172–74
    as proactive paralegal, 169–70
    questions to ask yourself, 171–72
    reasons for leaving job, 170–71
Charnley, Meg, 50, 126
Clements, Barbara, 121–22
Climbing the ladder, 74–78
    continuing education, 77
    handling resistance, 76–77
    master calendar, 75–76
    plan of action, 75
    supervising vendors, 77
    taking charge, 78
Coffee, getting, 61
Cohen, Herb, 111–12
Competing for Clients (Marcus), 179
Computer skills, 4, 46, 51, 164, 166
Confidentiality, 114
Conflict of interest, 47. *See also* Personal
    problems

Conflicts. *See* Office politics
Congratulations! You've Been Fired
        (Koltnow & Dumas), 165
Continuing education, 77
Corporate paralegal, 51, 128–29, 160,
        165
Corporate rates, 93
Cost-effective measures, 162–63
Cover letter, 19–22
Criticism, 30
Critics, 87–88
Cronkite, Walter, 68
Cross-training, 50, 61, 160–61
Culture (firm), 47, 139–41
Curtis, Patricia, 7
Cypert, Samuel, 62

Daly, Cindy, 114
Deadline deviants, 86
Deal, Terrence E., 61, 63
Decision-making process, 84–85
Deposition summarizing, 117
Discrimination, 137–41, 143
Ditonto, Douglas, 99, 102–3
Downsizing, 114–15
    and seniority, 155–57
    surviving in the 90's, 158–63
Dumas, Lynne S., 165
Dunbar, Dixie, 51, 190–92
Dysfunctional family unit, 27–28

Education, 38, 129–30, 199
Egan, Michelle, 126
Eighth year, 40–41
Elliott, Liz, 9
Employee benefit plan administration,
        117
Employee manual, 47, 59
Empowering your position, 57–67
    assignments, 63–64
    bending the rules, 63
    career advancement, 62–63
    career marketing, 59–60
    learning the ropes, 59
    managing your boss, 64–66
    "not my job" syndrome, 61
    risk-taking, 66–67
    vendor relationships, 66
End-of-year bonus. *See* Bonuses
Entertainment law, 51
Entrepreneurs, 179
Entry-level paralegals, 7
Estrin, Judy, 4, 6–7
Evaluation, 97–105
    appropriate basis for comparison,
        99
    improving process of, 103–4
    and office politics, 101–3
    paralegal role in, 104–5
    productivity, 100
    raise calculation, 100–101
    subjective qualities, 98–99
    tips for evaluators, 104
Experience, 7, 128
Experiment approach, 83–84
Eyres, Patricia, 188–89

Facilities management, 115–16
Family work atmosphere, 25–30
Fifth year, 40
Firings, 164–68
First year, 39
Foreign language skills, 50–51

Fortune, 61
Fourth year, 39–40
Friedman, Barry, 100

Gender, 143
George, Molly, 181–82
*Getting Past No: Negotiating with Difficult
        People* (Ury), 107
Gorkin, Mark, 27
Grajski, Barbara, 127, 157
Granat, Richard, 51
Greenberg, Debra, 101–3
Gretzky, Wayne, 66

Hardwick, Elizabeth, 7
Hill Street Blues, 34
Hiring, 137–28
Holtz, Herman, 179
Horizontal moves, 62
Horwitz, Wilma, 127
"Hot" practice areas, 160, 167
Howard, Rice, Nemerovski, Canady,
        Robertson & Falk, 120–21
*How to Succeed as an Independent
        Consultant* (Holtz), 179
Human resources, 116–18
Husnik, Nancy, 122–23

Iaccoca, Lee, 62
Infighting, 147–49
Information resources, 9, 17
In-house training, 130–31
Internships, 7
Interpersonal relationships, 146–47
Interview, 6–10
    insider tips for, 10–12
    top twenty turnoffs, 12
Interviews with paralegals
    career counselor (Andrea Wagner),
        193–94
    consultant and trainer (Patricia
        Eyres), 188–89
    entertainment paralegal (Dixie
        Dunbar), 190–92
    entrepreneur (Deanie Kramer),
        197–200
    legal placement specialist (Rose Ors),
        195–96
    marketing manager (Molly George),
        181–82
    senior legal assistant (Jon
        Montgomery), 183–87

Jackman, Michael, 73
Jenkins, William, 61, 63
Jet lag, 94
Job market, 166
Job search, 1–12
    career vs. transition positions, 4–6
    case study, 1–3
    computer skills, 4
    forty-seven ways to find a new job,
        13–18
    organizing plan for, 167–68
    what do firms want, 3–4

Kemp, Ann, 126
Kennedy, Sheila, 4
Khan, Naved, 127
Knowdell, Dick, 178
Koltnow, Emily, 165
Korda, Michael, 69–70
Kramer, Deanie, 197–200

Kudos letter, 22–23

L.A. Law, 34
La Panta, Michael, 100
Law Office Management &
          Administrative Report,
          116
Layoffs, 164–68
Learning the ropes, 59
Legal assistant committees, 131
Legal Assistant Management
          Association, 41
Legal Professional, 126–35
Letters of recommendation, 22
Leveraging your career, 79–81
Library services, 116
Licensing, 53
Lippmann, Walter, 137
Litigation paralegals, 36
Lunch invitations, 80

MacPherson, Holly, 120–21
Macro management, 83
Mail room, 116
Management, 62, 132–34
Management information systems
          (MIS), 114, 116
Managing the Hidden Organization
          (Jenkins & Deal), 61
Marcus, Bruce W., 179
Marketing services, 118
Master calendar, 75–76
Master plan, 80
McAuliffe, Claire, 126
McIntosh, Norma, 3
McKeown, Jeanine, 44
Media image, 34
Messenger service, 116
Micro management, 83
Mixed messengers, 87
Montgomery, Jon, 183–87
Musciannisi, Diana, 102

Nader, Cynthia L., 156
National Association of Temporary
          Services, 43
Negative reinforcement, 70
Negative reinforcement firm, 172
Networking, 52–55, 62–63
Newsletter, employee, 59
Ninth year, 41
Nonfirm work, 175–79
Nonlisteners, 85–86
"Not my job" syndrome, 61

Office politics, 47, 101–3, 146–49
          infighting among paralegals,
          147–49
O'Neill, Patricia, 114
Operations, 115–16
Orientation, 59
Ors, Rose, 195–96
Outsourcing, 113–19
          core functions of your firm, 118
          definition of, 113
          functions that can be reassigned,
          115–18
          impact of change, 114–15
Overtime, 109

Paralegal administrators
          of San Francisco, on personnel
          issues, 126–35
Paralegal of the Year Award, 71–72
Paralegal profession
          future of, 49–51
          pitfalls in, 137–41

trends in, 132–35
          what to expect in the first ten
          years, 38–41
Pendergrass, T.J., 44, 48
Performance review. See Evaluation
Perquisites, 110
Personality conflicts, 28
Personal problems, 150–53
Peterson, Mary Lou, 126
Pitfalls, 137-41
Pleasure packages, 92
Policy manual, 59
Politics. See Office politics
Polk, Tony, 113
Popham, Haik, Schnobrich, Kaufman
          & Doty, Ltd.,
          122–23
Positive emotional language, 30
Positive reinforcement firm, 172
Power, conduit to, 79
Power dynamics, 146–47
Proactive paralegal, 169–70
Productivity, 100
Project lawyers, 116–17
Promotion teasers, 87

Raises, 100–101
Real estate paralegal, 160, 165
Recession, 43, 50, 155–64
Recognition, 70–71
Recommendation, letters of, 22
Records management, 116
Recruiting, 127–28
Redacted writing samples, 24
Reporting structure, 143
Request for proposal (RFP), 118
Research skills, 8
Resistance, handling, 76–77
Restructuring. See Downsizing
Resume, 3, 79, 166
Retreats, weekend, 120–25
Reviews, 74
Risk-taking, 66–67, 69–70
Role models, 33–37
Rules, bending, 63

Salaries, 101, 128–29
          negotiating, 106–12
          deadlines for, 111–12
          doing your homework,
          107–8
          inappropriate techniques,
          111
          offer lower than expected,
          110
          overcoming objections, 111
          for perquisites, 110
          research for, 108–9
          when to discuss salary, 108
Salary surveys, 107
Sales representatives, 179
Schaerzle, Lois, 151–52
Scheele, Adele, 64–65
Schools, 38, 129–30, 199
Scott, Susan, 48
Second year, 39
Seigal, Benjamin, 99
Self-defeating behavior, 69–70
Self-promotion, 36
Seminars, 80
Seniority, 155–57
Senior-level paralegals, 7
Seventh year, 40
Sixth year, 40
Software, 4
Strategic bonding, 53
Success, 68–73

The Success Breakthrough (Cypert),
          62
Support Memo, 161
Sustainers, 64–65

Taking charge, 78
Tanaka, Dona, 28
Taxicabs, 91
Teamwork environment, 29
Temporary administrators, 117
Temporary agency, 44–46
Temporary legal assistants, 42–48,
          117, 166
Temporary secretaries, 114
Tenth year, 41
Third year, 39
Timesheet, 48
Time wasters, 86
Titles, 81
Training, 6–7, 129–31, 160–61
          in-house, 130–31
Transition jobs, 4–6
Travel, 89–94
          billing for, 93–94
          eating during, 91–92
          hotels for business, 91
          jet lag, 94
          saving on airfare and hotels,
          92–93
          taxicabs, 91
          travel agents, 91
          travel schedule, 93
Travel agents, 91
Trends, professional, 132–35
Trials of Rosie O'Neill, 35

Underground networking, 22
Ury, William, 107, 110

Value-added, 6
Vendors
          cost-cutting measures with,
          162–63
          relationship with, 66
          supervising, 77
          working for, 178
Vertical career path, 175
Visibility, 80

Wagner, Andrea, 50, 171, 193–94
Weekend retreat, 120–25
          Attorney General of California,
          121–22
          Howard, Rice, Nemerovski,
          Canady, Robertson &
          Falk, 120–21
          Popham, Haik, Schnobrich,
          Kaufman & Doty, Ltd.,
          122–23
          selling concept of, 123–25
White, Steve, 121
Widoff, Shelley, 51
Williams, Ralph, 82–83, 157
Wilson, Joyce, 2–3, 51, 156
Wisne, Patricia, 29–30
Women
          different expectations for, 142–45
          and success, 72
Working Woman, 27
Work plan, 103
Writing samples, 23–24

You Can Negotiate Anything (Cohen),
          111–12

Zammitti, Karen, 126